WE SURE CAN!

How Jams and Pickles are Reviving the Lure and Lore of Local Food

Sarah B. Hood

ARSENAL
PULP PRESS

ARSENAL PULP PRESS
Suite 101, 211 East Georgia St.
Vancouver, BC
Canada V6A 1Z6
arsenalpulp.com

The publisher gratefully acknowledges the support of the Government of Canada through the Canada Book Fund and the Government of British Columbia through the Book Publishing Tax Credit Program for its publishing activities.

Text and cover design by Lisa Eng-Lodge, Electra Design Group
Edited by Susan Safyan
Photo on cover by Reena Newman
Photos on pages 22, 24–25, 27, 29 30, 71, 75–77, 86, 97, 99, 101, 108, 157, 170, 175–176, 188, 217, 225, 242–243, and 249 by Sarah B. Hood

Printed and bound in Korea

Library and Archives Canada Cataloguing in Publication

Hood, Sarah B. (Sarah Barbara), 1958-
    We sure can! : how jams and pickles are reviving the lure and lore of local food / Sarah B. Hood.

Includes bibliographical references and index.
Issued also in electronic format.
ISBN 978-1-55152-402-3

        1. Jam. 2. Pickles. 3. Canning and preserving. I. Title. II. Title: Rediscovering the lure and lore of local produce through jams and pickles.

TX603.H66 2011   641.8'52   C2011-900492-5

Contents

This book is dedicated to my hardcore rock 'n' roll bike messenger, catnip king, compost artisan, and kitchen mentor, Jonathan St. Rose.

Introduction: Dammit, Jim, I'm a Writer, Not a Test Kitchen

The thing they may fail to tell you when you volunteer to write a cookbook is that you have to do much more cooking than writing. In fact, my original idea for this book was to write about the amazing resurgence of interest in home canning, with profiles of the people who are leading jam and pickle workshops, building online culinary networks, originating bold new approaches to traditional techniques, and re-educating people in their communities about local food preserving before a huge body of skills is lost. I thought I might toss in some instructions for a few staples like raspberry jam, Seville orange marmalade, and, possibly, dill pickles.

However, when I suggested it, Brian Lam at Arsenal Pulp Press was quick to say, "Great! We'll publish it ... But it needs 100 recipes. And they should come from all over North America." Thus began my Summer of Jars, which found me working at my desk every day and firing up the canner every night. I tried out 100 recipes and more in my 105-year-old house with six square feet of counter space and a stove with three burners that all need to be lit by hand. Somehow I suspect that Nigella Lawson never finds herself scrounging through the house for a pack of matches at two a.m. because she needs to relight the burner to heat up the canner one last time before getting to sleep.

I have never been more conscious of the seasons than while writing this book. Because I have tried to use only local ingredients whenever possible, I paid fourteen dollars for a tiny bunch of forced rhubarb; I hunted through markets all over town for local cranberries, golden raspberries, gooseberries, and red currants, as well as more exotic, imported fare like Kaffir lime leaves, lemongrass, Thai sweet basil, and guavas. (It's a blessing that I live in multicultural Toronto, with its eclectic food scene, because at least I know the ingredients are around somewhere; I just have to track them down.)

I begged neighbors for apples from their trees because local varieties don't arrive in stores until very late in the summer. I prowled my neighborhood for unsprayed dandelions, lilacs, roses, and wild violets, and raided my own community garden plot for chive blossoms, Chiogga beets, dill, sage, and thyme. I hounded culinary historians to help me source produce that's no longer commercially grown. I lost track of conversations I was having as I stared at the fruit or berries of some unfamiliar plant to wonder "Is that edible?" and "Could I make jam from that?"

I also scolded produce managers for failing to stock local peaches and berries in the height of the amazingly abundant and two-weeks-early Ontario growing season of 2010. There was also a dynamite recipe for kumquat marmalade that never made it into the book because I missed the kumquat window back in May. On the other hand, there was that wonderful September night when I arrived home to find a mysterious bag of quinces from an unknown benefactor sitting on my doorstep.

But I'm glad I did it. Apart from the fact that I've learned more about preserving than I ever guessed there was to know, all that testing turned out to be very useful. Some of the best cooks forget to write down the most crucial instructions, so I found myself tweeting, emailing, and phoning recipe contributors with all kinds of questions. "Do you strain the liquid?" "Should I peel the tomatoes?" "What size plums did you use?" "How many jars does it make?" I also learned early that recipe developers need to use waterproof pens.

Above all, the process has introduced me to a wonderful collection of talented, generous, and skilled people all over North America and in the UK who have opened their hearts, ears, and recipe files to help me compile this diverse collection of old and new canning recipes. I am honored to have entered their circle, and I look forward to trading jars with them in the future. Meanwhile, I owe a debt of thanks to the following people:

The patient and helpful Noreen Mallory, John Hood, Alexandra Hood, and Tanner Helmer, who have learned to understand over the past year that whenever they phone I'll be "jamming all through the night."

Niamh Malcolm for loving encouragement and fabulous photos.

Susan Safyan, Brian Lam, Shyla Seller, Cynara Geissler, and Robert Ballantyne at Arsenal Pulp Press, and Lisa Eng-Lodge of Electra Design Group.

My Twittering and blogging friends in Toronto and elsewhere, especially the Foodiemeet regulars and the participants in Tigress' Can Jam (especially Julia Sforza, Shae Irving, Audra Wolfe, and Tigress herself) for their inspiring enthusiasm and camaraderie.

All the recipe contributors: Audra Wolfe, Alec Stockwell, David Ort, Denise Gurney, Donna Julseth, Maggie Julseth Howe, Elizabeth Baird, Elsie Petch, Erin Scott, Gloria Nicol, Heather Kilner, Jennifer Mackenzie, José (Manny) Machado, Joel MacCharles, Dana Harrison, Julia Sforza, Julianna Carvi, Katie Quinn-Jacobs, Liako Dertilis, Pamela McDonald, Lorraine Johnson, Chef Mark Picone, Paige Bayer, Renée Joslyn, Risa Strauss, Roberta Schiff, Shae Irving, Shirley Lum, Sally McClelland, Tigress, Tom Boyd, and Yvonne Tremblay.

All those who helped me forage for recipes, contacts, ingredients, and jars, including: Emerie Brine of Bernardin; Fiona Lucas; Andrea Toole; Andrea Karpala and Jennifer Potvin of Faye Clack Communications; the gracious Paul and Rochelle Henbury, Melinda Polisella and Ashleigh McGaw at Blossom fruit stand; Anya Fernald of Yes We Can; Niya Bajaj for artisanal lavender; Lisa and Frank of Craven Road for apples; Cindy McGlynn, Ruby, and Violet for quinces; Julie Voulet of Voulez Vous Café in Toronto for plums; Anna and Rob Hubble of Ivy Avenue for raspberries; Alexandra Hood and Tara for crabapples; Heather McDonald and other members at Ashbridge's Community Organic Garden for zucchini, rhubarb, and raspberries; the National Watermelon Board for watermelon; the Ontario Tender Fruit Producers for peaches and plums; National Produce for mangoes; the Ontario Apple Growers for apples; and Willow Moonbeam and Nicole of Craven Road for jars.

The numerous food writers and researchers—many of them women—who have been laying the groundwork for projects like this for so long, including the members of the Culinary Historians of Ontario and the Women's Culinary Network. Gratitude and thanks to you all, and to anyone I may have neglected to mention!

Note: Recipes marked with have won ribbons in competitions.

1: The Pendulum Swings

Once upon a time, so the Brothers Grimm tell us, there was a good and beautiful girl named Katrinka who lived in a little cottage with her cruel, selfish stepmother and her stepsister Dobrunka. The two were always making impossible demands upon Katrinka, and one day they sent her out into the teeth of a January blizzard with the command not to return unless she brought them a bouquet of violets.

Katrinka wandered in the frozen woods—finding no violets, of course—until at length she came upon twelve majestic men seated around a towering bonfire. Three of them wore cloaks that were as green as grass in springtime, three were dressed in red like summer berries, three in golden cloaks like ripe wheat, and three in white like the snow that flew about the shivering girl. When she told them her tale, they were, at first, stern, but then took pity upon her. The men were, of course, the twelve months, and when Brother March, dressed in green, stirred the fire, the snow melted, birds sang, and Katrinka was able to gather her violets.

Needless to say, Dobrunka and the stepmother were not satisfied with the miraculous flowers, but sent Katrinka out twice more, first to gather fresh strawberries and then ripe red apples. But Katrinka was aided by Brother June and Brother September and brought home the fruits her demanding relatives required. Inevitably, the greed of her stepmother and stepsister knew no bounds, and they set off themselves, imagining that Katrinka was hiding some wonderful greenhouse full of always-ripe fruit.

They did encounter the twelve mysterious men, but addressed them most rudely. Instead of producing flowers and berries for them, Brother January stirred the fire himself, whereupon Dobrunka and her mother disappeared in a great winter storm and were never heard from again. As for Katrinka, she inherited the little cottage, where she lived to a great age, in harmony with the seasons.

Saving the Seasons

"The Twelve Months" has always been one of my very favorite fairytales, and it's a great parable for the developed world right now. Its message is clear to any child: those who have the presumption to disrespect the rules of nature do so at their very grave peril. But for a growing group of home cooks, it has more specific relevance. This is the burgeoning crowd of food experimenters who are relearning the art, craft, and science of home food preserving, teaching each other in classes and workshops in community kitchens, gourmet food shops, grade schools, cafés, and churches. Through this gateway, a generation of cooks is rediscovering the value of fresh local produce and relearning its seasonal planting and harvest cycles.

Home cooks are boldly trying all kinds of techniques; they're salting and pickling charcuterie, drying and dehydrating fish and fruit, fermenting sauerkraut, kimchi, and even basic cheeses, and pressure-cooking soups and sauces. But most often they're hot water-bath canning, an activity more commonly known as putting up food in jars. In general terms, this produces two types of food: jams and jellies preserved in sugar, and pickled or fermented fruits and vegetables preserved in vinegar and salt. And when you let an inquisitive and resourceful group of web-savvy kitchen scientists loose on a body of traditional lore, the creative possibilities are apparently endless.

So is the roster of blogs devoted entirely or in large part to food preserving: Food in Jars, Anarchy in a Jar, Put Up or Shut Up, Putting By, Put a Lid On It, Kitchen Jam, Tigress in a Jam, Tigress in a Pickle, Pickle Freak, A Bit of a Pickle, Hot Water Bath, Well Preserved, Saving the Season, Creative Canning, Frugal Canning, Canning with Kids, Canning Jars Etc., The Practical Preserver ... the list is formidable (see Jamming Online, p. 258).

And these neo-canners are not just communing virtually. They're also meeting face-to-face to exchange skills, like the participants in Yes We Can, a community canning project started in 2009 by sustainable food consultant (and *Iron Chef America* judge) Anya Fernald in San Francisco. Fernald, who founded and now works with an organization called Live Culture Company to "develop and activate powerful ideas in food and agriculture," began her career by helping artisan cheese makers in Sicily develop their businesses. She later directed programs for the Slow Food Foundation in Italy before returning to her California home to spearhead all kinds of creative food activism projects, including a massive 2008 San Francisco event called Slow Food Nation.

In 2009, Yes We Can supported local farmers by buying large quantities of fresh local fruit and vegetables in season (3,000 lb/1,360 kg of tomatoes, for instance). The participants got together to make apricot jam, dill pickles, and canned tomatoes, and then they shared the jars. The following year, under the name "Commando Canning," the group expanded its activities and took some projects out to local farms, cooking peach jam or grape jelly over an open fire.

"It's a really big mix, really diverse in terms of ages," says Fernald. "We purposely price it so it's not super-expensive. Last year, you worked and paid less, or didn't work and paid more. We changed it this year, because everybody wanted to work. A lot of people say, 'My grandmother did this, but I never learned.' Some people want to go home and start canning right away; some people want to have a lovely day and a nice meal outside. In general, there is a feeling that these are useful skills and we need to relearn them."

In the opposite corner of North America, in the area around Ithaca, New York, people with an interest in food preserving of all kinds meet online and in person through a website called IthaCan that was started by software developer Katie Quinn-Jacobs. Only eighteen months after going live in early 2009, the group had attracted about 260 members, all from the local area. "We do two things," says Quinn-Jacobs. "We have an online social network for home food preservers. People share information about drying, fermentation, root cellaring, sugar and honey and, of course, canning. We also have events: we have pesto and pickling coming up; people are learning pressure canning, cob-oven building, pig butchering, and we've got a summer cookout planned." The group has also given birth to Harvestation, a brand-new online farmer's market for bulk buyers.

The IthaCan mix includes folks from around Cornell University, Ithaca residents, and people who live in the surrounding countryside of rural Tompkins County. "We have people who live downtown who are very committed to living in a sustainable way, people whose grandmothers used to can but they

Sharon Kaplan and Andria Crowjoy of IthaCan, packing jars.

Packed jars: IthaCan handiwork. Photos: Sharon Berger

Anya Fernald, founder of Yes We Can.
Photo: Aya Brackett

Gloria Nicol of the blog Laundry Etc. (and author of the preserving cookbook *Fruits of the Earth*) was the sole British participant in Tigress' Can Jam.
Photo: Gloria Nicol

don't know how, and very strong back-to-the-landers, do-it-yourself types. I think we're in the middle of a back-to-the land movement, but we don't really know it yet," says Quinn-Jacobs. "We also have people who are locavores; we have a very strong local food movement."

Among this growing new breed of food preservers, a leading voice is the collective of writers, cooks, and other food professionals who have created the beacon blog Canning Across America. Although it's not very old, even by web standards (the first post materialized on July 16, 2009 under the title "This Can-volution Will Not Be Televised"), the group has attracted a lot of attention—not least for apparently coining the term "Canvolution."

Canning Across America is on a mission to promote safe food preservation. Well-known chefs and cookbook writers contribute recipes to the website. In July 2010, the group's second annual "Can-a-Rama" weekend inspired people across the US to get together to teach or learn about preserving. Reports came in from across the country: Illinois, Washington, California, Maryland, Massachusetts, Virginia, Montana, Arizona, Michigan, Oregon, Kansas ... and every participant had a story—or a collection of stories—to tell.

"H. Stiefel" of Chadds Ford, Pennsylvania: "My friend Joan and I have been canning for just two years. We have canned twice this year already and will be canning again July 24–26 to make use of the sixty-plus pints of blueberries that we bought on sale and then froze. We are inviting two other friends who are very interested but scared to try it on their own."

"Vicki H." of Lexington, Kentucky: "I plan to have some friends over, and my mother, who has canned vegetables for decades, will teach us all the basics. I am forty-one and grew up eating home-grown vegetables all the time. My dad manages the gardening and my mom does the canning, freezing, and preserving. During the summer, home-grown food is nearly all we ate! It is the healthiest lifestyle, and I look forward to sharing it with my friends and relearning the canning techniques I've forgotten."

"Marisa Z." of Boynton Beach, Florida: "Mango season is almost upon us. My friend's trees are so full of mangoes that I need to start my canning soon. A colder than normal winter delayed the ripening of fruit, as by this time of year I usually am elbow deep in mango jam, mango butter, and mango chutney. I think I will be able to have my canning party on July 24. I have two newbie canners this year, and I'll be teaching them the ropes."

"Robin B." of Burlington, Vermont: "I have two [canning] workshops scheduled for August 28th and September 28th through a local plant-start company. In addition, starting in September, I am going to do a series of free canning workshops at a local family and child center. The majority of folks who attend are food insecure and receive WIC [Women, Infants and Children Program aid] and/or food stamps. These workshops will allow them to save some of the produce that is often donated to the food bank here in the growing season."

"Shannon C." of Mint Hill, North Carolina: "I am on a local message board dedicated to mommies in the area called Charlotte Mommies. There is a forum there and tons of mommies are asking canning questions. I'm sure they would be thrilled to come over and discuss canning and learn from each other."

"Donna S." of Spotswood, New Jersey: "I would love to host a canning party on July 24 to help celebrate Canning Across America. I'll call it 'Getting Your Can On'; it's our going-to-the-county-fair canning party. Canning has been my passion since my husband's grandmother introduced me to the lost art. Guess she wanted to make sure this city mouse would keep her country mouse grandson healthy. It became an obsession. I would take vacations from my job around what I was canning. Then, on March 17, 2008, I got canned from my job. I turned to canning as my crutch to battle my anger. Thus [my blog] Just Got Canned was born."

This flood of activity was unleashed—or at least channeled—by a single tweet of July 15, 2009 from @kimodonnel, a.k.a. Seattle-based food writer Kim O'Donnel (a former online food columnist at *The Washington Post*), who, inspired by hearing about Yes You Can in San Francisco, tweeted "Hey Seattle, let's copycat this can-tastic idea." She could hardly have expected what was coming. "I was looking for canning partners. I had only canned once before; this is something I did not grow up with," says O'Donnel. "I was looking for likeminded folks who could tumble along with me or who could teach me a few tricks. The feeling I had that afternoon was that the Twitterverse lit up like a Christmas tree with people responding and sending all these direct messages."

O'Donnel's next tweet tore open the floodgates: "What if we set a date for a canning event in Seattle, but invited others to do the same across the country?" Shauna Ahern of the blog Gluten-free Girl was one of the first to organize a canning party in Seattle, but by the end of August 2009, events were springing up in Boston, Philadelphia, Chicago, and beyond. The Canning Across America website soon took on an exuberant life of its own, managed by Jeanne Sauvage of the blog The Art of Gluten-Free Baking (who tweets as @canvolution), with the help of contributors from all over the US.

"I would say that it's a collective in the truest sort of way," says O'Donnel. "There is a core group of eight to ten people, and everybody contributes in various ways, great and small. We have writers, business entrepreneurs, nutritionists, gardeners, bakers, and marketing people. It's a really interesting mix of people in Seattle, and we have what we call 'Friends of the Canvolution,' people scattered across the country who are creating events." These include online icons like Philadelphia's Marisa McClellan (Food in Jars) and Foodista.com editor Cathy Barrow of Washington, DC, who tweets as @mrswheelbarrow.

"This is a way of preserving food that dates back to the Napoleonic era, and here we are talking about it online and doing it with twenty-first-century technology," O'Donnel marvels. "I'm all for meeting in real time and in living color. I still put a really great value on traveling to places and understanding a sense of place and time, particularly as it relates to food. That aside, the stuff that's going on online relating to canning and preserving is very dynamic, and I think that social media has definitely had a powerful impact on keeping this thread alive."

The connections between virtual and face-to-face communication among canners became stronger in 2010 with the advent of a project called Tigress' Can Jam. Concert promoter Tigress (@hungrytigress) and her husband spend about half of each year in Long Island City in Queens, New York, and the other half on a twenty-acre farm with an 1850s-vintage farmhouse, where they have spent the past five years or so learning how to grow their own food. In the spring of 2009, she started writing two blogs—Tigress in a Jam and its salty sister site Tigress in a Pickle—to document her experiments with putting up food in jars.

In November of the same year, Tigress suggested to a few of the food-preserving bloggers she was getting to know online that they should get together in a year-long canning project that would challenge them to try canning one particular ingredient every month and write up the results online. Her offer was to read through each write-up and compile a monthly summary of all the posts on her own blog, with comments. Just as with O'Donnel and Canning Across America, the response was far beyond what she'd predicted.

"When I decided to do it, it was just in an effort to reach out to people who were into what I'm into and have some fun with it," she says. "I remember I said to my husband that if I found five people, I would be really happy." In fact, within two or three weeks, she heard from scores of people she didn't know who were eager to get in on the Can Jam.

"Before I knew it, there were a ton of people, and I had to put a deadline on it; there was no way for one person to be able to handle that," she says. By January (citrus month), 130 novice and experienced canners had signed up, and although there was some drop-off in subsequent months, by year's end about fifty people had canned their way through a rigorous schedule of carrots, berries, cucurbitae (the cucumber family), and nine other types of ingredients, posting photos, recipes, and lengthy tales about the learning process along the way.

In between reporting periods, participants exchanged lively conversation via Twitter, Facebook, Flickr, and the comment sections of their own sites. Friendships were also forged, meetups were organized, and jars flew cross-continent via the US Post Office.

"I would like to think that in the community of online preservers, the Can Jam was a way to make people come together even more," says Tigress, pointing out that this kind of network helps disseminate food-safety tips in an era when most cooks don't learn them in any other way. "If we're in a community and we're conversing with each other, there's a way to call attention to what we see; you don't have to scare the living daylights out of people, but there are rules about what's going on in those jars.

"People used to gather around the hearth and the kitchen, and that's where they shared and collected information," she says. "Now people are isolated; this seems to be a way to connect over food as people have done probably since the beginning of time."

Among the earliest to hop aboard the Can Jam train were dedicated Toronto-based food bloggers Joel MacCharles and Dana Harrison of the blog Well Preserved (@wellpreserved). Their site was born spontaneously on December 28, 2008. It began simply: "We had had the whole family over for Christmas, which is always a big thing for us to do; after they left, I was on the computer, and I said, 'Let's start a blog,'" says Harrison.

But, unlike most blogs, Well Preserved has maintained an incredible record of unbroken daily posts since that time. ("I generally get up an hour-and-a-half earlier every day than I used to," confesses MacCharles.) Although they are home cooks with day jobs, the couple has become well known to professional cooks and others involved in the local food community; it is a measure of the blog's reputation that they were invited in the fall of 2010 to stand shoulder-to-shoulder with the city's top chefs in a fundraiser for Slow Food Toronto called Picnic at the Brickworks to distribute portions of their preserving handiwork to 1,000 guests.

They settled on a menu of crackers handmade from local wheat, maple syrup, and dehydrated vege-tables; smoked field peppers; sundried tomatoes and home-canned tomato sauce. Ambitious, surely, but not a stretch for a pair who routinely take on projects like turning seventy-five lb (thirty-four kg) of apples into applesauce, canning eight to ten bushels of tomatoes, or (while on holiday on the Atlantic coast) cleaning, cooking, and freezing 160 lb (seventy-three kg) of fresh crab.

"Really, the common theme for everything we do is conscious food choices," says MacCharles. "We're trying to preserve traditions, trying to preserve food, for sure, and trying to preserve people and their work."

The Road to Jam-nation

Joel MacCharles comes from a family with a strong tradition of food preserving. Like him, quite a few of today's neo-canners are actually rediscovering skills that they absorbed in the steam of their mothers' and grandmothers' preserving kettles. I am not among them. Although my own mother grew up in a midsize town where lots of people made preserves, she hightailed it out as soon as she could to attend art college in Toronto. City life appealed to her. Except for a brief love affair with pie-baking in the late 1950s, she pretty much left traditional kitchen crafts behind her.

I had one mesmerizing glimpse of the lore she might otherwise have passed on to me when I was about six, during one of the summers we spent at the home of her great-aunt Lil, an intriguing antique house with a gigantic veranda, a birdbath, a tangle of berry bushes, and several climbing trees. Once—and only once, as far as I can remember—I followed my mother down into the cellar, which was gloomy, cool, and apparently hewn right out of bedrock, with walls that resembled those of a roughly carved-out cave. On the shelves at the bottom of the stairs were rows of somewhat cobwebby glass jars: containing what, I had no idea. Pickles probably, likely some jam, and maybe relishes, chilis, chutneys, chow chows?

That vision stayed with me. It felt like a glimpse into another world, or at least an earlier century. Which, in effect, it was; Aunt Lil would have been born about 1865. I found it immensely compelling and attractive. But it wasn't until much later that I found out how to make my own preserves.

For several years in the late 1990s, following what you might call a rough patch in my life, my home was an industrial warehouse unit in a one-time munitions factory. Behind it lay a tract of urban wasteland partly cut off from the rest of the city by two rail lines. It had been a huge factory complex, and before that, a notoriously punitive prison. The prison, which put its inmates to work in various productive enterprises, had possibly had an orchard, because there were untended apple trees all over the overgrown space.

Chef Chris Brown with Lucy Iervolino and a batch of pickled green tomatoes at the Stop Community Food Centre in Toronto.

With those apples, I made jelly. With no one to teach me how, I bought a book and read about boiling the jars in a pot to kill germs. For some reason, after the apples, I resolved to forage for other fruit. I made sour cherry jam and grape jelly (one of my greatest successes to date, actually) with fruit from people's backyards. I made a batch of jam with most of a crate of plums discarded outside a fruit shop. I begged roses from strangers with nice gardens, and made rose-petal jam. I filled a small cupboard with jars. All my family members received jam for Christmas that year. I didn't mention where I got the plums.

That winter, a friend who knew about such things introduced me to Seville oranges, and I made marmalade. From then on, I was hooked. I canned peaches and pears, jammed raspberries, strawberries, blueberries, red currants, gooseberries, cranberries, and rhubarb. I made herb jellies and citrus marmalades. I pickled carrots and cucumbers. But all this I did alone. It wasn't until about ten years later that I would get a chance to put up food with anyone who actually knew how to do it.

In 2009, I wrote an article, as an occasional columnist for Canada's *National Post* newspaper, about the Stop Community Food Centre, a groundbreaking Toronto social service agency that serves free meals to people who need them—not in itself that rare, except that the Stop serves great meals. They hire top chefs, and a sizable portion of their food is sourced from local farms or from their own community garden. On this particular occasion, I was invited to participate in a community canning day, putting up beets and green tomatoes to be used later in the year.

I was keen to do it, not least because I'd be working under Chris Brown, formerly the chef at Perigee, a very fine Toronto restaurant indeed (but now closed), which made a point of seating fewer than forty people at a time for meals that could easily cost upwards of $100 per person. (In fact, one of the Stop's ongoing fundraising initiatives is a high-end meal designed and cooked by Brown. It not only costs $100 to eat it, but people happily pay seventy-five dollars to work as part of the kitchen crew.)

I arrived a little early so I could interview Brown, a stocky, boyish-looking man who resembles something like a cross between Brendan Fraser and Michael Bublé. His energetic enthusiasm was palpable; he described unloading a shipment of produce and feeding local organic cherry tomatoes to the curious neighborhood kids who turned up to hang out and watch. "They weren't sure at first, but after they tried them, they were eating them like candy," he said. "Imagine it!"

In the kitchen, he was just as upbeat, mixing it up with volunteers Lucy Iervolino, Maria Marquesa, Silvia Esparza, and Opal Sparks, who arrived to help can the vegetables. He kept up a steady stream of Italian with Iervolino and Marquesa (apparently chefs, like opera singers, are apt to be fluent in foreign languages), while I stumblingly helped interpret for Esparza, the one Spanish-speaker in the group. Brown showed me the beets, which were new to me: gorgeous butter-colored Golden beets and lovely Chioggas, with their pink-and-white inner rings, which I fell in love with at once. (As with the Sevilles I encountered in the 1990s, this was another example of how canning tends to introduce one to new foods; until I made jam, I could barely recognize a gooseberry, let alone a white currant.)

The beets were boiled and scrubbed. The jars were washed and sterilized. Brown poured crimson vinegar and handfuls of spices into a pot, toasting the spices first in a frying pan to release their essence. The air filled with a delicious potpourri aroma. We filled the jars with beet chunks, then drowned them in fragrant vinegar. It fell to me to top the jars with the hot lids and fasten the screw-on bands, something I had done many, many times before. As I did my first one, spinning it gently with my fingertips (they shouldn't be closed too tight), I looked up to see Iervolino smiling and nodding. Even I could figure out what she was saying in Italian: "She knows how!"

It seems like a little thing, perhaps, but for me it was an emotional moment. For the first time in my life, I was canning food with people who knew how, and, seemingly, I was doing it right! It's fine to boil up a batch of jam, but, irresistibly, food preserving is also about community. It makes the most sense to do it with other people, to share skills, and, of course, to share the food. In rural societies, people have always combated isolation and the tedium of repetitive chores by getting together for food-preserving bees. Now, we're just as likely to meet online, via Twitter and the network of food blogs. But cooking is a visceral thing, and it demands face-to-face encounters too.

Filling jars with green tomatoes at a community canning session at at the Stop Community Food Centre in Toronto.

Audra Wolfe with a pantry full of her own canning handiwork. Photo: Andrew Chalfen

In the very early summer of 2010, I boarded a blue and yellow double-decker bus out of Toronto, heading for New York City. My ultimate destination, though, was Omega, a retreat center in the romantic, misty, spooky Hudson Valley, kind of a summer camp for grownups working on their spiritual growth. That's where Audra Wolfe, noted canvolutionary and Philadelphia-based author of the blog Doris and Jilly Cook, was offering a weekend-long workshop in various methods of food preservation. (Doris and Jilly, incidentally, are a pair of real live goats.)

I was interested in honing my own canning chops and learning about dehydrating, pressure canning, and lacto-fermentation (the process used to make kimchi and sauerkraut). I also wanted to find out who else is part of this canvolution. I was curious to know what would draw twenty or so others to travel to a three-day seminar in putting food up, even given the relatively modest fee for the classes and room and board. I was also, truth to tell, looking for a little canning company after so much lone jamming.

I spent a morning nosing around Manhattan, where the Union Square Greenmarket on the edge of Greenwich Village is a mecca for fresh-food aficionados. On that particular sun-washed morning,

Apples at the Union Square Greenmarket in Manhattan.

Just Food T-shirts at the Union Square Greenmarket in Manhattan.

amidst the tent-city of vendors offering fresh produce of all kinds, garden seedlings, baked goods, artwork, tie-dyes, and—yes—jams, jellies, and pickles, I was drawn right away to the Just Food table, where I resisted a "Beet the System" T-shirt but was unable to pass up "Yes We Can," partly because I liked the shirts and partly because I liked the cause; Just Food has been working in New York for the past fifteen years to bring fresh local produce to people who might otherwise not have access to it.

Clearly, Manhattanites are alive to the joys of seasonal foods. Literally emerging from the shadows of skyscrapers into the fresh spring sunshine, the lunchtime office crowd was eagerly snapping up bags of the new asparagus, rhubarb, and strawberries that were displayed alongside heaps of locally grown apples: burgundy Winesaps, bright yellow Gold Rushes, crisp Empires, and huge blushing Braeburns, as well as Jonagolds, Cortlands, Enterprises, Cameos, Galas, Spartans, Fujis, and the noble Northern Spy. From my Torontonian point of view, New York is generally a couple of weeks ahead in the growing season, so I was seduced by ravishing tables of strawberries, fragrant and tender: a delightful treat for a winter-weary northerner. I bought a pint and ate them all.

The Union Square Greenmarket runs year-round, and it's a beloved observance for hundreds of New

Yorkers. Later that weekend I would hear from one Manhattan-dweller that she makes a point of shopping there every single week, even in winter blizzards, "because if the farmers are going to bother to come, then I'm going to be there to support them."

As it turned out, in fact, Union Square was one of the magnets that drew people to Omega for the preserving weekend, which Wolfe titled "Join the Canvolution." Shopping at a farmer's market is one of the quickest ways to get addicted to the taste of fresh produce. From there, it's a natural progression to developing the desire to preserve that flavor in some way so you can enjoy at least a reasonable approximation—strawberry jam, if not fresh strawberries—for the six to ten months when it's not in season.

My fellow preserving students weren't only from the New York area; they were from all over New England. Most (but not all) were women, and in the forty-plus age group. All were interested in local, seasonal food. ("I will not buy tomatoes from grocery stores in the winter," as one person put it.) They also came together because they cared about nutrition and self-sufficiency. One of the women wanted to acquire the skills she'd seen her Italian mother-in-law practicing. One of the men had a special interest in wild edibles.

Most of us were also—in some cases, recently—growing a little of our own food. "I'm eating greens I never had before," one woman said. "I couldn't wait for ramps to get here, and I get really excited when asparagus comes in." Wolfe was up for fielding all their questions. With unobtrusive wire-rimmed glasses and a no-fuss short hairstyle of the type that was called a "pixie cut" when I was in grade school, she radiates cheerful efficiency, intelligence, and a passion for putting food by that she first explored as a girl on a midwestern farm.

These days, in urban Philadelphia, she still grows, bottles, cans, dries, and otherwise lays up a store of food through the summer months that makes her about as self-sufficient as a city-dweller can be. Her focus on getting the food into jars without unnecessary fuss has led her to develop quick-and-dirty methods for preserves that are safe, simple, and delicious. Her marmalade method (she would call it the goats' method) eliminates several of the most time-consuming steps in the standard process.

But there's nothing haphazard about Wolfe's approach to food safety. She's well-versed in the fine points of botulism prevention and has amplified her own expertise with a serious pursuit of the technical and scientific information that underlies the craft of canning. She also understands the social side; at her workshop I enjoyed the anticipated pleasure of standing over a cutting board, cheerfully chatting and chopping with my classmates, and sharing tastes of new-made jams and pickles. When the three days were up, I thought I was getting a sense of who's getting into canning, and why.

Making raspberry jam at Risa Strauss' canning workshop at the Kiever Synagogue.

But back in Toronto, I realized I had only seen the tip of the jamming and pickling iceberg; it's not only about middle-aged cooks, for instance. A bike ride in a crashing downpour later the same summer was the prelude to a class with quite a different demographic mix. The occasion was "Jam Making and Canning 101," one of eight courses offered by educator and environmentalist Risa Alyson Strauss in a Jewish Urban Homesteading Workshop Series at the Kiever Synagogue, a dynamic institution with a long history in Kensington Market, in the heart of Toronto's downtown core.

Strauss is the program director at Kavanah Garden, an educational organic garden in nearby Vaughan, Ontario. Boasting degrees in comparative religious studies and contemporary Jewish environmental ethics, she's instilling curiosity and cooking skills into a generation of downtowners who certainly didn't grow up making pickles at bubby's (grandmother's) knee. Slender, bright-eyed, and imbued with a passionate energy, Strauss says she sees several motivations in the urge to preserve food.

"[The participants] at most of our workshops are in their twenties and thirties, and they certainly have a do-it-yourself mentality," she says. "For me, growing up in a suburban community, everything came from somewhere else: your food, your clothes, your home were all made by someone else. For me, the whole thing in the past few years has been to go in the opposite direction. I think people are drawn to that because it's highly empowering."

Light on science and safety queries, this class was high on community spirit; Strauss led the eight participants in the tiny, steamy kosher kitchen through the making of raspberry and rhubarb jam while tales were told of brewing dandelion wine and of concocting red wine in the bathtub. Everyone went home with warm jars, some vowing to make more for themselves; others clearly more interested in the exploration than the destination.

Of course, in many places, home canning never went out of style. On farms and in small towns, canning competitions have always been part of the fall fair. Even some urban families still have their rituals, like my friend Elsie, who makes her Ukrainian family's dill pickles (p. 186) every year: now, pickling with her grandchild, she's working on a five-generation tradition. And if you grew up in farming country, preserving is in your blood.

In my curiosity to visit someplace where jams and jellies have never gone out of fashion, I found myself on a five-hour bus trip heading east out of Vancouver, British Columbia, en route to Summerland in the Okanagan Valley, fruit supplier to western Canada for the past century or so. For a central Canadian like me, the entire trip was exciting: my ears popped nonstop as we threaded our way up, over, and between impressive slopes that I would certainly call mountains (although the local passengers referred to them as "hills").

Paul and Rochelle Henbury.

There was no more awe-provoking scenery than the Okanagan itself; the deep glacial lake is a massive trench gouged out of the landscape as if by a titan's finger; the shore that rises up steeply on each side provides a unique climate for tree fruits and, most recently, the wine grapes that have caused the region to be recognized as one of Canada's rare wine appellations.

It was cherry season when I got there, and my friends Paul and Rochelle Henbury were (like the rest of the British Columbia population, apparently) snacking on buckets of them. Although they are also professional musicians, Paul and Rochelle moved from Vancouver to the Okanagan to pursue their careers in British Columbia's vibrant food and wine industries. (Rochelle is at Sumac Ridge, one of the larger wineries that bottles only local grapes with the VQA designation of quality.)

Blossom fruit stand in the Okanagan Valley: Melinda Polesello (right) and her mother Alice Polesello (left).

When I stepped into their home, they threw open a cupboard lined with jars—how could you live in a place literally surrounded by orchards and not catch the canning bug? Rochelle grew up on a Canadian prairie farm, but Paul was a Montrealer who wasn't really exposed to jamming and pickling until he began to work in restaurants. Now it's a big part of their lives, and at any meal, they're likely to pop open a lid to add some fresh-canned preserves to the list of ingredients.

Paul and Rochelle take me to the fruit stand known as Blossom, an Okanagan fixture since 1956, owned by the Polesello family, who grow cherries, apricots, peaches, plums, and a plethora of apples for sale, along with tomatoes, peppers, squash, and gourds. While young men harvest the cherries from a tree just outside the shop, daughter Melinda Polesello takes some time to speak to me, although the phone keeps ringing because her customers all want to know when the flats of strawberries will be arriving so they can make their jam.

"The older people never wavered," says Polesello. "But the forty-year-olds are now thinking they're all healthy—I call it the wannabe-a-foodie craze. They're just realizing for the first time that there are all those preservatives in their food—they're really educating themselves. Men as well as women are doing the preserving; it's a household thing, which I think is exciting, and the men are so proud of themselves ... it's really fabulous!"

I'm beginning to see the image, as each anecdote fills in a little bit more of the picture, of a real social sea change. Throughout the late twentieth century, while some people learned how to can fruit and vegetables from their mothers and grandmothers, and never stopped, many more lost the skill as they grew older, or never learned it at all. Just in the nick of time—as it was getting harder to buy crates of sauce tomatoes and buckets of cherries—the pendulum has swung back, and people are suddenly jamming and pickling with passion, for a whole series of convoluted (or should I say "canvoluted"?) reasons.

The evidence isn't merely anecdotal: in December 2008, the Nielsen Company reported "Canning Supplies" to be the fastest growing product category for big retailers like Walmart. From November 2007 to November 2008, US sales of canning and freezing supplies rose in dollar figures by 53.1 percent, from $6,570,566 to $10,062,285, and unit sales rose by 40.2 percent—that's a lot of Mason jars. In November 2009, Nielsen reported the figures had risen again, by 27.6 percent in dollar sales and by

10.7 percent in unit volume. This took place as the beginning of a worldwide recession was sending almost every other industry down the drain!

In fact, there may be a connection; in May of 2009, Nielsen's senior vice president for shopper and consumer insights, Todd Hale, wrote that: "The recession gripping the US has prompted many families to eat in and to entertain at home, and in many ways, return to basics in an effort to save money. Many analysts are predicting that the changes being witnessed in consumer behavior will be permanent."

In the same month, Julia Moskin of *The New York Times* dining section called attention to the growth in home canning with a piece that quoted preserving guru Eugenia Bone (author of a beloved cookbook called *Well Preserved*) as well as numerous other amateur and professional preservers across the US. She concluded that the new wave of canning popularity "fits neatly into the modern renaissance of handcrafted food, heirloom agriculture, and using food in its season. Like baking bread or making a slow-cooked tomato sauce, preserving offers primal satisfactions and practical results."

Canada's *Globe and Mail* published a similar piece by Hayley Mick in September of 2009, which found that, in Canada too, "the new breed of canner is driven by politics as much as practicality. A desire to eat locally and regain control over what goes into our food is fueling a resurgence in farmers' markets and backyard kitchen gardens. Many see canning as a necessary step toward having year-round access to produce from their own region." The following month, the venerable *Wall Street Journal* turned its eye to the subject with a piece by Ana Campoy in which she marveled at the numbers of people signing up for canning classes nationally and praised the flavor of a batch of peach preserves she made herself in a workshop.

Then, in March 2010 (to judge by numerous blog posts that followed), yet another Seattle food writer, Sara Dickerman, managed to peeve a number of dedicated jammers and picklers with an article on Slate.com that called home canning "ridiculously trendy" and quipped somewhat patronizingly that "[i]t's cute that a practice once associated with grandmothers, 4-H-ers, zealous gardeners with too many cucumbers, and the occasional survivalist, is now a litmus test for gourmandism." While admitting that homemade preserves can be pretty and appealing, Dickerman called pro-preserving rhetoric "overwrought," pointing out that many home canning projects end up being far from frugal, and that for the most part, canners only produce "high-sugar, high-acid foods like jellies, jams, chutneys, or pickles—in other words, condiments."

This argument fails to sway the enthusiasm of the thousands of canning converts who are relearning the seasonal cycles of winter citrus, summer berries, autumn apples ... and possibly even foraging like Katrinka for violets. (At least, this was the case for me and three of my Toronto friends when we discovered a sensational recipe for Wild Violet Jelly, see p. 96.)

But Dickerman does have a point. Even canning diva Eugenia Bone asks rhetorically (in the *NY Times* piece), "How much jam and dill pickles can a person get through?" There was a time, now long passed, when home food preserving was necessary for survival. But why should we be bringing it back in the twenty-first century?

Deep, deep in the human imagination lies the awareness that many of our favorite and most vital foods are available for only a few months, or weeks, or even days of the year. Many of our oldest myths, poems, songs, and stories revolve around this. It took tens of thousands of years of trial and error for humans to discover how to make fresh produce keep its flavor, color, and nutritional value in storage through the lean months.

The ancient Greeks and Romans knew all about preserving fruit in honey and wine. Europeans of the Middle Ages built on this knowledge and added new information about the salt curing of fish and meats. European settlers to North America apparently learned from the First Nations peoples how to make long-lasting cakes from fruit that was boiled and then spread out to dry, later to be reconstituted by cooking—sort of an early fruit leather. If so, they were actually reconnecting with much more ancient knowledge that could have arrived with the very earliest nomadic North Americans.

But since the Industrial Revolution, people have become somewhat cushioned from the anxious need to put food by. In most of the industrialized world, we've changed from being mainly rural to mainly urban dwellers. A century or so ago, it was normal for most people to know something about growing vegetables, catching fish, raising chickens, making jam, and so on; now these are almost lost arts. Today, most food production and processing is handled by large companies.

Over these past two centuries, we've eagerly explored the application of technology to the challenge of food preservation. There have been enormous gains along the way. Commercial food producers have helped reduce disease; they've made a wider variety of foods available to consumers, and they've made it feasible to feed large urban populations that simply can't produce all their own food for themselves.

We have confidence in processes like pasteurizing, vacuum-packaging, and freeze-drying; we have access to extremely efficient chemical preservatives. The enormous availability of relatively cheap electrical power gives most residents of the developed world an effective home refrigerator. We can transport huge quantities of food from remote places within hours (albeit at a huge cost to the environment), so that my local grocery store in Toronto routinely stocks apples, garlic, and other fresh produce grown in China.

How unimaginable would that have been at any other time from prehistory until the mid-twentieth century! Not so long ago, and for centuries, every household and community had to move fast to preserve fruits, vegetables, grains, meat, fish, and dairy foods in season, enough to last for the rest of the year or the length of a long-distance voyage. Until the 1700s, sailors at sea would start to die of scurvy—a dreadful disease—three months out of port, when their bodily store of vitamin C was depleted. We can be thankful that we live in a time when the importance of nutrition to health is better understood.

However, in losing the urgent need to put food by for later use, we've also lost touch with the personality and special characteristics of much of the food we eat. If you doubt this, try to name the dates when various fruits and vegetables come into season in your neck of the woods. I have handed city children fresh wild raspberries only to be asked whether it's safe to eat something that grew on a bush and might have dirt on it. This seems sad to me—I had so much fun foraging for wild blueberries and raspberries as a child. And if you've ever tasted tiny, tangy wild strawberries, it's hard to love the giant, misshapen, and bland commercial ones.

The best fruits and vegetables are generally the ones you pick and eat when they've just come to ripeness, preferably early in the morning when they're perky with dew, and before the sun has had a chance to fatigue them. Naturally, there are exceptions, like ice-wine grapes and certain apples that ripen in storage—which raises a key point: the more intimately you know your food, the better you'll eat. The convenience and efficiency of having someone else handle our food supply do not come without a cost.

From ancient times until the nineteenth century, except perhaps in the homes of the very rich, fruit and vegetable preserves were made within the household, generally under the supervision of the "lady of the house." During the nineteenth century, as the middle class grew, more families moved into the expanding cities. Household conveniences multiplied, and the male and female heads of the household gradually passed their roles as food preservers (and cooks, and cleaners, and keepers of animals) first to servants and then to businesses.

Between about 1850 and 1950, almost every formerly domestic task was taken over in one way or another by the companies that manufactured sewing and washing machines, factory-made clothing, packaged brand-name cleansers and other household products, and, of course, canned and bottled foods. Around 1900, with increasing improvements to commercial food manufacturing and rising concerns about public health, home preserving began to fall out of favor, especially in cities. The thrifty years of the Depression and the rationing of World War II brought some home preserving back in vogue. However, the convenience-and-technology-obsessed boom years that followed soon put home jamming and pickling equipment back on the shelf (so to speak). In the 1960s and '70s, back-to-the-landers revived these skills, but by the "me-first" '80s, home food production had dropped out of vogue for urbanites.

Now, the home-canning pendulum is swinging back again. On the west coast of North America, "there's definitely a growth in canning as an activity, a new enthusiasm for it," says Anya Fernald. "I think the drivers are taste and quality. We've all become interested in local food and supporting local farmers, but there's also the ability to take it to the next level. How do you make it more interesting and exciting? There's a desire to connect with food making."

"It's a logical progression with the whole local movement and people being interested in where their food comes from," says Tigress. "Even people who don't grow their own food want to eat in season and buy from farmers. That movement has been going on for at least a full decade, and if you're trying to eat in season or locally, how do you do that for the other six months out of the year?"

Growing up on a farm, Katie Quinn-Jacobs of IthaCan learned how to can foods. Now, as a community organizer, she uses that knowledge to help promote what she refers to as "energy defence." For her, preserving local food in season is one part of a whole series of activities that will help the world reduce unnecessary reliance on fossil fuels, with all their attendant ills. "Lowering our carbon footprint, and the fact that we're past the time when fossil resources like oil and gas are easily available—that's really what drives me to do this, because that's where we're going to go. If we can do this work now, it will make it easier later on down the road," she says.

In Toronto, Risa Strauss hopes to move out of the city and build a farming community with others who share her faith and values. "There's a line in [the Book of Genesis] where God told Adam that he must work the land and protect it," she says, quoting the words in Hebrew. "To me, anything that allows me to work the land more sustainably is observing that double commandment. You can take from the land, and you can also preserve it. To me, preserving food is honoring that commandment."

Dana Harrison of Well Preserved observes that "a lot of this has coincided with this horrible economic crap that everyone talks about. It's interesting, because I came out of school during a recession, and great things seem to come out of [recessions]; you have to be really creative. In 2000 or 2001, people were obsessed with beautiful boutique hotels and drinking Grey Goose vodka; I was doing work on condo marketing during the crazy housing boom. Then those things came to a halt, and when you take away some of the things that people can buy, you're left with authenticity and genuine experience. Economic crisis or whatever—I like it."

Joel MacCharles posits that "a lot of people probably got into [food preservation] at first thinking perhaps they could save some money and were then surprised that it became an entertainment. When I'm making a blueberry jam with maple syrup, I'm not saving money, but you can't buy it. In some cases, it's to achieve a taste that you can't get otherwise."

Kim O'Donnel is another canning proponent who believes the vaunted thriftiness of canning may be a red herring. "A lot of people have asked me over the last year, 'Do you think it saves money?', and I don't think it does, right off the bat," she says. "I think the savings are more long run than short run."

The benefits, in her view, are less tangible; she sees food quality as one of the strongest attractions of canning. "It allows more control over what you are eating," she says. "Here in the US we have a food-safety scare practically once a week, and people are more aware, or they are trying to reduce their sodium or their sugar or be as local as they can. This is their opportunity to know what's going into that jar."

Like Harrison and MacCharles, she also sees it as part of the broader yearning for a simpler life. "Canning forces you to slow down. You have no choice. You want to talk about slow food? This is it, kid," she says. "You need to block out three hours. There's no multi-tasking. Canning is not cooking; it's processing, so you can't wing it, and it requires your full attention. The TV must not be on, and it's probably a good idea to share the labor with another person or two.

"I think it's important to incorporate it into your life as a practice. I actually equate it with my yoga practice: it forces me to step away from my technology and connect with that moment in time when the berries are ripe or the cucumbers are there," she continues. "I think there's some huge, and not only therapeutic, benefit. A lot goes into that jar; you're capturing a moment, a feeling ... When you cook, you put the food out and it's consumed, but when you open that jar, you could be consuming a particular moment in time."

MacCharles would agree: "When I spend a fabulous weekend with the people that I love, that jar lasts a year, and when I open the jar, I think about Dana, our dog, our friends, and everything we did that weekend," he says. "It's a way to create a future memory, and that memory will tie in the warmth of summer with the cold of winter."

Gastronomical, economical, environmental, political, spiritual, and sensual: the reasons to take up canning are many and diverse. Which begs the question ...

What Kind of

Thrifty Householder. Your response to global recession—or your own household finances—has been to tighten your belt, but creatively. You've become the expert in repurposing everything from empty yogurt containers to worn-out jeans. You'll get a lot of satisfaction from collecting used jars and putting up Tomato Sauce (p. 172) for about a buck a quart. You'll enjoy salvaging something that would otherwise go to waste by making Pickled Watermelon Rind (p. 160), and you'll be pleased to create a delicious Mint Jelly (p. 144) with the one kitchen herb that literally grows like a weed.

Crafty DIYer. Your winter kit includes hand-knitted wrist warmers and way too many scarves. Every piece of furniture in the house has a homemade throw pillow, and you've tiled the kitchen backsplash ... twice. You'll not only want to make your own Candied Ginger (p. 233) to put into your Rhubarb Apricot Conserve (p. 88), but you'll beautifully decorate enough jars to give away as wedding favors (p. 252).

Foodie. Some of the vinegar you own is older than your mother, you can tell the difference between a terrine, a mousse, and a rillette, and you're badly hooked on David Lebovitz's blog about "living the sweet life in Paris." So you'll get a kick out of discovering the perfect cheese to pair with Lemon, Fig, and Lavender Marmalade (p. 227). You'll love to have a jar of Baco Noir Wine Jelly (p. 230) on hand to add body to a jus or reduction, and you'll start to get panicky if you don't make enough Vanilla Sour Cherry Preserves (p. 139) to use in all the clafoutis you intend to bake over the winter.

Culinary Historian. Your cooking repertoire includes syllabub, negus, and Simnel cake, and if you're not tending a Regency-style herb garden complete with dye plants, medicinal herbs, and edibles, it's only because your balcony just isn't big enough. You'll want to master Victorian-Style Seville Orange Marmalade (p. 190), the pioneers' ingenious Sumac Jelly (p. 145), and the traditional New England chutney known as Gen's Pickle (p. 168).

Canner Are You?

Veggie Gardener. If winter for you means perusing the seed catalogues, and spring sees you tending indoor seedlings, then summer probably means "Help! What do I do with all these zucchini?" Well, you could turn them into Indian Spiced Zucchini Pickle (p. 155). Meanwhile, you could can Pickled Beets with Fennel (p. 156) and turn those exciting Red Dragons into proper Fiery Carrots (p. 211).

Homesteader. If your goal is to get off the grid and live off the land, you'll want to be making your own Apple Pectin (p. 69) for jam while putting up large quantities of fruit Preserves (pages 135 to 141) and relying on classic no-fuss recipes like Dill Pickled Beans (p. 154) and Crabapple Jelly (p. 179).

Urban Forager. A city dweller with a pioneer heart, you can't believe how many edibles can be harvested in the nearest parking lot. You'll find it no chore to collect the flowers for Dandelion Jelly (p. 95), Wild Violet Jelly (p. 96), or Lilac Jelly (p. 98), or to get permission to pick fruit off your neighbor's tree for Apple Chutney (p. 166) or Cinnamon Yellow Plum Jam (p. 124).

Locavore. In your perfect world, farmers are paid decently to produce nourishing food that reaches people of all income levels with a minimal carbon footprint, and if it wasn't for coffee, you'd probably be living on the 100-Mile Diet. From April to October, all your produce comes from your local farmer's market or your CSA, if you don't grow it yourself. Depending where you live, you may be passionate about Pickled Fiddlehead Ferns (p. 105) or Saskatoonberry Jam (p. 121). You're likely devoted to the apple that reflects your particular zone—be that Idared, McIntosh, Ambrosia, or Cortland—for your annual dose of Applesauce (p. 183), and of course you'll source wine for jelly (pages 229 to 232) according to your own *terroir*.

Citizen of the World. You can name your favorite Buddhist vegetarian restaurant, the ingredients in callaloo, and a shop that sells *nam pla*. You won't have any trouble assembling the ingredients for Yuzu Marmalade (p. 199), Lemongrass, Ginger, and Kaffir Lime Jelly (p. 204), Thai-inspired Spicy Pickled Veggies (p. 164), or Buddha's Hand Marmalade (p. 202).

The Twelve Months

People are drawn to home canning for many reasons; clearly, an interest in local and seasonal foods is only one of them. However, almost everyone who develops an interest in making jams, jellies, and pickles ends up getting to know when their favorite produce is in season and would rather wait for local fruits to ripen than waste time canning food that was picked under-ripe and shipped across a continent on a truck.

So an interest in local food is a gateway to home canning, and vice versa. Let me go further, and be perhaps the first to propose a name for a new movement: sustainable shopping. Of course, I'm not the first to use it. By May of 2007 there was already a "Sustainable Shopping Guide" on Blogspot, and the general idea dates back much, much farther.

For instance, food historian Elizabeth Abbott describes in her book *Sugar: A Bittersweet History* how nineteenth-century British housewives helped close down the slave trade by insisting on purchasing only sugar produced without slave labor. I'm old enough to remember César Chávez and the 1970s boycott of California grapes to support farm workers in their protest against the use of toxic pesticides, as well as the boycott of South Africa's Granny Smith apples to protest apartheid. But sustainable shopping isn't only about refusing to buy certain products we're told to avoid: it's much more importantly about making conscious choices whenever we shop.

How far does your food travel to reach you? What conditions was it grown under? Who produced it, and how were they paid and treated? Did its cultivation leave the land or sea it came from in a spoiled and toxic state or refreshed and ready to grow again? And is that food fresh—is it nourishing, does it taste great?

When we start to ask these questions, we begin to effect change. We can truly vote with our grocery budget. In recent years, we've seen government regulators and corporations taking notice of the outcry against trans-fats and the desire to eat more organic food, more local food, and food with less packaging.

In June 2009, Ipsos Marketing reported on a survey of about 1,000 people in each of eighteen countries. When asked what priorities they wanted food producers to focus on, the respondents named fresher ingredients, extra health benefits, and more environmentally friendly packaging. We get what we ask for when we read labels and spend our money accordingly. When you start to ask where your strawberries were grown, when you stop buying tomatoes out of season, when you join a Community Supported Agriculture (CSA) program to buy food from a local farmer, when you pay a little more to buy organic produce, you are sending a message that will be heard.

In September 2010, Melissa A. Click of the University of Missouri and Ronit Ridberg of the Friedman School of Nutrition, Science, and Policy at Tufts University published a study in the journal *Environmental Communication* titled "Saving Food: Food Preservation as Alternative Food Activism." Click and Ridberg surveyed 143 men and 759 women in the US who were interested in food preserving. The subjects were recruited through online networks and organizations that promote food justice, slow food, and so on, so the study was bound to reach a somewhat specific niche (more than ninety percent were university-educated; more than half of these had done at least some graduate work, for instance). Still, the findings were interesting.

The respondents named three top motivations for food preserving: "to know and control what's in my food," "it tastes better," and "to eat more locally and sustainably." They also talked about the ways that food preserving offers other pleasures, like recreating food-related memories, spending intimate time with their families and friends, working with their hands and brains, enjoying the sight, smell and taste of their food, feeling pride in the results of their work, and feeling a stronger connection with the natural world, as well as with people in other countries and our shared human past.

The researchers concluded that "[t]he renewed interest in sustainable agriculture suggests we are in the midst of a food revolution ... Our examination of the practices of and motivations for food preservation, using survey and interview data, reveals that food preservation presents an opportunity to move alternative food practices away from an individualistic, consumer-oriented politics to a politics based upon relationships to self, others, and the earth, enabling activists to connect more deeply to the goals of food movements."

The effort it takes to put up a batch of preserves quickly turns a jammer or pickler into a discerning food shopper who's attuned to seasons for local and imported produce. Every recipe book ever written advises the home canner to use the very best possible fruit and vegetables. My friend Elsie won't make her excellent dill pickles unless she finds cucumbers that fit her definition of perfection in every way.

Every fall, Toronto's Italian and Portuguese produce vendors sell hundreds of crates of fresh tomatoes to families canning their own sauce. Not convinced? Try a batch of raspberry jam made in the afternoon with fruit picked that morning. Nothing else compares.

This is the heartbreaking beauty of fruit and flowers, berries, herbs, and vegetables: they are ephemeral and of their own seasons. This is the bittersweet truth that Katrinka understands, and Dobrunka tries to deny, to her peril. To learn about preserving food is one step in learning how precious and perishable it is. It helps us better appreciate the work of those who are trying to make food systems saner, whether they're doing it through organic and biodynamic growing practices, better food labeling, school nutrition programs, documentary filmmaking, or any one of a dozen more activist avenues.

Learning about safe food preserving also helps us realize that it would be a mistake to throw out the baby of regulated, large-scale food production with the bathwater of certain thoughtless and short-sighted corporate interests—because scale and efficiency do have their virtues. It would be crazy to dismantle all commercial food production, but we could sure go a long way in making it more sustainable.

Every batch of jelly, every conserve, and every chutney is a little meditation on the precise nature and characteristics of a particular variety of fruit or vegetables: what the scientists would call pH and Brix, and flavonoids, but which we think of as tartness, sweetness, and a range of less definable qualities that, in February, let the bouquet of a just-opened jar of strawberry jam take you back to a particular sparkling June day when you were eight and summer vacation seemed to last a little lifetime.

If for no other reason than the memories you can savor, it's worth learning how to can a basket of plums or tomatoes. We no longer need to do it in order to survive, but we may find there's more than sugar and fruit in a humble jar of jam. There's also flavor, of course, and satisfaction, and possibly (though not necessarily) thrift. There may even be a little bit of wisdom.

2: How to Stay Out of Hot Water: Basics of Hot Water Bath Preserving

A is for Acid: A Food Safety Primer

First, the tough stuff. There are only two ways to kill off the hardy bacterium known as *Clostridium botulinum,* which produces the potentially fatal botulism toxin and enjoys airless environments like the inside of vacuum-sealed glass jars. One way is to heat the entire contents of the jar to at least 240°F (115°C) for a certain period of time. This cannot be done in regular boiling water, which only reaches 212°F (100°C).

The other way is to make sure the contents of the jar are highly acidic. To be specific, they must have a pH level of 4.6 or less. (Higher pH is lower-acid and vice versa.) High-acid foods include most northern fruits, including apples, stone fruits, and most berries. (Citrus is also high-acid, but tomatoes are on the borderline of safety.) A recipe that combines high-acid fruits with sugar or vinegar is likely to be safe for hot water-bath canning, and should keep in a properly sealed jar for at least one year.

However, some tropical fruits and most vegetables are low-acid. They must be combined with higher-acid foods, or immersed in vinegar to bring up their acid levels. For this reason, it's safest to use commercially bottled types of vinegar or lemon juice for home canning, because these are less likely to vary in their acidity. (Read the label before you buy vinegar for pickles; it should be at least five percent acid.) It's also important not to change the proportions of high- and low-acid ingredients in any preserving recipe and to use up-to-date recipes that conform to the most recent scientific understanding of the situation.

Recipes that contain other ingredients, such as meat and oils, cannot be safely canned in a water-bath canner at all. There is another process called pressure canning, which heats food to a higher temperature, but this requires different and more costly equipment, and is a little trickier.

Now, the better news. Generally speaking, besides botulism, all the other organisms that are likely to be present in jars of food can be kept at bay with a few simple rules:

• Wash jars, lids, and produce before using them.
• Process filled jars by boiling them in hot water for the length specified in your recipe.
• Try to use up most food in sealed jars within one year.

Of course, if a jar has not sealed properly, or has been opened, it must be kept in the refrigerator and consumed within a few days or weeks, just like any other food in an open container.

The Magic of Boiling Water Canning

Here's how modern water-bath canning works: sterilized jars are filled with prepared food. A two-part lid is then screwed onto the jar, but only loosely. When the filled jar is placed in a pot of water that's brought to the boiling point, two things happen. First, most types of molds and bacteria in the jar are killed off by the heat. Second, the heated contents of the jar expand and push most of the air out (that's why the lid must be loose; if it's too tight, the jar can explode). When the jar is removed from the water, it cools, the contents contract again, and the lid is sucked down tightly and effectively vacuum-seals the jar so no new toxins can enter.

Although safe canning does mean following rules, would-be canners needn't be unreasonably fearful of poisoning themselves or others. On the whole, learning to can should be no scarier than learning to swim or change a light bulb. As California-based artisanal jam-maker June Taylor told the *Wall Street Journal,* "Once you know what you're doing ... the only way you're going to harm someone with jam is if you throw a jar and it hits them in the head."

What Kind of Equipment Do You Need?

Besides the jars themselves, with appropriate lids, not much equipment is needed for water-bath canning, and almost all of it (e.g., knives, spoons, dish towels, and measuring cups) can be found in any household kitchen. The most important specialized tool is a JAR LIFTER, which can be bought inexpensively at any hardware, houseware, or kitchen store that sells canning supplies. (Tip: Pick up the jars with the rubberized end of the lifter—a surprising number of very intelligent people have been known to use them backward for the first few years!)

It's often worthwhile to invest in the standard canning kit that includes the jar lifter plus a FUNNEL that fits the top of the jars, TONGS, and a doodad (usually called a "wand") with a magnet on the end for fishing jar lids out of hot water. I treasure my funnel (in fact, I have an elegant metal one instead of the standard-issue plastic), and I do use the tongs, but I don't use the wand because I put my bands and lids into a basket strainer before immersing them in the hot water. (Many people heat up their jar lids in a small pot of water.)

You also need a large pot called a CANNER. You can buy them in various sizes; they normally come with a lid and a WIRE RACK to protect the jars from excessive heat on the bottom of the pot and from getting knocked about. In theory, you could also lift the jars out with the rack, but I have never liked the thought of holding up a heavy wire rack of glass jars full of boiling water.

Anyone who cans a lot of food will want to own the biggest canner available for processing large batches of items like tomato sauce. However, to save energy, I often use a smaller enamel pot. If you have no wire rack, you can tie together a number of metal jar bands and set them on the bottom; you can even simply line the bottom of the pot with a dish towel or, in a pinch, a layer of metal cutlery. There are also soft plastic mats with fingerlike jar holders, but I've never used one.

For cooking the food itself before it's put into jars, you need a large NON-REACTIVE POT WITH A THICK BOTTOM that distributes heat well. Copper and heavy enamel both do this very well; aluminum, lightweight enamel, and glass do not. Stainless steel pots are best if they have a copper-lined bottom. Any size pot can be used, but a wide, shallow pot allows the food to cook more efficiently than a narrow, tall one. Sugar mixtures can almost double in size while they're boiling, so the pot must be bigger than you might think.

There are specialized pots for cooking up your preserves known as "preserving pans," "preserving kettles," or "Maslin pans" that flare from a narrow bottom to wider top, usually with a wire handle on top and a pouring lip. These are available through higher-end cooking equipment stores and are a nice luxury.

Since fruit preserves and pickles are highly acidic, any pot used to cook them should be made of a "non-reactive" material such as stainless steel or glass rather than cast iron, aluminum, regular steel, or uncoated copper. This is because acid and salt can damage the pot itself. Another side effect is that the metal may cause the food to change color.

Worse news: reactive pots can also release toxic substances into the food. Non-stick pots and enamel pots are fine as long as they're unscratched. Uncoated copper pans are safe with sugar-based foods, but can leach unsafe amounts of copper into brine and vinegar, so they should not be used for pickling. Modern copper pans are usually coated on the inside, so they are okay unless scratched, but it's best to err on the safe side.

Essential Canning Tools Checklist

- canner with inner wire rack, big enough to immerse at least six jars
- wide, deep non-reactive pot with a thick bottom
- glass jars with two-piece lids and bands
- jar lifter and/or tongs
- funnel that fits jar mouths
- strainer basket and small pot for heating jar lids
- dish towels
- measuring cups and spoons
- knives and cutting board for chopping fruit and vegetables
- wooden spoons
- large metal spoon or ladle or heatproof cup with handle
- assorted extra bowls and/or plates

(for some recipes)

- extra cooking pots
- grater(s) or zester
- wood or plastic knife or chopstick
- jelly bag, muslin or cheesecloth
- sieve(s) or strainer(s) or a food mill

Tools That May Come in Handy:

- colander
- kitchen scale
- rubber spatula
- magnetic lid wand
- candy thermometer
- fork(s)

- scissors
- carrot peeler
- cherry pitter
- nutcracker
- mortar and pestle or coffee/spice grinder

- cookie sheet(s) and muffin tins
- extra glass jars
- turkey baster (for making jelly)
- slow cooker (for chutney-style recipes)

- other types of chopping tools, such as a mezza-luna (a knife with a curved blade), a mandoline (a special type of slicer), or a food processor
- potholders

How to Sterilize Jars

These days, expert sources advise that it's okay not to sterilize your jars, but only if you fully process them once they've been filled with food. You should still wash all jars and lids before use. I sterilize mine in any case, because they still need to be heated up so they don't shatter when you fill them with hot food.

It's a good idea to sterilize a few more jars than you think you'll need. Try to include at least one that's a smaller size than the rest, in case you don't quite have enough preserves at the bottom of the pot to fill your last jar completely. Also, prepare a few extra bands in case one or two turn out to be slightly bent and refuse to screw neatly onto the jars.

- Wash the jars, bands, and lids in hot, soapy water. Rinse them and allow them to air-dry. Set clean, empty jars (without lids) upright on the wire rack in the canner. They shouldn't be stacked or crowded too tightly or they'll break.

- Cover the jars with water, to a level at least 1 in (2.5 cm) over the top of the tallest jar.

- Cover the canner with its lid and bring it to a boil. This may take as long as thirty minutes. To speed it up, start the pot with water that's hot from the faucet. However, never put cold jars into a very hot pot; they must warm gradually or they'll break. (This is a good time to start preparing the food to be preserved.)

- When the water has reached a full, rolling boil, start timing. Allow the jars to remain in the canner for a full ten minutes by the clock at a full, rolling boil. (Add one extra minute for every 1,000 ft/305 m above sea level.)

- The jars are now sterile. Place sufficient lids and bands into a pot of water and heat them up almost, but not quite, to the boiling point. Otherwise, put the lids into a basket strainer or some other con tainer that will allow them to sit in the hot (but not boiling) water in the canner itself.

- Put the lid back on the canner, turn off the heat, and finish preparing the food to be preserved.

How to Process Food in a Hot Water Bath

When your jam, jelly, chutney, pickle, or whatever else is ready, it must be processed in hot water. The amount of processing time depends on the size of the jars as well as the type and density of the food to be processed. Check the recipe to find out how long it should boil. Here's how you do it:

- Lift the sterilized jars carefully out of the hot water and pour the water out. Most of the water should go back into the canner, but when the filled jars go back in they'll take up more space than the empty jars, so you can usually pour at least one or two cups of water into the sink.

- Fill each jar with food, leaving between ¼ and ½ in (6 mm and 1 cm) of space at the top, according to the recipe. Avoid touching the rims of the jars. The proper funnel is invaluable here, as it makes it easy to keep the rims of the jars clean.

- Gently wipe any food spills off the rims with a clean, damp cloth so they don't spoil the seal, and place a lid on each jar. Avoid touching the lids; instead, use the magnetic wand or tongs if possible. Screw on the bands, but only fingertip-tight; hot air must be able to escape from the jars when they go back into the canner.

- Set the filled jars upright in the canner. Again, they should not be stacked or leaning, and they should not touch too closely. It is normal for them to release a lot of bubbles when they hit the water. This does not mean that the water is boiling.

- Adjust the level of the water so the jars are covered with at least 1 in (2.5 cm) of water, but the canner isn't full enough to boil over. Turn the heat up and replace the lid.

- When the water reaches a full, rolling boil, start timing, and boil the jars for as long as the recipe speci fies (which can be anywhere between about ten and ninety minutes). If you live 1,000 to 3,000 ft/305 to 915 m above sea level, add five minutes processing time. Above 3,000 ft/915 m, add ten minutes; above 6,000 ft/1,830 m, add fifteen minutes, and add twenty minutes for altitudes from 8,000 to 10,000 ft/2,440 to 3,050 m above sea level.

- Use the jar lifter to remove jars from the canner one at a time and place them on a heat-resistant surface, on a layer of newspaper or a dishtowel. Do not tilt the jars, and do not touch them or try to tighten the lids for at least twelve hours. (There's no need to dry them, as the pool of water on the lid will quickly evaporate.) Expect to hear a loud, startling pop (or "ping") from each jar as the cooling process sucks the lid tight against the jar.

- When the jars are cool, test the tops. If a top is loose or can be popped in and out, there is no seal. Refrigerate the jar and use it right away. (You can open it, check that the rim is clean and unchipped, and reprocess it. However, in the case of pickles, you may need to top up the brine. In the case of jam or marmalade, you risk changing the consistency if you reprocess it.)

- Remove the rings from the jars and wash both jars and rings to remove any food drips, which could cause mold under the ring later. Many people store jars without the rings so that they know for sure if the seal fails. Replace the ring or use a plastic lid after the jar has been opened.

- Label the jar with contents and date. Properly sealed jars will keep food fresh for anything from a few weeks to several years, depending on the contents. Most jams, jellies, and pickles will last for one year.

How to Choose Safe Recipes for Water-bath Canning

Many recipes that are unsafe in a simple water bath are fine after processing in a pressure canner. The problem is that, unless you are a qualified food scientist, you won't likely be able to guess how much vinegar will bring the onions, peppers, and mangoes in that online chutney recipe down to a safe pH. So when you want to start experimenting, how can you be sure you won't poison yourself and your loved ones?

There are two outstanding sources of completely trustworthy, safe canning recipes.

- The US National Center for Home Food Preservation, funded by the Department of Agriculture, maintains a comprehensive website with a wealth of essential canning information, including basic recipes, at *Uga.edu/nchfp.*

- Jarden, the company that manufactures most of the canning jars sold in North America, publishes a frequently updated guide called *The Ball Blue Book of Preserving* (in the US) and *The Bernardin Guide to Home Preserving* (in Canada), as well as a more extensive book of 400 recipes and safe canning instructions called the *Complete Book of Home Preserving* by Judi Kingry and Lauren Devine, which is sold under the Ball brand name in the US and the Bernardin brand in Canada.

Generally speaking, if you find a canning recipe in a recently published cookbook, it should be safe. But safety standards evolve, and many books still in circulation are perpetuating practices that are no longer considered advisable, like sealing jars with paraffin. Also, historical recipes in old books or family notebooks tend to assume the cook already knows the basic process, so they'll leave out important steps, like processing jars.

And you open yourself up to a world of risk if you start surfing the Internet for recipes. It's very important to remember that not all online canning recipes are tested and safe. Even the most experienced home cooks may not know enough about the chemistry of food preservation to concoct a blend that's sufficiently acid to prevent dangerous toxins from growing in the jars, and many jam, sauce, or pickle recipes are meant to be eaten right away, not stored for a long time. In fact, you'll notice that many reputable recipe sources, such as *jamieoliver.com*, don't even offer canning recipes. (Oliver's strawberry jam is a small-batch recipe that he recommends will "keep for about a week" in the fridge.)

Here are some tips for choosing safe recipes:

- If you're new to canning, don't use recipes from books published before 1990, or from great-aunt Julia's handwritten recipe book, and certainly don't experiment with recipes posted by individuals online, even if you take them from a big website like *Allrecipes.com* or *SimplyRecipes.com.* An exception to this general caution is canning information found on the websites of many North American university "extensions," such as the University of Georgia Cooperative Extension Service and the Oregon State University Extension Service, which are fine sources of scientifically sound canning advice.

- Even if you feel confident that you understand the basic rules of safe canning, you should compare the quantities and proportions of low- and high-acid ingredients in a new recipe to a similar recipe from one of the two reliable sources listed above. If the recipe you're thinking of using has propor tionally more low-acid or less high-acid ingredients, it may not be safe for water-bath canning.

- Don't put up food in jars unless the recipe specifically states that it's meant for water-bath canning. It should end with instructions like "seal the jars and process for fifteen minutes in boiling water."

- Don't try to process recipes containing meat, fish, fats, or oils in a water-bath canner.

- If you love a recipe but suspect it's not safe for canning, make a batch anyway, but don't seal and process the jars. Instead, keep it in the fridge and don't expect it to last more than a few days or (with jam) possibly weeks.

When Good Preserves Turn Bad

Children who grow up by the seaside learn to be aware of the dangerous ebb and flow of the tides; similarly, kids who grow up in a home with a root cellar tend to recognize the signs of spoilage. Toronto baker Kyla Eaglesham (proprietor of the delightful shop named Madeleines, Cherry Pie and Ice Cream) grew up in a small Ontario town where home canning was the norm. She says that, even as a young girl, she knew some jars just weren't safe to open, but she fears many urban dwellers have lost this skill. If you count yourself in this group, here are the main things to watch out for:

S: Smell. If the preserves smell bad in any way—if they remind you of rotten eggs or mold or any other unpleasant thing—get rid of them.

A: Appearance. If the preserves have blackened or dried out or in any other way changed in appearance since the jar was sealed, get rid of them. (However, it is normal for colors to fade evenly over time.)

F: Fizz, fuzz, and film. If the preserves seem fizzy or bubbly, if the brine is cloudy, or if they have developed any kind of moldy growth or fungus, get rid of them.

E: Easy-opening jars. You should encounter resistance when you pry off the lid and hear a sucking-in sound and a pop when it comes off. If air seems to leave the jar when you open it, or if the lid is not firmly sealed, get rid of the contents.

There are some exceptions to these rules (for instance, garlic often turns blue in vinegar), but these are generally noted in recipes. However, the golden rule of canning safety is always: *If in doubt, throw it out!*

It Must be Jelly 'Cause Jam Don't Shake Like That: How to Tell Whether Your Jelly Has Set

Apart from mastering the rules of food safety, the essential skill of a jam-maker is knowing how to tell when it's done. This is much more a matter of feel than timing. As the great chef Georges Auguste Escoffier so aptly put it, "the time allowed for cooking any jam can only be approximately decided, and it is a gross mistake to suppose the case otherwise." This is not just a superstitious remark but a scientific fact.

Normally, a fruit preserve must reach 220°F (105°C), or 8°F (about 5°C) above the boiling point of water (at sea level, water usually boils at 212°F [100°C]). For the same reason, as Annette Cottrell of the blog Sustainable Eats has noted, the weather can also affect how long it takes jams and jellies to hit the gel stage. She explains that, "During cloudy or stormy weather, atmospheric pressure decreases—which means a lower boiling point for water. Although it comes to a boil more rapidly, water boils at a lower temperature so food cooks slower. This explains the old adage that you can't make divinity [fudge] on a cloudy day." Making a larger-than-normal batch also affects the timing because it simply takes longer for the mass to heat; however, a taller, narrower pot allows for quicker boiling than a wider, shallower one. Cottrell says this is because, technically, the tall, thin pot "will increase the pressure placed on the water, giving you a higher boiling temperature." She adds that higher volumes of salt or sugar, or even using harder water, also raise the boiling temperature.

Photo: Niamh Malcolm

Escoffier advises that, whereas a jelly should be boiled down as fast as possible, it's better to cook a whole-fruit jam on lower heat to protect it from burning. It's such a delicate balance; the look, the texture, the taste, and presumably, the nutrients of the tender fruit are broken down if it's cooked too long at a lower heat, but they can also be spoiled by being heated to too high a temperature. Thus, once your jam starts to boil, you should experiment with your stovetop controls to see whether you can keep it boiling at a lower setting. (Fans of the laws of thermodynamics will note that the jam itself will stay the same temperature while it's boiling, but the *bottom of the pot* will heat up and scorch it.)

Certainly, it's worse to burn jam than to make it runny. If this ever happens, you will know right away, because you will smell a sharp caramel scent, and see the mixture start to turn brown before your eyes). It is possible to re-cook and reprocess unset jam that has already been sealed in jars, though there's a risk that this may cause the sugar to crystallize in the cooling jam. The alternative solution for loose jam or jelly is to call it syrup and use it on ice cream and waffles.

Most cookbooks suggest at least one of the following three methods to tell whether your jam, jelly, or marmalade has set and is ready to be funneled into the sterilized jars. I'm here to tell you that there are way more indicators that hardly anyone ever mentions.

The sheeting method: This is the one most cookbooks suggest, but I find it a bit tricky. Pour some of the boiling jam or jelly mixture off the side of your wooden spoon. If it's still liquid, it will drip back in separate droplets. When it has turned to jelly, it will "sheet": that is, the drops will join together and slide back into the pot in a sheet or "flake." The problem is that you need to do this quite a few times before you really feel confident about recognizing the sheeting. A helpful hint: if you have chunks of orange rind, raisins, or whole berries in the mixture, they will likely tend to stick to the spoon at the sheeting stage.

The chilled saucer method: This is probably the second most-frequently recommended way to test cooking jelly. Put a small plate or saucer in the freezer for a few minutes to chill. When it's cold, drop some jelly onto the saucer. It should quickly thicken up, and if you wait a moment or two then wiggle your finger in it, you should see the "skin" wrinkle up.

The temperature method: This is the scientist's way. Use a candy, jelly, or deep-fat thermometer to measure the temperature of the mixture. It should be 8°F (about 5°C) more than the temperature of boiling water at your altitude. As mentioned above, at sea level, water boils at 212°F (100°C), so if you're at sea level, the jelly should be at 220°F (104.5°C). However, barometric pressure changes the boiling point of water: for every 1,000 feet above sea level, water boils at about 2°F (about 1°C) less. It's a good idea to check the accuracy of the thermometer by testing it on boiling water first; remember not to hold it against the bottom of the pot, which will change the reading.

So much for the three usual methods. Here are seven more clues you've probably never heard about!

The volume method: Most good recipes will tell you roughly how many jars to prepare. If you seem to have way more jelly than the jars will hold, don't seal the jars! You probably need to reduce the mixture down quite a bit more.

The steam method: When you begin cooking the fruit-and-sugar mixture, quite a lot of steam will roll out of the pot. When it reaches the setting point, much of the water will have evaporated, and only faint puffs of steam will be released. Once you reach this stage, you shouldn't cook the jelly much longer, because you'll risk making it stiff and sticky when it sets.

The sinking fruit method: When you first mix fruit with sugar syrup, the fruit will float. As it loses moisture and the syrup thickens, the fruit begins to sink into the mixture. If you start to fill your jars but notice you have a bottom layer of syrup and a top layer of floating fruit, your jam may need to be cooked longer.

The surface appearance method: When you first bring jam or jelly to a boil, it looks more or less like boiling water. When it gets close to the setting point, though, the ripples become bigger and rounder, less scum rises up to the top, and the whole surface looks glassy, almost as though it were covered with a layer of clear varnish.

The pectin color method: Fruits that contain a lot of natural pectin tend to turn color when they're heated. They may start out pale green, like gooseberries, or yellow, like golden plums, but when they've cooked enough to turn to jelly, they take on a characteristic brick-pink color. Quinces will even turn a deep ruby red. If you see that change in color, you're probably good to go.

The random drips method: Have you dripped some jam on the counter? Did you skim some of the scum into a saucer? If your random drips and drops of jam have gelled as they cooled, the batch in the pot is probably ready too. But remember, that drip on the hot stove isn't an accurate indicator; instead, look for one that landed in a cool zone.

The best of all methods: My favorite way to test jam is to drip a bit into a clean teaspoon. When it's cool enough, I simply pop it into my mouth. Your tongue will tell you whether you're eating runny syrup or warm jam.

Of course, the most certain way to tell whether jam has reached the setting point is to make dozens of batches. Eventually, you just *know.*

Apple picking in Toronto. Photo: Reena Newman

Plums and cherries at the market in St. Jacobs, Ontario.
Photo: Heringa/Ontario Tourism 2003

About Choosing Fruit and Vegetables

When you are canning, you will generally look for the best and freshest produce you can find. However, in some situations (when making jelly, for instance), the fruit doesn't have to look perfect and can even have insect holes and bruised parts. Consider these points when choosing produce for canning, and balance them according to your priorities.

If you're making jam for gifts (or sale, if that's permitted in your jurisdiction), you probably do need to pick the best quality fresh, local fruit. However, a blend of just slightly underripe and fully ripe fruit will give the best balance of flavor and texture.

Organic produce is a great choice if you can afford it, but don't expect it to look as "perfect" as the commercially grown equivalent.

It's useful to find out what branding marks identify locally grown fruit in your area, read stickers on fruit to find out where produce was grown, and watch out for vendors who (carelessly or intentionally) display imported fruit under a sign that says it's "local."

Generally speaking, recently picked, underripe fruit contains the most pectin.

Photo: Renée Joslyn

Ripe tomatoes at Niagara on the Lake, Ontario. Photo: Ontario Tourism 1998

Farmers and market vendors will often give you a significant price cut if you offer to buy a large quantity of "seconds"—oddly shaped, blemished, overripe, or otherwise iffy produce.

It's a bad idea to buy more fruit or vegetables than you can cook within the next twenty-four hours. Better to pass up a bargain than to compost a bushel of rotting food.

When choosing whether a piece of fruit is good enough to can, ask yourself whether you would eat it as is. If so, there's no reason not to can it, says Audra Wolfe of the blog Doris and Jilly Cook.

Even in the city, you will find lots of fruit and flowers that can be made into jams, jellies, and pickles. However, be certain they have not been sprayed with chemical pesticides, and be extra careful washing them to remove toxins from urban air pollution. (That said, one must recognize that many farms are next to busy highways these days.)

Some citrus fruit is waxed to preserve it and make it look attractive on the fruit stand. Avoid buying waxed fruit if possible; it's very hard to scrub the wax off.

On the subject of worms: what your guests don't know won't hurt them.

The Best Things in Life are Free: About Foraging

Cookbook authors—particularly those from France and England—rhapsodize about gathering dew-kissed hips and haws from the hedgerows, and even residents of the most industrialized urban environments can have fun wild-gathering some edibles from the local landscape, even if it's only a handful of mint from an overgrown empty lot.

I have learned from experience that many homeowners are charmed when you ask permission to make jelly with apples from the tree on their property (jelly is a particularly good choice, because it doesn't call for perfect-looking fruit). Many folks don't realize that fruit from their ornamental crabapple or messy mulberry can be turned into delicious preserves, let alone those dandelions they wish would not bloom so plentifully on their front lawn.

I personally would never pick fruit from a public park, but numerous school, church, or business properties offer opportunities for urban harvesting (with permission, of course). Across North America, individuals and organizations are waking up to the untapped bounty of urban fruit trees, and groups are springing up whose sole purpose is to make that fruit available to city dwellers. Here in Toronto, the group called Not Far From the Tree organizes volunteers to pick fruit from trees on private property, with shares in the yield going to the pickers, the property owners, and local food charities.

Another amenity of my own city is a bylaw banning the use of chemical pesticides and fertilizers, which makes it easier for me to be certain I'm not going to poison anyone with my preserves (a definite faux pas).

Foraging Etiquette
- If someone gives you produce from their garden or property, give them some of the jam or pickles you make from it.
- In the wild, only gather a tiny sample of any plant you find growing.
- Leave some fruit for the birds.

Food Prep Tips

Some canning books, and most standard cookbooks like *The Joy of Cooking*, give detailed advice on peeling, chopping, and slicing all manner of fruits and vegetables. The following basic rules will see you through most operations, however.

- To skin peaches, tomatoes, almonds, onions, and similar foods, dip them into boiling water for about a minute, then into cold water. The skins should slip off easily.
- To skin garlic or cardamom pods, simply crush them under the flat of the knife first.
- The basic rule of chopping any fruit or vegetable is to slice it in half or shave a thin layer off one side first so you have a flat base to work on—then it's easy to cut the object into a series of slices or cubes, and there's less risk of cutting yourself if the item you're chopping stays still while you're slicing into it. Ginger may seem hard to chop, but if you start with a thumb-shaped piece and shave thin slices off each side until it's roughly squared off, then you can peel any remaining skin from each corner and chop as you like.
- If you're trying to achieve a very fine chop, slice the food into medium cubes, then, holding the knife handle with one hand and steadying the pointed end of the blade with the other, rock your knife back and forth over the pile until it reaches the texture you want.
- With fruits that have a large, solid stone (like peaches, plums, and mangoes), start by slicing off about one-third of the fruit, as close to the stone as possible. Then you'll either be able to pop out the stone or slice the remaining flesh neatly off in a few cuts.
- Cutting dried fruits like figs and apricots can be a sticky mess. Use kitchen scissors that have been lightly rubbed with vegetable or nut oil to make the job easier.
- If chopping onions makes you cry, it may help to run your hands and knife under cold water occasionally as you chop.
- You can't be too careful when working with hot peppers. Never touch your face (especially your eyes) while handling them, and don't expose your face to the steam rising from the cooking pot. Be certain the volatile oils have subsided before you bathe or touch anyone else's skin for an hour or two afterwards. Wearing disposable surgical gloves (available in most drugstores) is a good idea.

Slicing Citrus Rind: The Cheater's Way Versus the Stickler's Way

Slicing citrus is inevitable when making marmalade, and there are many ways to approach it. Here are two, which will suite very different kitchen personalities.

The Stickler's Way: Poach or parboil the citrus first. Cut each fruit in half through the middle, and use a spoon to scoop out the semi-liquefied flesh, membranes, pulp, and seeds (these can be saved, to be used later in the recipe). Cut the half-rind in half again. Flatten each piece of softened rind, remove the base of the stem, and slice into very thin shreds (you may wish to trim the longest shreds in half). You can use this technique with recipes like Victorian-Style Seville Orange Marmalade (p. 190), Grapefruit Marmalade (p. 192), and Lemon, Fig, and Lavender Marmalade (p. 227).

The Cheater's Way: Before cooking the fruit, cut it into quarters lengthwise. Cutting through two quarters at a time, slice off the "nose," or thin stem end, and then slice into very thin wedges, removing any seeds as they appear. Discard any pieces that are all rind with no flesh. You can use this technique with recipes like Tangerine Marmalade (p. 198), Strawberry Lemon Marmalade (p. 92), Blueberry Lemon Marmalade with Lavender (p. 117), and Plum Conserve for a Winter's Night (p. 127).

Safety First

Canning should not be rushed. If you are new to canning, allow yourself at least a four-hour window of time to try out a recipe. If the recipe states that something needs to cook for more than half an hour, add extra time. When you become accustomed to the process, you may find yourself whacking out batches of jam in ninety minutes, but rushing the job will only lead to spoiled batches, unhappy cooks, and the need to break out the first-aid kit.

Use well-sharpened knives, and don't get caught up in the fantasy that you are some sort of *Iron Chef* contestant who can do that choppity-chop thing and render down a turnip in a trice. This is how fingers are lost.

Maceration

In the fine French tradition of jam-making, fruits are often allowed to macerate overnight before being cooked. To macerate something is to allow it to soften in a liquid; if you toss berries or sliced fruits in sugar and let them sit overnight, a lot of juice will be extracted and the structure of the fruit will start to break down. This will make the fruit in the finished jam more concentrated, and will give it a brighter color. As you become familiar with jam-making, you might want to try macerating your fruit even if the recipe doesn't call for it.

Freezing Berries for Jam

If you acquire far more berries than you can deal with, you can store them in the freezer until you have time to put them up. You simply mix ¾ cup of sugar with 4 cups of washed berries (with any stems or leaves removed). Cut larger berries in half. They can be stored in covered containers (leave a little space for the frozen fruit to expand) or in freezer bags.

Although the quality of the fruit will diminish if you leave them there too long, a visit of up to two or three weeks will actually act like maceration, breaking down the berries' structure and releasing the juice into the sugar. Just remember to cut down the sugar in your recipe by the amount that's already in the fruit!

Sugar and Spice, When Heated, Are Nice

In any recipe that calls for adding sugar to a warm fruit mixture, it's a good idea to heat the sugar first, in a heatproof dish placed in an oven set to 250°F (120°C) until it has warmed through. This helps the sugar dissolve smoothly into the mix.

Similarly, when a recipe calls for the addition of spices (e.g., peppercorns, whole cloves, cinnamon sticks, or allspice berries), help to release the flavor into your food by gently toasting the spices first in an ungreased frying pan on medium heat. Keep a close eye on them and stir them frequently while they heat up, then take them off the heat as soon as they begin to release their aroma into the air.

Food Coloring

Many canning cookbooks suggest using artificial food coloring to bump up the color of preserves. For instance, it's common to find mint jelly recipes that call for green food coloring; otherwise the jelly will be a pale yellow-green. I can see the fun of making crazy-colored jellies for kids, but—apart from the question as to whether all commercial food colorings are safe to eat—I tend to prefer the paler, earthier colors of the uncolored jams and jellies.

If you're interested in experimenting, you might want to play with some natural coloring agents. Canadian food historian Elizabeth Driver has informed me that early Ontario settler and author Catherine Parr Traill colored her apple jelly by adding a few beet slices, though I imagine this would affect the flavor a little bit. Blueberries, strawberries, carrots, and the skins of red apples and dark grapes are among the other foods with strong color.

If you use slices of low-acid foods like carrots or beets in your jam mixture for their color, don't put them in the jars, as this could affect the safety of the recipe.

Size Matters

When I first started to experiment with preserves, I thought small-batch preserving was for losers and would make massive quantities at once. What this meant was that I'd battle for space in the canner and on the counter, fight constantly to keep pots of molten sugar from boiling over, and often had to wait as long as two hours for a batch to gel. This is no convenience.

Now that I'm a more experienced canner, I think a jam recipe that calls for 4 to 6 cups of fruit is ideal; for jelly, 6 to 8 lb (2¾ to 3½ kg) of fruit is sufficient. If you really want to can 25 lb (11 kg) of fruit in a day, you can; just run it through in smaller batches. That way, there's less risk of spoiling all your fruit if one batch doesn't turn out as planned. And if you're wise, you'll call up a couple of friends to split the labor and share the profits.

Don't Stir the Edges of Your Pot

The great chef Escoffier explained that the scum that forms when cooking fruits can cause jams to crystallize later—and so can sugar from the edges of the pot or the stem of the spoon, if it gets stirred back into the jam. Therefore, one must resist the thrifty urge to scrape the sides of the jam pot while it's cooking. When filling the jars, I lift the jam from the center of the pot with a spoon or ladle. It also probably doesn't hurt to clean your stirring spoon from time to time.

About Jelly Bags

The most beautiful jellies are crystal clear, with no sediment or uneven thickening, which is why fruit juice for jelly is strained through fine cloth first. You can use a purpose-bought jelly bag, which is often made with an elasticized edge so it will fit snugly over a funnel or container.

The classic old-fashioned method is to use several layers of cheesecloth or muslin; a wide-weave dishtowel works too. It should, of course, be clean, and if new, it's best if it's been washed a few times to remove any residual dye, bleach, or sizing in the fabric. (Another great choice? A worn-out T-shirt.)

Depending on the quantity of fruit pulp, it's often a good idea to run the mixture through a coarse strainer or food mill first, to remove large undissolved chunks, stems, seeds, and so on. Then you may lay the fabric into a large sieve or colander over a bowl, or tie the fruit up into a bundle and suspend it with sturdy kitchen cord from a handy overhead rack or shelving unit or hanging basket. There are also inexpensive stand-up wire or plastic devices designed to suspend jelly bags over bowls.

Whichever approach you use, remember to dampen the fabric first; otherwise a large amount of precious juice will get sucked into the fabric instead of the bowl. If you intend to reuse your jelly bag, wash, rinse, and air-dry it very carefully after each use. Ideally, you should boil it like your jars to sterilize it before each new use.

Ten Tips for Prize-winning Jelly for the County Fair

1. Never, never squeeze the jelly bag.

2. Don't start cooking the jelly until the jars are ready to fill, since it will thicken up in an unattractive way if it sits too long in the pot waiting for the jars.

3. If you use apple pectin, remove it from the jar with a turkey baster, so you don't get any sediment in the jelly.

4. Skim off any foam early and often; be careful not to ladle leftover foam or scum into the jars when you fill them.

5. Use a candy thermometer to test for set (220°F/105°C).

6. When the jelly reaches the setting point, turn off the heat and allow it to relax for about a minute, stirring occasionally, to reduce bubbles.

7. When filling jars, pour the jelly along the sides of the funnel's interior and let it slide in; if you drop it straight in, you'll create a lot of bubbles.

8. It's better to overfill the jars and then remove some jelly to adjust for the correct headspace; if you try to top up the jelly at the end, you'll create a noticeable blobby bit in the center of the jar.

9. Don't process jelly for longer than necessary. When the jars have been processed, remove the canner lid, turn off the heat, and let the jars relax for five minutes in the water bath.

10. Be resigned to having one last jar that looks blobby and messy, because you won't want to waste any. Scrape the bottom of the pot into that last jar and use it up yourself.

The Pectin Controversy

Jammers are more or less polarized along pectin lines. Some refuse to add commercial pectin to their jams and jellies; others always do, even when they don't need to. On the face of it, you might think that pectin is an inoffensive commodity to have sparked such debate; it's simply a fiber that occurs naturally in plants. In combination with sugar and acid, it's what causes fruit to gel into the pleasing consistency that makes jam or jelly stick to toast.

Pectin also eases nausea and stimulates the digestive process (at the risk of offering Too Much Information, it's a gentle laxative). So the Victorians knew what they were doing when they recommended jellies as food for invalids.

The skins of apples—particularly underripe, tart ones—and the pith and seeds of citrus fruits are naturally rich in pectin. Many other fruits—plums, cranberries, quince, guavas, and gooseberries, for instance—contain more than enough pectin to turn into jam or jelly without any outside help. But if you want to make jelly from flowers or herbs, or get a rich jam from pectin-poor fruits like watermelons or pears, you'll probably want to pump up the pectin somehow.

This is when the old-school jammer reaches for a package of commercial powdered or liquid pectin, which is inexpensive and widely available in grocery stores large and small. One package typically delivers the right amount of extra pectin to cause the average pot of fruit to gel successfully. It is normally derived from citrus peel or apple pomace (what's left after juicing), and, because it's commercially formulated in large batches, it's always consistent and predictable. So what's the problem?

First, some would say, the quality. I find powdered pectin has a tendency to impart a slight graininess to the texture of jam and jelly—though I've also noticed that it seems to dissipate after a couple of months in the jar. More serious: when you add pectin, you also have to increase the sugar in the recipe, by quite a lot. However, as mentioned in the sugar discussion on p. 71 to 73, you can use pectin products that allow you to cook with less sugar.

For vegans, it's important to know that although lactic acid is listed as an ingredient in some commercial pectins, this does not mean that dairy products have been introduced into the mix; lactic acid can be produced by fermenting vegetable products.

The best argument against adding commercial pectin to your homemade jam is what you don't know about it. Why would anyone bother to spend extra money on high-quality fruit (possibly local, perhaps even organic), only to toss in a box of pectin made from unidentified fruit by unknown methods in an unspecified location? Furthermore, the production of commercial pectin calls for the use of chemicals such as ammonium hydroxide and alcohols like ethanol and isopropanol. How much ends up in your jam? It's hard to say.

If you read the label on the box of whatever pectin brand is available in your neighborhood, you will probably see several ingredients listed, but ethanol is unlikely to be one of them. This is because manufacturers don't generally have to list every substance used to make their products. For instance, you might see "Oreo cookie crumbs" listed as an ingredient on a dessert package, but not the quantities of flour, salt, and so on present in those crumbs.

Similarly, if one of the ingredients on your grocery store pectin box is simply "pectin," the company that manufactures the brand you've bought has likely purchased pectin from another supplier farther up the production chain, and they're not required to list everything that went into it. This is not to say that commercial pectin necessarily contains anything unpleasant or harmful, just that it would be difficult to find out what it does contain.

If you want to avoid commercial pectin, you can harness the pectin from apples or citrus fruit to set your jams or jellies. This will slightly change the flavor; apples generally give a subtle flavor, a gentle, springy texture, and a clear jelly, while citrus fruits tend to give a sharper, more aromatic flavor, a harder set, and often a slightly milky look.

{ **Tip:**
If you peel and pare a lot of apples for some other recipe, you can keep the leftover skins and cores in the refrigerator for a few days and use them to make pectin at a later date.

Apple Pectin

One cup of this liquid is enough to gel at least 2 cups of fruit combined with about 3 cups of sugar and 2 tbsp of lemon juice. It also makes a lovely jelly if it's well strained. See pp. 143–45, 181, and 230–32 for several jelly recipes using apple pectin. It's fine to make a double batch, a half-batch, or a one-third batch.

Immature green apples will work well—they don't have to be pretty—but apples lose pectin as they age in storage, so this recipe may not give good results between about mid-March and the arrival of new apples in late summer. If you're lucky, you'll get a big bag of apples from a neighbor who has a tree, in August when they're still slightly too tart to eat out of hand.

{ **Note:**
It's best
to start this
recipe early in
the morning.

Makes 7–8 cups.

5 lb (2.2 kg) apples (10 heaping cups of small to medium apples, quartered)

10 cups water

Wash the apples and quarter them, leaving skins on. Remove large bruised pieces and any evidence of bugs, but don't worry about minor imperfections.

In a non-reactive pot, combine the water and apples, and bring the mixture to a boil. Turn heat to low and allow the mixture to simmer, stirring occasionally, until the apples have broken down (about half an hour).

Strain out the solids (if possible, strain first through a strainer with large holes, then a finer one).

Put the apple mixture into a jelly bag, two or three layers of cheesecloth, or a wide-weave dishtowel. Hang it over a bowl to drip; this will take several hours. (Do not squeeze the bag or the jelly will be cloudy.)

If you have the patience, put it through the jelly bag a second or even a third time.

Store the apple pectin in the refrigerator if you plan to use it within a few days; otherwise, freeze it.

Let the apple pectin sit overnight in the refrigerator in tall jars before using it. Then use a turkey baster to extract the liquid from the top of each jar (or pour very carefully) to avoid using the fine sediment at the bottom.

Orange Pectin

From Julia Sforza of the blog What Julia Ate

Originally posted at *Whatjuliaate.blogspot.com/2010/03/strawberry-and-orange-pectin-jelly. html*

This thrifty pectin, made from orange pith collected from fresh oranges over several weeks, can be frozen. See p. 94 for Julia's recipe for Strawberry and Orange Pectin Jelly; she continues to experiment with this technique and posts successful recipes on her blog from time to time.

**Makes about
4 cups.**

**2½ lb (1.13 kg) of
white pith
of citrus fruits**

1 cup lemon juice

9 cups water

Day 1:

Chop up all the pith into small, uniform pieces (a food processor makes this task easier).

In a non-reactive pot, combine pith, lemon juice, and water and let sit overnight.

Day 2:

In a medium-sized pot, bring the mixture to a boil on high heat. Let boil for ten minutes. Cool and strain, as for the apple pectin recipe, p. 69.

Store the mixture in the refrigerator if you plan to use it within a few days; otherwise, freeze it.

> **{ Tip:**
> Wet the jelly bag
> or cloth with
> water first so it
> doesn't soak up
> a lot of valuable
> juice.

Testing for Pectin Content

If you're trying to make jam or jelly with offbeat ingredients and you can't find a source to tell you whether your Madagascar Boo-Boo Berries are supposed to have enough pectin to gel, you can do a simple test to find the answer. Assuming you have a pot of boiling Boo-Boos on the stove, pour one tablespoon of rubbing alcohol into your smallest canning jar. Then drop one teaspoon of the juice into the jar, screw the lid on, and shake it gently. (If you can rustle up a lab coat and some thick glasses for this exercise, you'll feel very scientific indeed, I can assure you.)

If there's a little pectin in the mixture, you'll only see a faint cloudiness in the jar. If there's a lot, the juice will thicken up as soon as you drop it in, like an egg dropped into hot water. If you see significant thickening, you don't have to add extra pectin. Perhaps needless to say, you must be very careful that no one tries to eat your poisonous test sample. Get rid of it and wash the jar carefully right away so it cannot possibly get mixed up with the edible fruit.

Some final tips:

- If you use commercial pectin, make sure there's a best-before date on the box, because it's not supposed to last more than a couple of years.
- If you experiment with unusual fruit or low-sugar recipes, remember that some jam will continue to set days, weeks, or even months after it's sealed in the jar, so you shouldn't worry if it looks runny the morning after you make it. And you can always re-label it as "syrup"!
- Remember that you can actually defeat pectin by boiling it too long, so if your jam is taking an unusually long time to set, sometimes the best choice is to give up, can it, and wait to see what happens in the jar.

Photo: Shae Irving

Sweet on You: About Sugar and Its Substitutes

The single most common explanation people give when they say they don't make jam is: "I don't eat it; it's too sugary." A fair objection, because the basic ratio for most jam, jelly, and marmalade recipes is more or less equal parts fruit and sugar (or much more sugar in recipes calling for added pectin). These days, most beginning jam-makers are likely to question whether they want to use so much sugar in their recipes, or if they can substitute something else. In fact, there are several alternatives to sugar, though each one slightly changes the final product.

Sugar, when combined with pectin and acid, causes fruit liquids to gel. It's also a preservative that discourages mold and gives jams and jellies their gorgeous bright jewel-like colors. The ahead-of-his-time foodie Jean Anthelme Brillat-Savarin wrote in 1825 in his book *Physiologie du goût (The Physiology of Taste)*, "Mixed with fruits and flowers, [sugar] gives jams, marmalades, conserves, pastes and crystallized fruits a technique of preservation that allows us to delight in the perfume of these fruits and flowers long after the lifetime nature has allotted them."

On the other hand, sugar, like alcohol, is a dangerous pleasure that contributes to numerous health problems, and its history, bound up with slavery and international conflict, is a dishonorable one. Also, today there are way too many opportunities to eat sugar; people around the world can buy cheap sugary snacks everywhere, and almost every prepared food, from breakfast cereal to bread to soup to spaghetti sauce, has at least some sugar in the mix.

You can generally cut up to about one-quarter of the sugar in a traditional recipe that does not call for added pectin and still produce a successful jelly or jam, but you may have trouble getting it to gel in a satisfactory way, the color will be duller, and it will not keep as long once the jar is opened. If you cut the sugar even further, the color will dull within a few weeks, and you may lose some of the jam to mold. Recipes made with reduced sugar tend to look more like a compote (a sweetened cooked fruit) than a classic jam.

The traditional jams and jellies came from a time when sweet treats were scarcer and when people used up a lot more calories doing everyday work without conveniences like cars, escalators, washing machines, and hot running water. In the Middle Ages, marmalade was considered a precious sweetmeat to be served at the very end of a meal, like chocolate truffles or dessert wine.

If you choose to make traditional jam or jelly with sugar, savor and treasure it. Use it in small quantities. Remember how long it took to cut up all that orange peel into thin slices, or to top and tail all those gooseberries. In that context, the sugar content becomes less of an issue. If you object to sugar more on environmental and political grounds than nutritional, remember that it is becoming possible to buy organic and fair trade sugar, though it's more costly than what you'd normally pick up at the grocery store. Raw sugar can be used without causing a noticeable difference to the finished product.

Alternative Sweeteners

For flavor, ethics, and food safety, honey is the first choice as a cane sugar substitute in jamming. Most people can buy local honey, and it does have similar preservative properties to sugar; however, it doesn't cause exactly the same kind of gelling and may change the color of the product. Before beet and cane sugars were known in Europe and around the Mediterranean, honey was the primary agent for sweetening and preserving fruit.

A pale-colored honey will behave more like sugar than a dark one, and you will still need some sugar to achieve the expected result. Substitute between $7/8$ and 1 cup of honey for each cup of sugar in any recipe calling for added pectin, but do not replace more than half the total volume of sugar, or more than 2 cups (whichever is less). If the recipe does not call for added pectin, honey can replace up to half the sugar, even if the total volume is more than 2 cups.

Corn syrup is another substitute for sugar; its main virtue, for most people, is that it may be sourced locally. In jams and jellies made with added pectin, corn syrup can replace up to half the sugar, to a maximum of 2 cups. In recipes that don't call for added pectin, it can replace up to a quarter of the sugar.

Every fruit will respond a little differently, so if you're interested in reducing the sugar content of your favorite traditional recipes, you will probably need to experiment until you find the right proportions. The alternative is to use a low-ester pectin, which is a pectin product that can gel with a relatively small proportion of sugar (as little as twenty percent sugar to eighty percent fruit). Pomona's Universal Pectin is probably the best known brand name in North America; one box will make several batches of jam. It comes with an extra envelope of calcium powder, which is mixed with water and added to the jam or jelly to allow the pectin to do its work. (You can keep the calcium water in a jar in the fridge between batches.)

Each package of Pomona's includes recipes, and there are more on the company website. They provide options not only for cooking with reduced sugar and honey, but also with other sweeteners such as stevia, agave, and Sucanat. The company that makes Pomona's, Workstead Industries, operates a "jamline" to handle customer queries, and they are fairly prompt and thorough in their responses. The company recommends that properly processed jams and jellies made with their pectin will keep for a year, but admits they will turn moldy more quickly than high-sugar products once they've been opened (within about three weeks). The color will also fade quite a bit.

Like natural citrus pectin, Pomona's gives a slightly milky look to jellies. The set is firm, but anyone who is used to cooking with other types of pectin will be surprised to find that the jam or jelly will still seem quite liquid when it goes into the jar; it doesn't tend to thicken completely for several hours or even days. Among the recipes in this book are several using Pomona's Universal Pectin: Pineapple Jam with Honey (p. 208), Chardonnay Wine Jelly (p. 229), Lemongrass, Ginger, and Kaffir Lime Jelly (p. 204), and Blackberry Lime Jam (p. 112).

Patents and Pickle Jars

Modern home canning is a tale of many jars. In the early days, preserves were sometimes kept in metal or ceramic containers, but glass jars finally advanced to the front of the pack because they're so stable and don't interact with the contents. Preserve cooks have used an ingeniously wide range of methods to seal the jars. At first, this was probably done as much with the intention of keeping insects and rodents away from the contents as to prevent spoilage, because the sealed jars were not processed in boiling water or made airtight, and, in any case, the practice of keeping food in jars long pre-dates any understanding of the scientific principles that explain why you don't have to worry that your next bite of a dill pickle will be fatal.

Some of the methods that have been used throughout history include sealing with rendered sheep suet (like what's done with meat-based pâtés and terrines), paper soaked in brandy or egg-whites, and pigs' bladders. At Toronto's Fort York historic site, I had a chance to attend a workshop where a volunteer historic cook (suitably clad in gown, apron, and mob-cap) demonstrated most of these techniques in the Officer's Mess, which looks much as it would have around 1800, down to the copper pots simmering on the open hearth. Back in the day, these sealing techniques were so well-known to cooks, she pointed out, that most recipes of the eighteenth and nineteenth centuries don't waste any time explaining them. Just as today's cookbooks say things like "whites of three eggs," without describing how to separate them, antique cookbooks most often offer instructions in shorthand, like this one from Elizabeth Raffald in a marmalade recipe, dated 1769, from *The Experienced English Housekeeper:* "When it is cold, put it into jelly or sweetmeat glasses, tie them down with brandy papers over them."

Seville orange marmalade cooking in a copper kettle on an open hearth at Fort York in Toronto.

Escoffier, writing a century and a half later, is somewhat more helpful. He instructs that the cook should pour the preserves into pots and, "the following day, set a round piece of white paper saturated with rectified glycerine or wax on each pot, and drop these pieces of paper directly on the jam. Rectified glycerine will be found preferable by far to the commonly used sugared brandy. Then close the pots with a double sheet of paper, fastened on with string, and set them somewhere dry."

He doesn't mention whether the paper should first be moistened with egg-white, which, as we saw in the Fort York workshop, dries to a satisfyingly airtight seal. So does a pig's bladder—though it's a big job to remove all the damp and nasty bits. The rounds of prepared bladder need to be soaked in brine, then worked and stretched like particularly feisty pizza dough before they can be tied over the jars—a job that's almost too much for just one pair of hands.

Photo: David Ort

Photo: Shae Irving

An old method that persists even now is to seal over the top of the pre-serves with wax or paraffin. This is no longer recommended as a perfectly safe way to preserve food, because the edges of the seal have a tendency to pull away from the jar and allow air to flow in and food to flow out. Nonetheless, every little hardware store stocks paraffin next to the jam jars at the height of preserving season. No doubt hundreds of thousands of pints of paraffin-sealed jam have been consumed without resulting in fatalities, but it's wiser to use the approved methods.

The big breakthrough in home canning technology—the sturdy glass jar with the reusable, screw-on lid—seems to have developed more or less simultaneously in two different places. In the UK, the company founded by Yorkshireman John Kilner started manufacturing a glass fruit jar with a glass stopper in 1842. Today, in the UK, many home canners still use a variation on the Kilner jar that has a hinged glass lid with a wire bail closure.

In the US, New Yorker John L. Mason introduced his jar in 1858. The first Mason jars had a threaded top that mated with a zinc lid; the join was sealed originally with wax, and later with a rubber ring gasket. These days, the name "Mason" stamped on a jar still means it's designed to be processed without breaking even in a pressure canner.

A parallel technology emerged in 1882, when Henry W. Putnam of Bennington, Vermont, invented the "Lightning" jar, with a glass lid held in place by a wire bail. These were also very popular, and were manufactured by numerous companies in the US and Canada.

Ball jars, a Mason-style jar still manufactured today, were patented around 1898 by a family of five brothers from Buffalo, New York, after the original Mason patent had expired. Their Ball Brothers Glass Manufacturing Company, which operated in Muncie, Indiana, from the 1880s to the 1960s, soon expanded and acquired other firms, like Alexander H. Kerr's Hermetic Fruit Jar Company. It was Kerr who, in 1915, developed the first practical version of the two-part metal lid and band that's still in use. Ball also acquired Toronto's Bernardin company, the only comparable jar and lid manufacturer in Canada.

Old-fashioned methods of sealing jars: with paper and egg whites, suet or pigskin, as demonstrated at the Culinary Historians of Canada's annual Mad for Marmalade event at Fort York in Toronto.

Collecting Antique Jars

I treasure my two dozen or so old-fashioned jars, picked up from where they'd been left on someone's front lawn many years ago. However, I find them tricky to work with, so I mainly use them for storing sugar and rice. They have glass lids and metal bands that require rubber rings. The rings are still commonly available in hardware and kitchen stores, but the glass lids are not. When I see extras in antique stores, as I sometimes do, I pick them up because they're apt to break occasionally.

Some of my jars are made of pale turquoise-blue glass, which I understand was meant to protect the contents from light. Canning jars have also been manufactured in dark blue, amber, yellow, or green glass, but I've seldom run across them. A charming detail of some of my own jars is that they have the year of manufacture printed in raised letters on the bottom, so I know some of them date from as early as the 1920s.

Serious collectors can revel in many small differences like this: older jars may be printed with various brand names and logos or come in obsolete shapes and sizes. Some discontinued brand names include Knox, Lamb, Drey, Presto (which now makes pressure canners), Foster, Root, Perfection, Improved, Ideal, Eclipse, Universal, and, in Canada, Crown and Imperial. (And doesn't that just encapsulate the difference between the two countries!)

Today, most of the canning jars in North America are made by one company, called Jarden Home Brands, the descendant of Ball Brothers. Their jars are sold in the US under the brand names Ball, Kerr, and Golden Harvest, and in Canada as Bernardin. All these jars come in standard sizes with either a narrow-mouth opening of just under 2½ in (6½ cm), or a wide-mouth openings of about 3 in (8 cm). The narrow mouth is most often used, but the wide mouth is handy for larger fruit preserves and pickles.

Standard Canning Jar Sizes

The standard canning jar sizes are as follows (conversions are approximate):

¼ pint or 125 mL or ½ cup or 4 fl. oz. This size is good for gift or sample-sized batches of jams, jellies, and preserves, or for very concentrated condiments like hot-pepper jellies that don't get eaten in large quantities.

½ pint or 250 mL or 1 cup or 8 fl. oz. This is a standard jam-jar size, useful also for condiments like cranberry sauce and for gift or sample sizes of the smallest pickles like cornichons or pickled onions.

1 pint or 500 mL or 2 cups or 16 fl. oz. This is a family-sized jam jar, which would be convenient for households that eat jams and jellies for breakfast on most mornings. It can also be used for most pickles, or for small batches of tomato sauce.

1 quart or 1 L or 4 cups or 32 fl. oz. This is a dill pickle-sized jar, and also a good size for tomato sauce.

½ gallon or 2 L or 8 cups or 64 fl. oz. This jar holds a serious quantity of food; think of the big jar of pickled eggs that you might see at a bar. It's a bit large for the average home cook to deal with conveniently because it takes up so much room and requires very long processing. Also, it's not recommended for canning anything but high-acid juice by the US National Center for Home Food Preservation, so it's best left to true homesteaders and large-scale commercial producers.

Alternatives to the Two-Part Lid

Those who find it unsettling that the entire canning phenomenon is essentially dependent upon the products of a single company may be interested to know that there are alternatives to the standard snap-lid jar.

The European-style bail-closure Kilner jars can be bought in North America through Amazon and other outlets. For instance, they are manufactured under the brand name "Fido" by an Italian company called Bormioli Rocco with offices in New York. Some of these are gorgeous in an opulent way, with embossed fruits on the side. They can be sealed airtight in a hot-water bath; however, an important sign of spoiled food is a lid that stops holding its seal. Because these jars have a wire bail that holds the glass lid on tightly, they could mask food spoilage. The US National Center for Home Food Preservation recommends that they should only be used to store dry foods, not for canning.

A company called Weck in Crystal Lake, Illinois, is popular with many online canners; their pear-shaped and straight-sided jars are pricy, but have a pleasingly contemporary look. Weck jars have glass lids sealed with rubber rings and attached with a clamp, but the clamp is designed to be removed; the jar is sealed only by air pressure, and any build-up of gases in the jar caused by spoilage is obvious.

Another company, SKS Bottles and Packaging of Watervliet, New York, has a line of preserving jars—including some very pretty hexagonal ones—with one-piece lids. Audra Wolfe of the blog Doris and Jilly Cook tried them out and reported that the SKS jars are not appropriate for pressure canning, and are a little bit fussy to handle, but that they make a professional-looking and satisfactory alternative to snap-ring jars.

A German company called Leifheit also manufactures pretty, teardrop-shaped jars with one-piece lids that are sold as canning jars. However, the US National Center for Home Food Preservation does not yet recommend any one-piece lids as safe for canning.

Reusing Jars

Because canning jars have been standardized for a long time, a thrifty cook can collect used jars from many sources, ranging from websites like Craigslist and Freecycle to garage sales and second-hand shops. In my own municipality, where we enjoy curbside pickup of recyclable glass and plastic once a week, I occasionally spot free jars on my own block. And etiquette dictates that recipients of gift preserves should return the empty and washed jar to their jamming benefactor.

Many commercial soups and sauces are sold in 1-qt or 1-L jars that are compatible with snap-rings. Not all of these are true preserving jars (apparently, even some of those marked "Mason" are not genuine), but I've never had a problem with processing or sealing reused soup or sauce jars by hot-water bath canning. However, it would be wise never to use jars of dubious origin in a pressure canner.

Also, you should never reuse the screw-top lids that come with commercial jars of soups and sauces for home canning. Likewise, when reusing snap-lid jars, never reuse the lids. They can be inexpensively replaced, in little boxes of twelve, anywhere that other canning supplies are sold. The screw-on bands can be reused until they become dented, bent, or rusty. These can also be replaced; they come with lids. (But I find I always have way too many of them!)

If you collect and reuse jars, check for and discard any that are cracked or chipped. In *The Old Ontario Cookbook*, writer Muriel Breckenridge recalls that glass canning jars were once considered so precious that home cooks would patch them up with a mixture of plaster-of-Paris, resin, and lard when they cracked. She even provides the recipe—but this is not a recommended practice for twenty-first-century preservers.

BPA and Canning Lids

Recently, some people have become concerned about the presence of the chemical known as Bisphenol A (BPA for short) in canning lids. BPA is an endocrine disruptor that's believed to be capable of causing harm to the brain and reproductive system. It's found in many food containers, such as reusable water bottles and the lining of aluminum cans. A study by Health Canada's Food Director-ate concluded that exposure to BPA through food packaging was "not expected to pose a health risk to the general population, including newborns and infants." However, in June 2009, the Canadian government moved to prohibit the sale of plastic baby bottles that contain BPA, as part of a policy to reduce infants' exposure to the chemical as much as possible.

In January 2010, the US Food and Drug Administration changed its past position that BPA was not a risk for consumers, stating instead that it had "some concern about the potential effects of BPA on the brain, behavior, and prostate gland in fetuses, infants, and young children." It also stated that it would support voluntary efforts on the part of the food industry to stop using BPA in infant food packaging and to limit its use in food packaging for adults.

The winter 2009–10 issue of *Organic Gardening* magazine and various websites have looked into the BPA situation as it relates to canning lids. While they surmise that food in jars normally doesn't touch the lid, and that therefore the transfer of BPA into the food would be negligible, they suggest that parents whose infants eat food from these jars might like to be cautious. As of March 2010, the Jarden website, *freshpreserving.com*, carried a statement that, although all four of their jar brands use BPA in the lids, they conform to FDA standards.

Weck jar lids are made of glass and use no BPA. There is also a reusable white plastic jar lid made from a food-grade product known as Polyoxymethylene Copolymer (POM) or Acetal Copolymer that is FDA-certified for contact with food and BPA-free. Sold under the brand name Tattler, it's made by a company in Fruita, Colorado, that advertises it as safe for water-bath and pressure canning. Well-known canning blogger Marisa McLellan of Food in Jars has tried these out; she says the trick is to tighten, then slightly loosen the lids before the jars go into the canner and then to tighten them again when they come out. (She and other bloggers also point out that, at about eighty cents per lid, they won't be using any on the jars they give away.)

Other alternatives probably exist, but this is likely an issue that will continue to develop; one may hope that the food packaging industry will eventually be able to find a safer alternative to BPA.

3: The Recipes

The following collection of recipes is really an anthology. I developed about half of them, but the other half come from generous and skilled home cooks, chefs, cookbook authors, and food bloggers in three countries. What this means for anyone who's still learning the craft of canning is that these recipes present a wide variety of different tastes, methods, and techniques, some simpler and some trickier, some more laid-back and some more persnickety.

Once you've grown used to the basics of canning, you might like to mix methods from different recipes. When making marmalade in the winter, for instance, you might prefer to poach citrus fruit in the oven to warm the house, but in summer you could use Audra Wolfe's method of chopping citrus, bringing it to a quick boil, and steeping it overnight, to use a minimum of extra heat.

If you've signed up to make a very big batch of jam, you may want to pick a quick-and-dirty recipe that gives you eighty percent of the result for twenty percent of the effort. On the other hand, if you're spending a month on retreat in a solitary beach house, you may prefer to pick the most painstaking recipe in the book and do it with complete attention, as a kind of meditation on the food.

Many of the recipes were originally published on blogs (a few were in cookbooks). If you're trying one of the previously published recipes, you'll enjoy having a look at the original source, where you're sure to find a few extra nuggets of wisdom and possibly some gorgeous pictures of the finished product.

A few notes:

- In these recipes, "sugar" means granulated white sugar, unless otherwise noted.
- Various types of vinegar (white, cider, malt, red wine, white wine, rice wine) are mentioned in the recipes. Each one will impart a different color and taste to the recipe. However, as long as they contain at least five percent acid, you may use them interchangeably.
- The amount of time it takes for jam or jelly to set is influenced by many factors, including the condition of the fruit, the size and shape of the cooking pot, and even the weather. Therefore, times are not specified in the recipes that follow, but you should expect most jams and jellies to set somewhere within about fifteen to twenty-five minutes. The few cases where the process may take much less or more time are noted.
- You should use coarse pickling or kosher salt, not table salt, in pickling recipes. Table salt contains iodine and anti-caking additives that will darken your pickles and make your brine cloudy.
- When you release trapped air bubbles from a jar of fruit or vegetable pieces in brine, as the recipes note, you should use a non-metallic knife or chopstick. This is because a scratch or nick from a metal implement can cause the jar to break when it is immersed in boiling water.

Which Jam I Am

When is a jam not a jam? There is a certain amount of confusion about the names of various types of preserves, and when you start to explore the world of antique cookbooks and old family recipes, the situation only grows more muddled. To begin with, you could call almost any food stored in a jar a "preserve," but it can also be used in a more specialized way, as you will see following.

Chutney: A fairly thick savory sauce made from fruit and vegetables, sugar, vinegar, and spices; the term came into English from Hindi in the nineteenth century. Mango chutney is the classic, but these days the term is most often used when a recipe contains dried fruit (like raisins) along with fresh ingredients.

Compote: Halfway between a jam and a fruit preserve, a compote is usually a thick sweetened or unsweetened reduction.

Conserve: A sweet, jam-like concoction that usually contains dried fruit, nuts, and/or some kind of liquor (typically rum or brandy) along with fruit and sugar.

Jam: A sweet mixture of fruit (or sometimes vegetables) with sugar, thickened with pectin to achieve a spreadable jelly-like consistency.

Jelly: A sweet mixture of fruit, flower, herb and/or vegetable juice with sugar, thickened with pectin to achieve a translucent, semi-solid but still spreadable gel.

Marmalade: In the past, marmalades were made with all kinds of fruit (especially quinces), but today, only a sweet jam made with citrus peel is generally called a marmalade.

Pickle: This can be a catch-all term for almost any food (whole or in pieces) preserved in a vinegar and salt brine. Something called a pickle in an old-fashioned recipe might today be called a relish or chutney.

Preserve: These days, the term preserve generally refers to whole, halved, or quartered fruits preserved in sugar syrup, juice, or water.

Relish: A savory sauce made with fairly finely chopped vegetables and/or fruit with vinegar and sugar. The old-fashioned term "chowchow" is more or less a synonym.

Salsa: This could be any sauce, but most often it's a tomato-based savory sauce containing hot peppers and other strong spices.

Photo: Collette Pryslak

Photo: Julia Srorza

Recipes for Spring

The impatiently awaited stars of the North American spring are rhubarb, strawberries and asparagus. Urban foragers can preserve some of the spring flowers that pop up in every backyard and park, while their rural counterparts may be able to find fiddleheads—the bud of the wild fern before it unfurls—or the tender woodland garlic *Allium tricoccum*, better known as ramps or wild leeks.

Rhubarb Apricot Conserve

This intensely orange-flavored conserve is gorgeous with roast pork. You can buy candied ginger or make your own (see p. 233). Normally this would be a spring recipe made with fresh-picked rhubarb, but you could freeze a bag of rhubarb to make a tangier version in January or February when Seville oranges are available instead.

Makes about 4½ cups.

2 oranges

4 cups rhubarb, chopped

12 dried apricots, very finely chopped

3 cups sugar

3 tbsp lemon juice

½ cup chopped walnuts

¼ cup finely cubed candied ginger

2 tbsp orange liqueur

Sterilize jars and warm lids. (See full instructions, p. 49, or Bare-bones Cheat Sheet, on flap.)

Scrub the oranges in warm, soapy water to remove any wax, pesticides, or dirt. Zest them, reserving the zest. Then cut them in half and juice them, reserving the juice.

In a wide, deep non-reactive pot with a thick bottom, combine the orange juice and zest, rhubarb, apricots, sugar, lemon juice, walnuts, and ginger. Stir together and allow to macerate for at least 20 minutes or as long as overnight.

Bring the mixture up to a full, rolling boil that cannot be stirred down and continue to boil, stirring frequently, until it reaches the setting point.

Turn the heat off, add the orange liqueur, and allow the mixture to rest for 5 minutes, stirring occasionally.

Ladle into sterilized jars, leaving ¼ in (6 mm) of headspace, seal with warm lids and process for 10 minutes at a rolling boil (15 minutes for pint/500 mL jars).

Remove the canner lid, turn off the heat, and allow the jars to sit in the hot water for another 5 minutes to cool down.

Rhubarb Strawberry Jam

From Risa Alyson Strauss (Toronto; not previously published.)

Rhubarb and strawberry are an unbeatable combination, and the pineapple is a very compatible third companion. Take note that this recipe uses far less sugar than many of the jams in this book and therefore has an earthier color and won't last as long—but it has a delicious tanginess.

Makes about 3½ cups.

1 cup sliced strawberries

4 cups chopped rhubarb

1 cup chopped pineapple

1⅓ cup raw or light brown sugar

Sterilize jars and warm lids. (See full instructions, p. 49, or Bare-bones Cheat Sheet, on flap.)

Gently wash the strawberries and hull them, then crush them with a potato masher or the back of a slotted spoon.

In a wide, deep non-reactive pot with a thick bottom, combine the strawberries with the rhubarb and pineapple. Heat them just to the boiling point, then turn the heat down and simmer until the mixture breaks down into a thick paste (some of the pineapple may remain chunky). You can help the process along by crushing larger fruit pieces with a spoon.

Add the sugar, stirring well until it dissolves completely.

Bring up to a full, rolling boil that cannot be stirred down and continue to boil, stirring frequently and skimming off foam, until it reaches the setting point. (It may be tricky to recognize the gel stage with this thick and pasty jam, but don't stop cooking until it has reduced by about half.)

Ladle into sterilized jars, leaving ¼ in (6 mm) of headspace, seal with warm lids and process for 15 minutes at a rolling boil (20 minutes for pint/500 mL jars).

Remove the canner lid, turn off the heat, and allow the jars to sit in the hot water for another 5 minutes to cool down.

Refrigerate jars or use them up within 8 to 12 weeks; discard if you see any signs of mold.

Devonshire Scones (p. 235), filled with (clockwise, from upper left): Strawberry Jam with Black Pepper and Balsamic Vinegar (p. 93), Strawberry Lemon Marmalade (p. 92), Easy Victorian-Style Strawberry Jam (p. 91), and Strawberry and Orange Pectin Jelly (p. 94).

Photo: Niamh Malcolm

Easy Victorian-Style Strawberry Jam

Rich, sweet strawberry jam is the classic condiment for a Devonshire Cream Tea (p. 255) with scones and clotted cream. If it's cooked carefully, it should still have almost-whole strawberries suspended in it. No jam smells sexier when it's cooking, like the essence of early summer made into a perfume.

Makes about 6 cups.

8 cups strawberries

4 tbsp lemon juice

7½ cups sugar

Sterilize jars and warm lids. (See full instructions, p. 49, or Bare-bones Cheat Sheet, on flap.)

Gently wash the strawberries and hull them.

In a wide, deep non-reactive pot with a thick bottom, heat the strawberries and lemon juice just to the boiling point.

Add the sugar, stirring well until it dissolves completely.

Bring up to a full, rolling boil that cannot be stirred down and continue to boil, stirring frequently and skimming off foam, until it reaches the setting point. Ideally, some strawberries will still hold their shape at this point, but if any are bobbing above the surface, this jam is not yet ready to set.

Ladle into sterilized jars, leaving ¼ in (6 mm) of headspace, seal with warm lids and process for 10 minutes at a rolling boil (15 minutes for pint/500 mL jars).

Remove the canner lid, turn off the heat, and allow the jars to sit in the hot water for another 5 minutes to cool down.

Strawberry Lemon Marmalade

From Audra Wolfe of the blog Doris and Jilly Cook (Philadelphia)

Originally published at *dorisandjillycook.com/2010/01/21/strawberry-lemon-marmalade*

This fabulously fresh-tasting preserve—amazing with goat cheese—is made with a minimum of fuss and bother. It works just as well with frozen strawberries in sugar (¾ cup of sugar to 4 cups of strawberries stored in a freezer-safe container). This means you can make fresh strawberry jam in December if you want. Just remember to cut the sugar in the recipe down to 3 cups if you do!

Makes about 5–6 cups.

4 medium lemons

about 3 cups water

4 cups whole strawberries

3¾ cups sugar

Day 1:

Scrub the lemons in warm, soapy water to remove any wax, pesticides, or dirt. Slice them as thinly as possible, then chop them into pieces.

In a wide, deep non-reactive pot with a thick bottom, cover the lemons with water, bring to a boil, and simmer for 5 minutes. Turn off the heat and let the pan cool, then cover and let stand overnight.

Meanwhile, if you are using frozen berries, take them out of the freezer.

Day 2:

Sterilize jars and warm lids. (See full instructions, p. 49, or Bare-bones Cheat Sheet, on flap.)

Crush the strawberries with a potato masher or the back of a slotted spoon.

Add the strawberries and sugar to the lemon mixture. Bring it to a full, rolling boil that cannot be stirred down, and continue to boil until it reaches the setting point (watch out, because the lemons have lots of pectin, and the gel stage may arrive rather suddenly!).

Ladle into sterilized jars, leaving ¼ in (6 mm) of headspace, seal with warm lids and process for 10 minutes at a rolling boil (15 minutes for pint/500 mL jars).

Remove the canner lid, turn off the heat, and allow the jars to sit in the hot water for another 5 minutes to cool down.

Strawberry Jam with Black Pepper and Balsamic Vinegar

From Alec Stockwell (Toronto; not previously published.)

A darker, more complex-tasting strawberry jam in the French style, best with goat cheese or slightly heated and poured over vanilla ice cream. (Alec says: "Do not touch it for at least a month—then it's heaaaven!" Use small jars to make the most of this jam; because it's mainly fruit, it's more costly than some.)

Makes about 2–3 cups.

4 heaping cups strawberries

1½ cups sugar

3 tbsp lemon juice

¼ cup balsamic vinegar (at least 5 percent acid)

¼–1 tsp cracked, not ground, black peppercorns

> **Tip:**
> You can use a mortar and pestle to crack the peppercorns, or just cover them with a dishtowel and tap them with a hammer.

Day 1:
Wash, then hull the strawberries. If small, leave whole. If large, cut in half.

In a non-reactive bowl, combine berries, sugar, and lemon juice. Cover with cloth and allow to macerate about 24 hours.

Day 2:
Sterilize jars and warm lids. (See full instructions, p. 49, or Bare-bones Cheat Sheet, on flap.)

In a wide, deep non-reactive pot with a thick bottom, bring berry mixture to a full, rolling boil that cannot be stirred down.

Remove strawberries and continue to boil the liquid until it begins to thicken. Then return the strawberries to the pot, and bring it back up to a boil. Continue to boil, stirring frequently and skimming off foam, until it reaches the setting point. (Some berries will still hold their shape at this point.)

Add vinegar and pepper to taste; a full teaspoon will make quite a hot flavor—even ¼ tsp will give a good hint of pepper.

Let the jam rest on a low heat briefly and test to be certain you have reached the setting point, but be careful not to burn the jam.

Ladle into sterilized jars, leaving ¼ in (6 mm) of headspace, seal with warm lids and process for 10 minutes at a rolling boil (15 minutes for pint/500 mL jars).

Remove the canner lid, turn off the heat, and allow the jars to sit in the hot water for another 5 minutes to cool down.

Strawberry and Orange Pectin Jelly

From Julia Sforza of the blog What Julia Ate (Esopus, New York)

Originally published at *whatjuliaate.blogspot.com/2010/03/strawberry-and-orange-pectin-jelly.html*

Julia is one of the bloggers who has been experimenting with ways to avoid using commercial pectin in her jam recipes. In this case, the low-pectin strawberries get a helping hand from pectin extracted from orange pith. The resulting firm jelly has a dark color and a delicious aromatic flavor.

Makes 2 cups.

2 cups orange pectin (see p. 70)

2 cups mashed strawberries

2 cups sugar

Sterilize jars and warm lids. (See full instructions, p. 49, or Bare-bones Cheat Sheet, on flap.)

In a wide, deep non-reactive pot with a thick bottom, combine orange pectin, strawberries, and sugar; bring the mixture to a full, rolling boil that cannot be stirred down. Continue to boil, stirring frequently and skimming off foam, until it reaches the setting point.

Ladle into sterilized jars, leaving ¼ in (6 mm) of headspace, seal with warm lids, and process for 10 minutes at a rolling boil (15 minutes for pint/500 mL jars).

Remove the canner lid, turn off the heat, and allow the jars to sit in the hot water for another 5 minutes to cool down.

Dandelion Jelly

From Erin Scott of the blog Yummy Supper (Berkeley, California)

Originally published at *yummysupper.blogspot.com/2010/03/dandelion-jelly.html*

This golden jelly is a rustic French tradition that commemorates the 365 suns that have risen and set since last year's spring. In Berkeley, California, Erin was able to pick the dandelions on the first day of spring (March 20), but in my more northerly zone I had to wait until May Day (May 1), which is almost as good. Erin writes: "This jelly is delicious, with a bright springy flavor very reminiscent of local honey." It tastes great with spring lamb. The set may be iffy; if it's too liquid to be called jelly, call it Dandelion Nectar or Dandelion Honey instead.

Makes about 6 cups.

365 ripe yellow dandelion flowers

6 cups water

3 tbsp lemon juice

6 cups sugar

8 tsp powdered pectin

Day 1:

Find a protected patch of dandelions that have not been sprayed with pesticides. Pick 365 blossoms. Wash thoroughly. Snip off green base of each flower so that you have only petals for the jelly.

In a wide, deep non-reactive pot with a thick bottom, combine the flowers, water, and lemon juice. Bring to a full, rolling boil that cannot be stirred down.

Transfer the mixture to a bowl, cover with wax paper, and refrigerate overnight.

Day 2:

Sterilize jars and warm lids. (See full instructions, p. 49, or Bare-bones Cheat Sheet, on flap.)

Return the mixture to the pot. Add the sugar and bring to a full, rolling boil for about 10 minutes. Remove from heat. When it is cool enough to handle, strain out and discard the petals.

Add the pectin and return the liquid to a boil until it reaches the setting point.

Ladle into sterilized jars, leaving ¼ in (6 mm) of headspace, seal with warm lids and process for 10 minutes at a rolling boil (15 minutes for pint/500 mL jars).

Remove the canner lid, turn off the heat, and allow the jars to sit in the hot water for another 5 minutes to cool down.

Wild Violet Jelly

From mother Donna Julseth and daughter Maggie Julseth Howe of the blog Prairieland Herbs (Iowa)

This sure-fire recipe produces a great set and the most beautiful color ever! It's very exciting to see the indigo-blue liquid change to heavenly violet-pink when you add the lemon juice. It can be adapted for other flowers and herbs, including rose, lavender, lemon balm, cinnamon, basil, dandelion, and mint.

Makes about 6 cups.

2 cups fresh violet petals

2 cups water

¼ cup lemon juice

4 cups sugar

1 pouch (3 oz/85mL) liquid pectin

Wash petals well.

In a non-reactive bowl or pot, pour boiling water over petals and let steep for at least 2 hours (up to 24).

Strain through a fine sieve. (The violet liquid can then be refrigerated for up to 24 hours.)

Sterilize jars and warm lids. (See full instructions, p. 49, or Bare-bones Cheat Sheet, on flap.)

In a wide, deep non-reactive pot with a thick bottom, combine the violet liquid with lemon juice and sugar, stirring well until the sugar dissolves completely. Bring to a full, rolling boil that cannot be stirred down.

Add the liquid pectin and cook at a rolling boil, stirring frequently and skimming off foam, until it reaches the setting point (about 2 minutes).

Ladle into sterilized jars, leaving ¼ in (6 mm) of headspace, seal with warm lids and process for 10 minutes at a rolling boil (15 minutes for pint/500 mL jars).

Remove the canner lid, turn off the heat, and allow the jars to sit in the hot water for another 5 minutes to cool down.

{ **Tip:**
Look for fully opened flowers, for better color and more intense flavor. Be sure only to gather flowers that have not been sprayed with chemicals.

{ **Variation:** Add a heaping tablespoon of dried lavender or rosemary to the petal mixture, and a second tablespoon to the liquid after it's been strained. The lavender jelly is lovely with chicken, while the rosemary rocks with pork.

Lilac Jelly

From Julianna Carvi of the blog Egg Day—The Brunch Project (Columbus, Ohio)
Originally published at *eggday.blogspot.com/2010/04/lilac-jelly.html*

In perfume, lilac is considered one of the most elusive and difficult-to-capture scents. As Julianna writes, this jelly tastes mostly of sugar, although "there is a subtle floral taste, which is lovely." For the best results, try to find the most aromatic lilac tree in your neighborhood, and get permission to pick young blossoms that have not quite finished opening. Pale flowers will produce a yellowish or even tan-colored jelly, while darker blossoms turn out more pink or mauve. Try a blend of variously colored flowers.

Makes about 4½ cups.

2 cups lilac blossoms

2 cups boiling water

3 tbsp lemon juice

1 pouch (3 oz/85mL) liquid pectin

4 cups sugar

Day 1:
Rinse flowers very gently, then pick the individual blossoms off the stems, removing as much green from the flowers as you can.

In a non-reactive bowl or pot, cover the lilacs with boiling water and steep, covered, for 24 hours.

Day 2:
Sterilize jars and warm lids. (See full instructions, p. 49, or Bare-bones Cheat Sheet, on flap.)

Strain blossoms. If you like, save a few flowers to put into the jars.

In a wide, deep non-reactive pot with a thick bottom, combine lilacs, lemon juice, and pectin. Bring to a boil.

Turn down the heat and add the sugar, stirring well until it dissolves completely.

Bring to a full, rolling boil that cannot be stirred down and continue to boil, stirring frequently and skimming off foam, until it reaches the setting point (about 5 to 10 minutes).

Add a few flowers to each jar.

Ladle jelly into sterilized jars, seal with warm lids and process for 10 minutes at a rolling boil (15 minutes for pint/500 mL jars).

Remove the canner lid, turn off the heat, and allow the jars to sit in the hot water for another 5 minutes to cool down.

Ashbridge's Garden Chive Blossom and Sage Jelly

{ **Note:**
This jelly may take a day or two to reach a full set.

This delicately onion-flavored jelly could be used with goose, turkey, pork, or hamburgers. It cooks up into a lovely pale peachy-orange color, and the whole chive blossom holds its shape well. It would also look pretty to separate the blossom into separate flowerettes and put them into the jars instead.

Makes about 4½ cups.

2 cups chopped chive blossoms and stalks (no leaves) plus 1 whole blossom for each jar

½ cup crumbled dried sage leaves

2 cups water

¼ cup white wine vinegar (at least 5 percent acid)

4 cups sugar

1 pouch (3 oz/85mL) liquid pectin

Day 1:

Wash chives well before chopping.

Trim whole blossom stems to about 3 in (8 cm) in length and stand like a bouquet of flowers in a glass of cool water overnight.

In a non-reactive pot, combine chopped chive blossoms and stalks, sage, and water and bring to a boil. Turn the heat down and let steep for 2 to 4 hours.

Add the vinegar and steep, covered, overnight.

Day 2:

Sterilize jars and warm lids. (See full instructions, p. 49, or Bare-bones Cheat Sheet, on flap.)

Strain the chive mixture through a jelly bag.

In a wide, deep non-reactive pot with a thick bottom, combine the strained liquid with sugar. Bring to a full, rolling boil that cannot be stirred down.

Turn down the heat, add the liquid pectin, and bring back up to a full, rolling boil that cannot be stirred down. Continue to boil, stirring frequently and skimming off foam, until it reaches the setting point (about 5 to 10 minutes).

Snip stems off whole chive blossoms and place one in each sterilized jar.

Ladle jelly into sterilized jars, seal with warm lids and process for 10 minutes at a rolling boil (15 minutes for pint/500 mL jars).

Remove the canner lid, turn off the heat, and allow the jars to sit in the hot water for another 5 minutes to cool down.

Photo: Renée Joslyn

You either love it or you hate it, and although there may have been a time when haters prevailed, these days, garlic lovers abound. Whether as a subtle hint in a pasta sauce or boldly munched as whole cloves, the taste of garlic inspires devotion ... and festivals—lots of them.

In my province of Ontario, I can attend the Perth Garlic Festival or one in Stratford; on Canada's west coast, British Columbia boasts the Hills Garlic Festival in New Denver and the South Cariboo Garlic Festival in Lac La Hache. Across the US, you can find the Hudson Valley Garlic Festival in Saugerties, New York, the Southern Vermont Garlic and Herb Festival in Bennington, Vermont, the Elephant Garlic Festival in North Plains, Oregon, and the

great-granddaddy of them all, the famous Gilroy Garlic Festival in Gilroy, California.

With so many North Americans celebrating the pungent allium in everything from chili to ice cream, you'd think the continent would have a goodly supply of its many different varieties— but not so fast!

Over seventy-five percent of the world's garlic is produced in China, and the average North American grocery store is more likely to stock imported Chinese garlic, to the exclusion of local varieties.

There are hundreds of types of garlic, grouped into categories with names like Porcelain, Rocambole, Artichoke, Silverskin, Creole, and

Garlic will grow well in a fairly wide range of climates, from scorching California summers to snowbound Canadian winters. Few insects or microscopic organisms prey on it, and its odor even helps protect nearby plants from pests, so gardeners may enjoy experimenting with some unusual types beyond what's normally available to them.

Garlic is an essential ingredient in dill pickles and a useful flavor addition to almost any pickle. If it's canned in vinegar, it tends to turn blue due to a normal chemical reaction that doesn't make it unsafe to eat. However, it's a very low-acid food, so if you're planning to can it by itself, it should be entirely immersed in vinegar, and if you're thinking of adding an extra quantity to a chutney or sauce that will be canned, you'll need to bump up the acid level of the recipe to compensate for it.

A great book about garlic:

A Garlic Testament: Seasons on a Small New Mexico Farm by Stanley Crawford (an inspiring consideration of food and *terroir* and the process of coming to know one particular plant intimately).

Turban, and ranging in color from white to pink to purple. They fall into two basic types: hard-neck, or top-setting, garlic, which can reproduce itself fairly efficiently, and soft-neck garlic, which has become somewhat dependent on human cultivation. (Neither elephant garlic nor garlic chives are true garlic, by the way.)

Top-setting garlic sends up a shoot from its buried bulb every year, which produces a cluster of seed-like bulbils at the end. Each of these numerous bulbils, if it hits the ground, will in two years become a new garlic bulb. As for soft-neck garlic, if you've ever seen a household garlic bulb start to sprout, you know that each clove can become a new plant. However, if the bulb is left in the ground, the resulting dozen or so new bulbs will eventually crowd one another out.

Pickled Onions and Green Garlic "al Balsamico"

From Renée Joslyn of the blog Flamingo Musings (South Miami, Florida)
Originally published at *flamingomusings.com/2010/03/can-jam-3-alliums.html*

Renée (a.k.a. @RJFlamingo on Twitter) describes herself as "a middle-aged South Florida Jewish woman who has never had any 'work' done," but this hardly describes the lively humor of her popular blog. She writes: "I made two batches of this: one with the regular aged balsamic vinegar, and the other with the fig balsamic ... it was simply delish with my homemade Italian bread and parmesan breadsticks." She recommends using the pickling liquid for cooking, too.

Makes 4 cups.

6 spring onions

4 green garlic heads, washed well and thinly sliced (white and light-green parts only)

1 cup red wine (Renée uses a Montepulciano)

1 cup water

1 tsp kosher or pickling salt

¾ cup balsamic vinegar (at least 5 percent acid)

Sterilize jars and warm lids. (See full instructions, p. 49, or Bare-bones Cheat Sheet, on flap.)

In a wide, deep non-reactive pot with a thick bottom, combine onions, green garlic, red wine, water, and salt. Bring to a boil, then lower the heat and simmer until the vegetables soften slightly (about 5 minutes).

Add the balsamic vinegar and return to a simmer for another 5 minutes.

Fill jars with onions and garlic to within ¾ in (2 cm) of the top, and top up with vinegar/wine mixture to within ½ in (1 cm) (this is double the headspace for jams or jellies). Run a plastic or wooden knife or chopstick around the inside of the jar to release any trapped air bubbles. Top up the vinegar/wine mixture if necessary.

Seal the jars with warm lids and process for 10 minutes at a full, rolling boil.

Remove the canner lid, turn off the heat, and allow the jars to sit in the hot water for another 5 minutes to cool down.

Wait at least a week before eating to allow flavors to develop fully.

Use a plastic lid after the jar is open to keep the vinegar from corroding the metal one.

Pickled **Fiddlehead Ferns**

From Lorraine Johnson (Toronto; not previously published.)

Lorraine is the author of the inspiring *City Farmer: Adventures in Urban Food Growing* and numerous books about native plants. A Toronto local hero, in this recipe she shares her love of one of the favorite spring delicacies of temperate North America: the fiddlehead fern.

Makes 3 pint (500 mL) jars.

2 lb (1 kg) fiddlehead ferns

1 tbsp salt for boiling fiddleheads

1 tbsp kosher or pickling salt for vinegar mixture

2¼ cups white wine vinegar (at least 5 percent acid)

1 tbsp whole black peppercorns

Sterilize jars and warm lids. (See full instructions, p. 49, or Bare-bones Cheat Sheet, on flap.)

Trim and clean fiddleheads, removing all chaff and trimming off fibrous stems.

Place fiddleheads in a large pot of boiling, salted water and cook for 5 minutes. Drain.

In a wide, deep non-reactive pot with a thick bottom, combine salt and vinegar, and bring to a boil until the salt has dissolved.

Pack fiddleheads into the warm sterilized jars.

Add a third of the peppercorns to each jar. Top up with vinegar mixture to within ½ in (1 cm) (this is double the headspace for jams or jellies). Run a plastic or wooden knife or chopstick around the inside of the jar to release any trapped air bubbles. Top up the vinegar/wine mixture if necessary.

Seal the jars with warm lids and process for 15 minutes at a full, rolling boil.

Remove the canner lid, turn off the heat, and allow the jars to sit in the hot water for another 5 minutes to cool down.

Wait at least 4 weeks before eating to allow flavors to develop fully.

Use a plastic lid after the jar is open to keep the vinegar from corroding the metal one.

Pickled Asparagus and Fiddleheads

From Heather Kilner of the blog Backyard Farms (Toronto)

Originally published at *backyardfarmsto.blogspot.com/2010/05/can-jam-5-gus-and-barb. html*

Heather, who has been canning since she was a young girl, grows much of her own food in an urban garden and teaches canning workshops around Toronto. This recipe combines two of spring's most beloved crops.

Makes 4 pint (500 mL) jars.

8 cups white wine vinegar (at least 5 percent acid)

3 cups water

5 tbsp sugar

1 tbsp each mustard seeds, coriander seeds, black peppercorns, allspice berries, and dried chilis

3 tsp kosher or pickling salt

1 medium onion, thinly sliced

1 lb (500 g) fresh fiddleheads, cleaned (about 30)

4 lb (1.8 kg) fresh asparagus (about 60 spears)

Sterilize jars and warm lids. (See full instructions, p. 49, or Bare-bones Cheat Sheet, on flap.)

In a wide, deep non-reactive pot with a thick bottom, combine vinegar, water, sugar, spices, and salt, bring to a boil, and boil on moderate heat for about 10 minutes.

Divide slices of onion evenly among the jars, then place a layer of fiddleheads on top of the onions. Trim the asparagus to the height of the jar, less ¾–1 in (2–2.5 cm). Pack them in with the cut end facing down.

Top up the jars with vinegar mixture to within ½ in (1 cm) (this is double the headspace for jams or jellies). Run a plastic or wooden knife or chopstick around the inside of the jar to release any trapped air bubbles. Top up the vinegar/wine mixture if necessary.

Seal the jars with warm lids and process for 20 minutes at a full, rolling boil.

Remove the canner lid, turn off the heat, and allow the jars to sit in the hot water for another 5 minutes to cool down.

Wait at least 4 weeks before eating to allow flavors to develop fully.

Use a plastic lid after the jar is open to keep the vinegar from corroding the metal one.

Pickled Wild Leeks or Ramps

From Joel MacCharles and Dana Harrison of the blog Well Preserved (Toronto)

Originally published at *wellpreserved.ca/2010/04/01/preserving-spring-wild-leeks-or-ramps/*

Well Preserved has quickly become one of the most consulted food preserving blogs, and Joel and Dana's passion for the subject is evident. They write: "When you pick a wild leek, it does not grow back ... Ethical harvesting of wild leeks is tricky business—guidelines recommend that you harvest less than 5 percent of a patch, which is fine as long as someone doesn't arrive after you and pick another 5 percent and so forth." Joel and Dana advocate buying from an ethical source and using the rest of the plant as well; they "dehydrate the roots for winter salad topping and freeze a pesto from the leaves for soups, stews, and sauces." That said, wild leeks are worth the effort and care: Joel and Dana say these pickles are great alone or with cheese.

Makes 5–6 cups.

3 cups white vinegar (at least 5 percent acid)

½ cup water

1 tsp kosher or pickling salt

1 cup sugar

4 loosely packed cups of chopped, cleaned leeks

4 tsp mustard seeds

2 tsp celery seeds

Sterilize jars and warm lids. (See full instructions, p. 49, or Bare-bones Cheat Sheet, on flap.)

In a wide, deep non-reactive pot with a thick bottom, combine vinegar, water, salt, and sugar, and simmer on medium-high heat for 3 minutes (begin timing when you hit a solid simmer).

Add leeks to liquid; bring back to a gentle simmer and time for 5 minutes from that point.

Divide the leeks and spices evenly and pack them in the warm jars.

Top up with vinegar mixture to within ½ in (1 cm) (this is double the headspace for jams or jellies). Run a plastic or wooden knife or chopstick around the inside of the jar to release any trapped air bubbles. Top up the vinegar/wine mixture if necessary.

Seal the jars with warm lids and process for 10 minutes at a full, rolling boil.

Remove the canner lid, turn off the heat and allow the jars to sit in the hot water for another 5 minutes to cool down.

Wait at least 6 weeks before eating to allow flavors to develop fully.

Use a plastic lid after the jar is open to keep the vinegar from corroding the metal one.

Recipes for Summer

Summer is the glory time for home canning. Mounds of tender berries and luscious stone fruits beckon enticingly from every shop and farm stand, and the only question is how much time you have to put them up before the season is over.

Easy Victorian-Style Raspberry Jam

My very favorite of all the berries, raspberries combine a rich, aromatic fragrance with a gorgeous ruby-red color (or you may be lucky enough to find the rarer golden raspberries). They're very tender and will get crushed if carried in a paper bag, so I collect the smallest size of plastic, clamshell-style berry containers in case I plan to buy berries at a farmer's market or roadside stand.

Bakers from the French tradition consider raspberry jam indispensable for cake fillings. You can make it with frozen berries (don't quite thaw them—they can still have some ice crystals when you begin to heat them), but the ultimate jam is made from raspberries that you've picked within the past 3 or 4 hours.

Makes about 6 cups.

Sterilize jars and warm lids. (See full instructions, p. 49, or Bare-bones Cheat Sheet, on flap.)

6 cups raspberries

Gently wash the berries.

6 cups sugar

In a wide, deep non-reactive pot with a thick bottom, heat the berries just to the boiling point.

{ **Tip:** When washing tender berries, pour a small amount at a time into a strainer and immerse them in a large container full of clean, cool water. Agitate them gently for a very short time.

Remove from the heat and add the sugar, stirring very gently until it dissolves completely.

Return the mixture to the heat, bring it up to a full, rolling boil that cannot be stirred down and continue to boil, stirring frequently and skimming off foam, until it reaches the setting point. (Ideally, some berries will still hold their shape at this point.)

Ladle into sterilized jars, leaving ¼ in (6 mm) of headspace. Seal with warm lids and process for 10 minutes at a rolling boil (15 minutes for pint/500 mL jars).

Remove the canner lid, turn off the heat, and allow the jars to sit in the hot water for another 5 minutes to cool down.

Golden Raspberry Jam with Spearmint and Lemon Balm

If you have a shady backyard that grows nothing but mint and lemon balm, this is the recipe for you! (You could substitute regular red raspberries if you can't find the golden ones.) This delicate combination smells like summer.

Makes 3 cups.

6 cups golden raspberries

½ cup fresh lemon balm (or 2 tbsp dried)

½ cup fresh spearmint (or 2 tbsp dried)

4 cups sugar

Sterilize jars and warm lids. (See full instructions, p. 49, or Bare-bones Cheat Sheet, flap.)

Gently wash the berries.

If using fresh herbs, chop them finely. Tie the chopped fresh or dried herbs into a jelly bag or a piece of cheesecloth.

In a wide, deep non-reactive pot with a thick bottom, combine the berries and the bag containing the herbs, and heat just to the boiling point.

Remove from the heat and add the sugar, stirring very gently until it dissolves completely.

Return the mixture to the heat, bring it up to a full, rolling boil that cannot be stirred down, and continue to boil, stirring frequently and skimming off foam, until it reaches the setting point.

Remove the herbs and ladle into sterilized jars, leaving ¼ in (6 mm) of headspace. Seal with warm lids and process for 10 minutes at a rolling boil (15 minutes for pint/500 mL jars).

Remove the canner lid, turn off the heat, and allow the jars to sit in the hot water for another 5 minutes to cool down.

Blackberry Lime Jam with Pomona's Pectin

From Shae Irving of the blog Hitchhiking to Heaven (Fairfax, California)

Originally published at *hitchhikingtoheaven.com/2010/07/blackberry-lime-jam-with-pomonas-pectin.html*

This tart-sweet jam is my mother's favorite from among all the recipes in this book. Perhaps that's because the recipe's creator, Shae Irving, loves blackberries and has tweaked this recipe to just the right balance of flavors.

Makes about 6 cups.

2 tsp Pomona's calcium water (or 3 tsp if half the blackberry seeds are removed)

4 cups crushed blackberries

2 tsp Pomona's Pectin powder (or 3 tsp if half the blackberry seeds are removed)

2 cups sugar

zest of 3 limes, minced

¼ cup lime juice

Sterilize jars and warm lids. (See full instructions, p. 49, or Bare-bones Cheat Sheet, on flap.)

Prepare calcium water in a small jar with a lid (½ tsp calcium powder from the Pomona's Pectin kit to ½ cup water). Store in the fridge between uses, but shake well to mix before using.

Rinse the blackberries only if necessary to remove dust or insects.

Optional: If you wish to reduce the number of seeds in the jam, use a food mill to remove the seeds from 2 cups of berries. To get the maximum pulp from the berries, let the food mill sit over a bowl while you prepare other ingredients. Scrape pulp off the bottom and give it another crank every few minutes. Use the full 3 tsp of pectin and calcium water if you remove some of the seeds.

Gently crush the remaining berries with a potato masher or the back of a slotted spoon—or your hands, if you don't mind the stains.

In a bowl, combine the pectin and sugar and set aside.

In a wide, deep non-reactive pot with a thick bottom, combine all 4 cups of berries, lime zest, lime juice, and calcium water. Bring the mixture to a boil.

Add the pectin-sugar mixture and stir vigorously for 1 to 2 minutes to dissolve the pectin.

Return the mixture to a boil and remove it from the heat immediately. Skim the foam.

Ladle into sterilized jars, leaving ¼ in (6 mm) of headspace. Seal with warm lids and process for 10 minutes at a rolling boil (15 minutes for pint/500 mL jars).

Remove the canner lid, turn off the heat, and allow the jars to sit in the hot water for another 5 minutes to cool down.

{ Tip:
Jams and jellies made with Pomona's Pectin continue to set for several hours or even days after processing, so don't worry if they look soft when they first cool.

Blackberry-Raspberry Jam

Raspberries are my favorite, so I overload this gorgeously colored jam with them, but if you come across some especially delicious blackberries, feel free to reverse the proportions. This jam is a classic in tarts (see p. 236).

Makes 3 cups.

3 cups raspberries

1 cup blackberries

3 tbsp lemon juice

3 cups sugar

Sterilize jars and warm lids. (See full instructions, p. 49, or Bare-bones Cheat Sheet, flap.)

Gently wash the berries.

In a wide, deep non-reactive pot with a thick bottom, combine berries and lemon juice. Crush berries with a potato masher or the back of a slotted spoon, then heat just to the boiling point.

Remove from the heat and add the sugar, stirring very gently until it dissolves completely.

Return the mixture to the heat, bring it up to a full, rolling boil that cannot be stirred down, and continue to boil, stirring frequently and skimming off foam, until it reaches the setting point.

Ladle into sterilized jars, leaving ¼ in (6 mm) of headspace. Seal with warm lids and process for 10 minutes at a rolling boil (15 minutes for pint/500 mL jars).

Remove the canner lid, turn off the heat, and allow the jars to sit in the hot water for another 5 minutes to cool down.

Vanilla Blueberry Jam

The beautiful color makes this jam an exciting choice to stir into yogurt for breakfast or dessert. But watch out while handling the berries; they can turn your fingertips gray!

Makes 6 cups.

6 cups blueberries

¾ cup water

3 tbsp lemon juice

1 vanilla bean

1 box (2 oz/57 g) powdered pectin

6 cups sugar

> **{ Tip:**
> Since vanilla beans don't come cheap, you may wish to save the one you fish out of the pot. Rinse and dry it, then poke it into a sugar bowl to add flavor to morning coffee, or into a bag of sugar that will be used for baking cookies.

Sterilize jars and warm lids. (See full instructions, p. 49, or Bare-bones Cheat Sheet, flap.)

In a wide, deep non-reactive pot with a thick bottom, crush the blueberries (a potato masher or slotted spoon is an ideal tool for this job). Add the water, lemon juice, and vanilla bean. Bring to a boil.

Remove from heat, then add the pectin and stir in until completely dissolved in the fruit mixture.

Return to stove on low heat and simmer for 5 minutes. Remove from heat, cover, and let stand for 30 to 60 minutes.

Return to stove and bring up to a boil. Once again, remove from heat and add the sugar, stirring well until it dissolves completely.

Bring to a boil again and cook at a rolling boil, stirring frequently and skimming off foam, until it reaches the setting point.

Remove the vanilla bean and ladle into sterilized jars, leaving ¼ in (6 mm) of headspace. Seal with warm lids and process for 10 minutes at a rolling boil (15 minutes for pint/500 mL jars).

Remove the canner lid, turn off the heat, and allow the jars to sit in the hot water for another 5 minutes to cool down.

Gooseberry Ginger Jam

After making this jam with ginger, I will never make plain gooseberry jam again; ginger wakes up the distinctive gooseberry taste and gives it a delicious fullness and bite. This recipe won first prize for berry jam at Toronto's Royal Winter Agricultural Fair.

Makes 5–6 cups.

6–7 cups gooseberries

about 3 cubic in (49 cubic cm) candied ginger (p. 233) or peeled fresh ginger

1¼ cups water

6 cups sugar

Sterilize jars and warm lids. (See full instructions, p. 49, or Bare-bones Cheat Sheet, on flap.)

Wash the gooseberries and remove the stems and woody tufts from tops and tails.

Peel then chop the ginger finely.

In a wide, deep non-reactive pot with a thick bottom, combine the gooseberries, ginger, and water, and bring to a boil. Turn the heat down and simmer for about 30 minutes, stirring occasionally, until the mixture resembles pea soup.

Remove from the heat and add the sugar, stirring well until it dissolves completely.

Return the mixture to the heat, bring to a full, rolling boil that cannot be stirred down, and continue to boil, stirring frequently and skimming off foam, until it reaches the setting point.

> **{ Tip:**
> The gooseberry mixture will gradually change color in the pot from greenish gray to a pinkish gold.

Ladle into sterilized jars, leaving ¼ in (6 mm) of headspace. Seal with warm lids and process for 10 minutes at a rolling boil (15 minutes for pint/500 mL jars).

Remove the canner lid, turn off the heat, and allow the jars to sit in the hot water for another 5 minutes to cool down.

Blueberry Lemon Marmalade with Lavender

This tasty marmalade is my homage to Audra Wolfe and the goats. It seemed to yield a lot of marmalade per cup of fruit, so it almost qualifies as a thrifty recipe.

Makes 10 cups.

3 lemons

2 tbsp dried lavender

2 cups water

6 cups blueberries

6 cups sugar

Day 1:
Scrub the lemons in warm, soapy water to remove wax, pesticides, or dirt. Slice them as thinly as possible, then chop into pieces.

Tie the lavender into a jelly bag or a piece of cheesecloth.

In a wide, deep non-reactive pot with a thick bottom, cover the lemons with the water and add the lavender. Bring to a boil, and simmer for 5 minutes. Turn off the heat and let the pan cool. Cover and let stand overnight.

Day 2:
Sterilize jars and warm lids. (See full instructions, p. 49, or Bare-bones Cheat Sheet, on flap.)

Add the blueberries to the lemon mixture and crush them with a potato masher or slotted spoon.

Add the sugar to the mixture, stirring well until it dissolves completely.

Bring the mixture to a full, rolling boil that cannot be stirred down, then continue to boil until it reaches the setting point (watch it carefully—the lemons have lots of pectin, and the gel stage may arrive rather suddenly).

Remove the bag of lavender from the pot.

Ladle into sterilized jars, leaving ¼ in (6 mm) of headspace. Seal with warm lids and process for 10 minutes at a rolling boil (15 minutes for pint/500 mL jars).

Remove the canner lid, turn off the heat, and allow the jars to sit in the hot water for another 5 minutes to cool down.

Photo: Briand/Ontario Tourism 2001

We Sure Can ... Blueberries and Their Relatives

They inspire affection out of all proportion with their small size and modest appearance. But for the Native and earliest European settlers to North America, plants of the genus *Vaccinium*—blueberries, cranberries, bilberries, huckleberries, and lingonberries—offered tasty and nutritious food in the poorest of growing conditions. (I know from experience that blueberry bushes in particular will thrive on solid rock with the barest litter of pine needles; to maintain their peak fruiting capabilities, they even like to be burned back every few years.)

The huckleberry may be the friendliest of all US native plants. In literature, its associations are uniformly folksy and cheerful: from Huckleberry Finn to Huckleberry Hound to "Huck,"

the name of the farmhand played by Ray Bolger in *The Wizard of Oz*, whose alter ego is the Scarecrow. And the term "huckleberry friend" (best known from the song "Moon River") means a buddy from your childhood.

Cranberries (along with maple syrup) are loved by central and east-coast Canadians as national icons almost on a par with hockey, the beaver, and "Canadian" back bacon. That love is apparently shared by New Englanders in the US, and cranberry sauce is, of course, a *sine qua non* of Thanksgiving and Christmas turkey dinners.

For a while, most people weren't eating many *vaccinia* on other occasions, but over the past decade or so both cranberries and blueber-

deep indigo to vivid red. Their pectin content is somewhat low, however, so they generally need help from another source.

Since the word "antioxidant" became a household term, wild organic blueberries have become one of the costliest fruits at the market, so if you get an invitation to pick some on a friend's property when they ripen in early summer, you should leap at the chance.

Some great books about *vaccinium*:

The Cranberry Connection: Cranberry Cookery with Flavour, Fact, and Folklore and *The Blueberry Connection: Blueberry Cookery with Flavour, Fact and Folklore*, both by Beatrice Ross Buszek (enormously chatty, reproduced directly from handwritten manuscripts, and filled with odd facts).

Cranberries: Recipes from Canada's Best Chefs by Elaine Elliott and *Blueberries: Recipes from Canada's Best Chefs* by Elaine Elliot and Virginia Lee (very pretty little books with lots of tempting photography of food and fruit)

Huckleberry Cookbook by Stephanie Hester and Alex Hester (includes lots of lore about this beloved American berry).

ries have risen in prominence because of their health benefits (they're high in antioxidants and vitamins), and are being avidly consumed in baked goods, as juice, and in dried form (as "craisins," in the case of cranberries). I do wonder how much nutritional benefit one might derive from drinking a "crantini," but the humble *vaccinium* has also taken its place on the bartender's shelf.

All the members of the genus are useful in canning, and the cranberry in particular, rich in both pectin and acid, will gel if you so much as wave a cup of sugar in its direction. Blueberries are one of the classic jam fruits, and although they don't have the intoxicating aroma of raspberries or citrus, they are remarkable for the astonishing color range of their juice, from

Red Currant Jelly

Red currant jelly is what I treat myself to in the winter when I'm feeling low; currants have a lot of vitamin C and a delicious tangy scent that'll perk you up.

Makes 2 cups.

Sterilize jars and warm lids. (See full instructions, p. 49, or Bare-bones Cheat Sheet, on flap.)

4 cups red currants

Wash the red currants and separate them from their stems.

2–3 cups sugar

In a wide, deep non-reactive pot with a thick bottom, heat the currants until they break down and come to a boil. Turn the heat down and simmer until the berries have broken down completely, skimming off scum as it forms.

Remove from the heat and strain first through a strainer or food mill, gently squeezing out the juice with the back of a spoon, and then through a jelly bag. Do not squeeze the jelly bag.

Measure juice, return it to the pot, add an equal amount of sugar (should be about 2–3 cups), and stir well, until the sugar dissolves completely.

Return the mixture to the heat, bring it to a full, rolling boil that cannot be stirred down, and continue to boil, stirring frequently and skimming off foam, until it reaches the setting point.

Ladle into sterilized jars, leaving ¼ in (6mm) of headspace. Seal with warm lids and process for 10 minutes at a rolling boil (15 minutes for pint/500 mL jars).

Remove the canner lid, turn off the heat, and allow the jars to sit in the hot water for another 5 minutes to cool down.

Saskatoonberry Jam

From David Ort of the blog Food With Legs (Toronto) Originally published at *foodwithlegs .com/?p=480*

A dedicated local food forager and preserver, David gets the berries for this recipe from a tree on family property. He writes: "Serviceberries *(Amelanchier alnifolia and Amelanchier canadensis)* go by many names. On the [Canadian] prairies, they're known as Saskatoon berries (the city is named after the bush, not the other way around); in the northern United States as Juneberries, where they can be counted on to ripen during that month, and as shadberries in places where the rivers are full of migrating shad fish when the flowers appear ... They blow blueberries out of the water in terms of magnesium, calcium, potassium, and fiber."

Makes 3–4 cups.

finely chopped peel, flesh, and whole seeds of 1 lemon

about 2½ cups whole Saskatoon berries

about 5½ cups crushed Saskatoon berries

2 tbsp lemon juice

1 cup sugar

Day 1:

Tie the lemon peel, flesh and seeds in a jelly bag or muslin or cheesecloth. Put the bag into a non-reactive bowl with the whole and crushed berries and lemon juice. Refrigerate overnight.

Day 2:

Sterilize jars and warm lids. (See full instructions, p. 49, or Bare-bones Cheat Sheet, on flap.)

Strain the contents of the bowl and squeeze the jelly bag or fabric to collect all the liquid. Reserve the fruit and allow it to stand for 15 to 20 minutes.

In a wide, deep non-reactive pot with a thick bottom, bring the strained liquid to a boil on medium-high heat. After the juice has reduced slightly (about 5 minutes), add the sugar and the reserved fruit pulp, stirring well until the sugar dissolves completely.

Return the mixture to a full, rolling boil that cannot be stirred down, and continue to boil, stirring frequently, until it reaches the setting point.

Ladle into sterilized jars, leaving ¼ in (6 mm) of headspace. Seal with warm lids and process for 10 minutes at a rolling boil (15 minutes for pint/500 mL jars).

Remove the canner lid, turn off the heat, and allow the jars to sit in the hot water for another 5 minutes to cool down.

Wait about a month before eating to allow flavors to develop fully.

Sour Cherry Jam

This jam makes a quickie dessert when spooned into ready-made mini tart shells or (even better) baked into fresh ones (see p. 236).

Makes 3½ cups.

Sterilize jars and warm lids. (See full instructions, p. 49, or Bare-bones Cheat Sheet, on flap.)

6 cups sour cherries

Wash and stone the cherries.

4 cups sugar

¼ cup lemon juice

In a non-reactive bowl, combine all ingredients and allow them to macerate for at least two hours.

¼ tsp vanilla extract

In a wide, deep non-reactive pot with a thick bottom, bring the mixture up to a full, rolling boil that cannot be stirred down, and continue to boil, stirring frequently and skimming off foam, until it reaches the setting point.

Ladle into sterilized jars, leaving ¼ in (6 mm) of headspace. Seal with warm lids and process for 10 minutes at a rolling boil (15 minutes for pint/500 mL jars).

Remove the canner lid, turn off the heat, and allow the jars to sit in the hot water for another 5 minutes to cool down.

{ Tip:
Be very careful not to overcook cherry jam, as it can become unmanageably stiff when it sets.

Apricot Jam Five Ways

From Alec Stockwell (Toronto; not previously published.)

Alec's decadent French-style jams are greatly coveted by his friends and neighbors. This one is an absolute classic, from maceration to the choice of various flavorings. The slivered almonds stand in for the traditional apricot kernel (see p. 133). Use apricot jam on toast, to glaze a fruit tart, or as filling for a layer cake.

Makes 5–6 cups.

4 cups pitted and finely chopped apricots

about 4 cups sugar (if you have a kitchen scale, weigh the prepared apricots and use an equal weight of sugar)

(optional) ½ cup slivered toasted almonds

(optional) 1 sprig rosemary or ¼ cup organic lavender flowers (dried or fresh) or 1 vanilla bean or ½ stick of cinnamon (any of these is nice; the jam is also delicious without extra flavoring)

Day 1:

In a non-reactive bowl, layer the apricots and sugar, and leave them to macerate overnight.

Day 2:

Sterilize jars and warm lids. (See full instructions, p. 49, or Bare-bones Cheat Sheet, on flap.)

In a wide, deep non-reactive pot with a thick bottom, add the apricots and sugar and bring to a boil, stirring frequently.

After about 15 minutes of boiling, when the mixture has turned darker, add the slivered almonds (if using) and your choice from among the optional seasonings.

Continue to boil, but keep the heat as low as possible, stirring continuously until it reaches the setting point.

Remove optional seasoning, if used.

Ladle into sterilized jars, leaving ¼ in (6 mm) of headspace. Seal with warm lids and process for 10 minutes at a rolling boil (15 minutes for pint/500 mL jars).

Remove the canner lid, turn off the heat, and allow the jars to sit in the hot water for another 5 minutes to cool down.

Wait about a month before eating to allow flavors to develop fully.

Cinnamon Yellow Plum Jam

A comforting, gentle jam that's easy to make and delicious on toast or cereal.

Makes 3½ cups.

Sterilize jars and warm lids. (See full instructions, p. 49, or Bare-bones Cheat Sheet, on flap.)

4 cups halved and stoned yellow plums

In a non-reactive bowl, combine the plums, sugar, and lemon juice, and allow them to macerate for at least 2 hours.

3 cups sugar

¼ cup lemon juice

In a wide, deep non-reactive pot with a thick bottom, add the plum mixture and cinnamon sticks, on medium heat, and stir well until the sugar dissolves completely.

3 whole cinnamon sticks

Bring the mixture to a full, rolling boil that cannot be stirred down, and continue to boil, stirring frequently and skimming off foam (there will be a lot of foam; skim it off thoroughly), until it reaches the setting point.

Remove the cinnamon sticks and ladle into sterilized jars, leaving ¼ in (6 mm) of headspace. Seal with warm lids and process for 10 minutes at a rolling boil (15 minutes for pint/500 mL jars).

Remove the canner lid, turn off the heat, and allow the jars to sit in the hot water for another 5 minutes to cool down.

Persian-Inspired Yellow Plum Jam

This jam is exotically flavorful and has a very pretty greenish-yellow hue. You may finely grind the cardamom seeds, but whole ones look nice in the jar.

Makes 4 cups.

Sterilize jars and warm lids. (See full instructions, p. 49, or Bare-bones Cheat Sheet, on flap.)

6 cardamom pods

4 cups halved and stoned yellow plums

3 cups sugar

¼ cup lime juice

about 2 cubic in (33 cubic cm) candied ginger (p. 233) or peeled fresh ginger

In a hot, ungreased skillet, toast the cardamom pods until they are fragrant, being careful not to scorch or burn them. Remove from skillet, then crush them under the flat of a knife and release the dark seeds inside; discard the shells.

In a wide, deep non-reactive pot with a thick bottom on medium heat, combine the plums, sugar, lime juice, ginger, and cardamom, stirring well until the sugar dissolves completely.

Bring the mixture to a full, rolling boil that cannot be stirred down, and continue to boil, stirring frequently and skimming off foam, until it reaches the setting point.

Ladle into sterilized jars, leaving ¼ in (6 mm) of headspace. Seal with warm lids and process for 10 minutes at a rolling boil (15 minutes for pint/500 mL jars).

Remove the canner lid, turn off the heat, and allow the jars to sit in the hot water for another 5 minutes to cool down.

Ontario Tutti-Frutti Jam

Three gorgeous summer stone fruits, all in season at the same time!

Makes 5 cups.

Sterilize jars and warm lids. (See full instructions, p. 49, or Bare-bones Cheat Sheet, on flap.)

1½ cups water

2¼ cups sugar

In a wide, deep non-reactive pot with a thick bottom on medium heat, combine the water, sugar, and cinnamon sticks, stirring well until the sugar dissolves completely.

2 cinnamon sticks

Bring the mixture to a boil, and continue to boil for about 2 minutes.

2 cups skinned, stoned, and chopped peaches

Remove from the heat and add the fruit. Return the mixture to the heat, bring to a full, rolling boil that cannot be stirred down, and continue to boil, stirring frequently and skimming off foam, until it reaches the setting point. Remove the cinnamon sticks.

4 cups halved and stoned yellow plums (unpeeled)

Ladle into sterilized jars, leaving ¼ in (6 mm) of headspace. Seal with warm lids and process for 10 minutes at a rolling boil (15 minutes for pint/500 mL jars).

2 cups quartered and stoned apricots (unpeeled)

Remove the canner lid, turn off the heat, and allow the jars to sit in the hot water for another 5 minutes to cool down.

{ Tip:
Skin the peaches by immersing them in boiling water for about a minute, then plunging them into cold water; the skins will slip off easily. Remove the stones and chop the fruit roughly.

Plum Conserve for a Winter's Night

Although plums are summery, this conserve is perfectly suited to savoring on a dark winter night, to be eaten before a roaring fire with nuts, strong cheese, gingerbread, and other warming treats.

Makes 4–5 cups.

4 lb (1.8 kg) blue plums (about 24), washed, pitted, and halved

3 limes, washed, quartered lengthwise, seeded, and cut into very fine slices

4½ cups sugar

¾ cup golden raisins

¼ tsp each ground cloves, nutmeg, and cinnamon

about 2 cubic in (33 cubic cm) finely chopped candied or peeled fresh ginger (optional)

¾ cup finely chopped walnuts

6 tbsp brandy

Sterilize jars and warm lids. (See full instructions, p. 49, or Bare-bones Cheat Sheet, on flap.)

In a wide, deep non-reactive pot with a thick bottom, combine all ingredients except the walnuts and brandy, bring them to a full, rolling boil that cannot be stirred down and continue to boil, stirring frequently and skimming off foam, until the mixture reaches the setting point. (The plum skins may dissolve or may roll up like thin cigars. I like the way they look in the jars, but you may choose to remove some.)

Turn the heat off, add the walnuts and brandy, and allow the mixture to rest for 5 minutes, stirring occasionally, until the walnuts begin to blend into the mixture.

Ladle into sterilized jars, leaving ¼ in (6 mm) of headspace. Seal with warm lids and process for 10 minutes at a rolling boil (15 minutes for pint/500 mL jars).

Remove the canner lid, turn off the heat, and allow the jars to sit in the hot water for another 5 minutes to cool down.

Photo: National Watermelon Promotion Board

Watermelon Cranberry Sauce

From the National Watermelon Promotion Board

Originally published at *watermelon.org/recipe_detail.asp?recipeDisp=232*

An interesting alternative to traditional cranberry sauce. The watermelon retains its crunch, but anyone who tastes it will probably guess it's cucumber. Meanwhile, the cranberry gives up a lot of its bitterness, although there's not very much added sugar. This would make a good addition to the menu for a New Year's celebration since it contains ingredients from spring (maple syrup), summer (watermelon), fall (cranberry), and winter (lemon).

Makes about 4½ cups.

4 cups fresh or frozen cranberries

½ cup sugar

1 teaspoon vanilla extract

juice and zest of 1 lemon

½ cup maple syrup

¼ tsp ground cinnamon

2 cups minced watermelon flesh

Sterilize jars and warm lids. (See full instructions, p. 49, or Bare-bones Cheat Sheet, on flap.)

In a wide, deep non-reactive pot with a thick bottom, heat cranberries, sugar, vanilla, lemon juice, and zest to the simmering point. Simmer gently, stirring occasionally, until cranberries are tender, about 15 to 20 minutes.

Reduce heat to low and add the maple syrup and cinnamon. Simmer for another 2 to 3 minutes. Remove from heat and allow to rest for 10 minutes. Stir in watermelon and allow the watermelon juice to blend into the rest of the mixture.

Ladle into sterilized jars, leaving ¼ in (6 mm) of headspace. Run a plastic or wooden knife or chopstick around the inside of the jar to release any trapped air bubbles. Top up with more sauce if necessary.

Seal with warm lids and process for 15 minutes at a rolling boil.

Remove the canner lid, turn off the heat, and allow the jars to sit in the hot water for another 5 minutes to cool down.

Guava Jelly

Guava jelly is a beloved staple in places like India and the Caribbean, and it turns out to be loaded with pectin that produces a pleasant, firm, slightly milky set that complements the delicate flavor. Guavas somewhat resemble pears in texture. They should yield to the touch and smell fragrant when they are ripe.

Makes 2–3 cups.

Sterilize jars and warm lids. (See full instructions, p. 49, or Bare-bones Cheat Sheet, on flap.)

3 lb (1.5 kg) guavas (about 20)

6 cups water

3 tbsp lime juice

about 3 cups sugar

In a wide, deep non-reactive pot with a thick bottom, combine guavas and water and bring to a boil. Turn heat to low and allow the mixture to simmer, stirring occasionally, until the fruits have broken down (about 30 minutes). You can help it along by mashing it with a potato masher or the back of a spoon.

Strain the guava pulp by pushing it with the back of a spoon through a wide-mesh strainer (it will be thick and pulpy). Strain a second time, but without forcing it through.

Put the strained juice into a wet jelly bag or two or three layers of cheesecloth or a wide-weave dish-towel. Hang it over a bowl to drip for about 1 hour. (Do not squeeze the bag or the jelly will be cloudy.) If you have the patience, pour the juice through a clean jelly bag to remove the last of the sediment.

Measure the liquid (there should be about 3 cups).

In a wide, deep non-reactive pot with a thick bottom over medium heat, combine the guava liquid with the lime juice and 1 cup of sugar for every cup of juice, stirring well until the sugar dissolves completely.

A quartet of Asian-inspired jellies. Left to right: Guava Jelly (p. 130), Lemongrass, Ginger and Kaffir Lime Jelly with Pomona's Pectin (p. 204), Masala Chai Tea Jelly (p. 223), and Watermelon Jelly with Thai Sweet Basil Ribbons (p. 146).

Photo: Niamh Malcolm

Boil gently, stirring frequently and skimming off foam, until it reaches the setting point. (Guava seems to produce a very thick foam.)

Ladle into sterilized jars, leaving ¼ in (6 mm) of headspace. Seal with warm lids and process for 10 minutes at a rolling boil (15 minutes for pint/500 mL jars).

Remove the canner lid, turn off the heat, and allow the jars to sit in the hot water for another 5 minutes to cool down.

We Sure Can ... Peaches and Other Drupes

Many places claim peaches as their own special fruit: Georgia, of course, and the Okanagan Valley near Canada's west coast, as well as the Niagara region of Ontario, and no doubt numerous other locales. The melting, seductive texture and flavor of the peach makes it among the sexiest of all fruits, but it takes a certain flair to make it into a great preserve.

Although there are numerous varieties of peaches ripening in different months, differing slightly in coloring, and ranging in size from not much bigger than a golf ball to baseball size or bigger, commercial producers tend to downplay the variety names. Instead, they market peaches as either "freestone" or "clingstone."

In general, the clingstone peaches arrive earlier in the summer; the name refers to the fact that their flesh sticks stubbornly to the stone.

Freestone peaches are far easier to work with for pickles and jams because the stones pop right out and you don't risk crushing the fruit into ragged pieces in the process of removing it. Although I'm a fan of clingstone peaches for eating out of hand, for canning purposes, I think it's worth waiting until August for the freestones. (Tip: if peaches have a stem, they've been picked before they were completely ripe.)

For folks from the southern US, pickled peaches are the classic peach preserve: spiked with cloves and bathed in a vinegar-sugar syrup, they're cracked open for Thanksgiving

apricot jam is beloved in France, where it is used to glaze fruits tarts and to ice the insides of layer cakes. You'll notice that many traditional recipes (including those of the great chef Escoffier), suggest adding the inner "almonds," the kernels found inside the apricot stones, to the jam. These kernels actually have an almond taste. As any murder-mystery reader might be able to guess, this is because they contain the poison cyanide, as do the seeds and stones of many fruits, including apples, peaches, cherries, nectarines, and plums.

The quantity of kernels required to harm an adult would be fairly high; however, a child could apparently die from eating only a handful. Heat is said to destroy the enzyme that allows the cyanide to form, but if you have young children in the house, you should probably not cook with apricot kernels.

Great books about peaches:

Apples, Peaches and Pears: Great Canadian Recipes by Elizabeth Baird (a cookbook that is very informative about characteristics of the types of peaches grown in Canada).

Stone Fruit: Cherries, Nectarines, Apricots, Plums, Peaches by Cynthia Nims (part of a series about local foods of the Pacific Northwest).

dinner. Many people also love peach jam, but I find that the slippery texture and somewhat bland taste need to be bumped up a little; also, peaches are fairly low in pectin, and may not gel nicely on their own. Luckily, their taste blends well with a variety of herbs (e.g., rosemary, lavender) and other fruits.

Stone fruits like peaches are technically known as drupes; others include the plums, cherries, apricots, nectarines, and hybrids like apriums and plumcots. Of these, plums are the pectin champions: they gel up readily with no fuss. The rest of the stone fruits are iffy gellers; sour cherries in particular seem to come to a syrupy set on their own.

Apricots can be coaxed to a decent gel, and

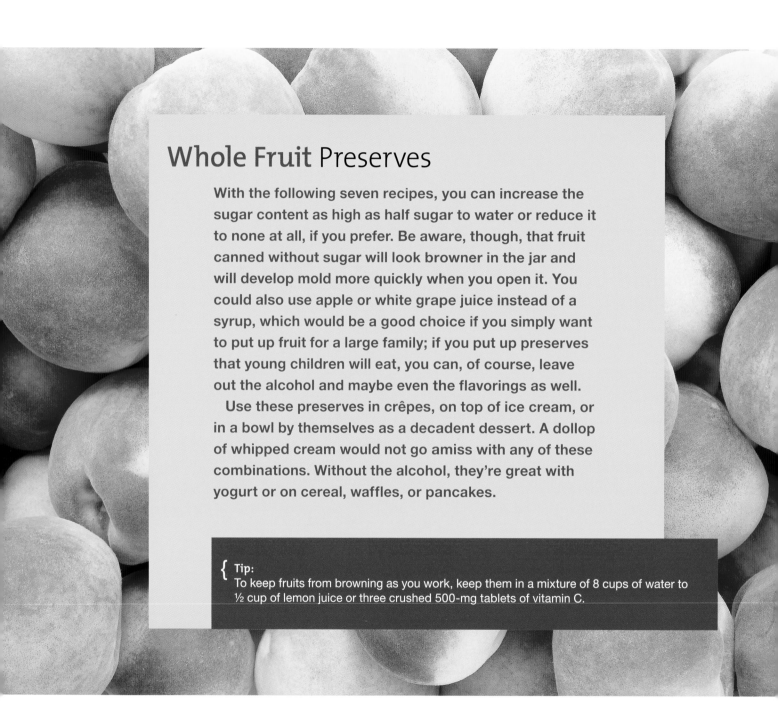

Whole Fruit Preserves

With the following seven recipes, you can increase the sugar content as high as half sugar to water or reduce it to none at all, if you prefer. Be aware, though, that fruit canned without sugar will look browner in the jar and will develop mold more quickly when you open it. You could also use apple or white grape juice instead of a syrup, which would be a good choice if you simply want to put up fruit for a large family; if you put up preserves that young children will eat, you can, of course, leave out the alcohol and maybe even the flavorings as well.

Use these preserves in crêpes, on top of ice cream, or in a bowl by themselves as a decadent dessert. A dollop of whipped cream would not go amiss with any of these combinations. Without the alcohol, they're great with yogurt or on cereal, waffles, or pancakes.

{ **Tip:**
To keep fruits from browning as you work, keep them in a mixture of 8 cups of water to ½ cup of lemon juice or three crushed 500-mg tablets of vitamin C.

Almond Apricot Preserves

Fills 6 pint (500 mL) jars.

about 48 small apricots (golf-ball size or smaller)

1¾ cups sugar

4 cups water

¾ cup kirsch

1½ tsp almond extract

Sterilize jars and warm lids. (See full instructions, p. 49, or Bare-bones Cheat Sheet, on flap.)

Halve and pit the apricots.

In a wide, deep non-reactive pot with a thick bottom on medium heat, combine the sugar and water, stirring well until the sugar dissolves completely, then heat to the boiling point.

If you have been keeping the apricots in vitamin-C water (see p. 134), strain first, then add them to the sugar syrup. Bring the pot back to the boil for about 1 minute, then turn off the heat.

Put 2 tbsp of kirsch and ¼ tsp of almond extract into each jar.

Fill jars with apricots to within ¾ in (2 cm) of the top, and top up with syrup to within ½ in (1 cm) (this is double the headspace for jams or jellies). Run a plastic or wooden knife or chopstick around the inside of the jar to release any trapped air bubbles. Top up the syrup if necessary.

Seal the jars with warm lids and process for 25 minutes at a full, rolling boil.

Remove the canner lid, turn off the heat, and allow the jars to sit in the hot water for another 5 minutes to cool down.

Wait at least 6 to 8 weeks before eating to allow flavors to develop fully.

Brandied Sweet Cherry Preserves

**Fills 6 pint
(500 mL) jars.**

**about 8 cups
fresh cherries**

1¾ cups sugar

4 cups water

¾ cup brandy

Sterilize jars and warm lids. (See full instructions, p. 49, or Bare-bones Cheat Sheet, on flap.)

Pit the cherries with a cherry or olive pitter, or by poking the pits out with a narrow chopstick.

In a wide, deep non-reactive pot with a thick bottom on medium heat, combine the sugar and water, stirring well until the sugar dissolves completely, then heat to the boiling point.

Put 2 tbsp of brandy into each jar.

Fill jars with cherries to within ¾ in (2 cm) of the top, and top up with syrup to within ½ in (1 cm) (this is double the headspace for jams or jellies). Run a plastic or wooden knife or chopstick around the inside of the jar to release any trapped air bubbles. Top up the syrup if necessary.

Seal the jars with warm lids and process for 25 minutes at a full, rolling boil.

Remove the canner lid, turn off the heat, and allow the jars to sit in the hot water for another 5 minutes to cool down.

Wait at least 6 to 8 weeks before eating to allow flavors to develop fully.

Cinnamon Plum Preserves

**Fills 6 pint
(500 mL) jars.**

**about 48 small blue,
green, or yellow
plums (about golf-
ball size)**

1¾ cups sugar

4 cups water

¾ cup rum

36 allspice berries

**3 cinnamon sticks,
broken in half**

Sterilize jars and warm lids. (See full instructions, p. 49, or Bare-bones Cheat Sheet, on flap.)

Halve and pit the plums, or leave them whole, but prick the skins.

In a wide, deep non-reactive pot with a thick bottom on medium heat, combine the sugar and water, stirring well until the sugar dissolves completely, and heat to the boiling point.

If you have been keeping the plums in vitamin-C water (see p. 134), strain and add them to the sugar syrup. Bring the pot back to the boil for about 1 minute, then turn off the heat.

Put 2 tbsp rum, 6 allspice berries, and half a cinnamon stick into each jar.

Fill jars with plums to within ¾ in (2 cm) of the top, and top up with syrup to within ½ in (1 cm) (this is double the headspace for jams or jellies). Run a plastic or wooden knife or chopstick around the inside of the jar to release any trapped air bubbles. Top up the syrup if necessary.

Seal the jars with warm lids and process for 20 minutes at a full, rolling boil.

Remove the canner lid, turn off the heat, and allow the jars to sit in the hot water for another 5 minutes to cool down.

Wait at least 6 to 8 weeks before eating to allow flavors to develop fully.

Lavender Peach Preserves with Kirsch

Fills 6 pint (500-mL) jars.

about 30 medium peaches (about tennis-ball size)

1¾ cups sugar

4 cups water

¾ cup kirsch

¾ cup very fragrant dried lavender flowers (or, even better, 12–24 fresh flower stalks)

Sterilize jars and warm lids. (See full instructions, p. 49, or Bare-bones Cheat Sheet, on flap.)

Blanch peaches in boiling water for a few moments, then plunge them into cold water. Their skins should slip off easily. When peaches are cool, run a knife around them, following the natural seam. If you have a fully ripe freestone peach, you should be able to twist the knife and pop the peach in half while neatly removing the stone. Otherwise, you may want to quarter them and coax the stone out with a small paring knife.

In a wide, deep non-reactive pot with a thick bottom on medium heat, combine the sugar and water, stirring well until the sugar dissolves completely, and heat to the boiling point.

If you have been keeping the peaches in vitamin-C water (see p. 134), strain them and add the peaches to the sugar syrup. Bring the pot back to the boil for about 1 minute, then turn off the heat.

Put 2 tbsp of kirsch and 1–2 tbsp of dried lavender or 2–3 flower stalks into each jar.

Fill jars with peaches to within ¾ in (2 cm) of the top, and top up with syrup to within ½ in (1 cm) (this is double the headspace for jams or jellies). Run a plastic or wooden knife or chopstick around the inside of the jar to release any trapped air bubbles. Top up the syrup if necessary.

Seal with warm lids and process jars for 30 minutes at a full, rolling boil.

Remove the canner lid, turn off the heat, and allow the jars to sit in the hot water for another 5 minutes to cool down.

Wait at least 6 to 8 weeks before eating to allow flavors to develop fully.

Vanilla Sour Cherry Preserves

Fills 6 pint (500-mL) jars.

about 8 cups fresh or frozen (thawed) sour cherries

1¾ cups sugar

4 cups water

¾ cup kirsch

3 vanilla beans or 1½ tsp pure vanilla extract

Sterilize jars and warm lids. (See full instructions, p. 49, or Bare-bones Cheat Sheet, on flap.)

Pit the cherries with a cherry or olive pitter, or by poking the pits out with a narrow chopstick.

In a wide, deep non-reactive pot with a thick bottom on medium heat, combine the sugar and water, stirring well until the sugar dissolves completely, and heat to the boiling point.

Put 2 tbsp of kirsch and half a vanilla bean or ¼ tsp of vanilla extract into each jar.

Fill jars with cherries to within ¾ in (2 cm) of the top, and top up with syrup to within ½ in (1 cm) (this is double the headspace for jams or jellies). Run a plastic or wooden knife or chopstick around the inside of the jar to release any trapped air bubbles. Top up the syrup if necessary.

Seal the jars with warm lids and process for 25 minutes at a full, rolling boil.

Remove the canner lid, turn off the heat, and allow the jars to sit in the hot water for another 5 minutes to cool down.

Wait at least 6 to 8 weeks before eating to allow flavors to develop fully.

Star Anise Plum Preserves

Fills 6 pint (500 mL) jars.

about 48 small blue, green, or yellow plums (about golf-ball size)

1¾ cups sugar

4 cups water

¾ cup rum (dark or light)

6 whole star anise

Sterilize jars and warm lids. (See full instructions, p. 49, or Bare-bones Cheat Sheet, on flap.)

Halve and pit the plums or leave them whole, but prick the skins.

In a wide, deep non-reactive pot with a thick bottom on medium heat, combine the sugar and water, stirring well until the sugar dissolves completely, and heat to the boiling point.

If you have been keeping the plums in vitamin-C water (see p. 134), strain them. Add them to the syrup. Bring the pot back to the boil for about 1 minute, then turn off the heat.

Put 2 tbsp of rum and 1 star anise into each jar. (Place them so you can see the pretty stars on the outside of the jar.)

Fill jars with plums to within ¾ in (2 cm) of the top, and top up with syrup to within ½ in (1 cm) (this is double the headspace for jams or jellies). Run a plastic or wooden knife or chopstick around the inside of the jar to release any trapped air bubbles. Top up the syrup if necessary.

Seal the jars with warm lids and process for 20 minutes at a full, rolling boil.

Remove the canner lid, turn off the heat, and allow the jars to sit in the hot water for another 5 minutes to cool down.

Wait at least 6 to 8 weeks before eating to allow flavors to develop fully.

Vanilla Pear Preserves

**Fills 6 pint
(500-mL) jars.**

**about 24 firm small
to medium pears**

1¾ cups sugar

4 cups water

¾ cup brandy

**3 vanilla beans or
1½ tsp pure vanilla
extract**

Sterilize jars and warm lids. (See full instructions, p. 49, or Bare-bones Cheat Sheet, on flap.)

Halve or quarter the pears, whichever will make the most even pieces according to their shape, and core them. (Some pears are almost round; some have very long thick necks. Round pears quarter well; the others don't.)

In a wide, deep non-reactive pot with a thick bottom on medium heat, combine the sugar and water, stirring well until the sugar dissolves completely, and heat to the boiling point.

If you have been soaking the pears in vitamin-C water (see p. 134), strain and add them to the sugar syrup. Bring the pot back to the boil for about 1 minute, then turn off the heat.

Put 2 tbsp of brandy and half a vanilla bean or ¼ tsp of vanilla extract into each jar.

Fill jars with pears to within ¾ in (2 cm) of the top, and top up with syrup to within ½ in (1 cm) (this is double the headspace for jams or jellies). Run a plastic or wooden knife or chopstick around the inside of the jar to release any trapped air bubbles. Top up the syrup if necessary.

Seal the jars with warm lids and process for 25 minutes at a full, rolling boil.

Remove the canner lid, turn off the heat, and allow the jars to sit in the hot water for another 5 minutes to cool down.

Wait at least 6 to 8 weeks before eating to allow flavors to develop fully.

A romantic, Victorian-style jam; if you use some deep-red rose petals, it will be an extravagantly beautiful pink color. This jam is a knockout in sandwich cookies with a (heart-shaped) cut-out window, and is ideal for a Valentine's Day or Mother's Day breakfast, served on mini-scones. It has a Middle-Eastern quality that also allows it to stand out in combination with almonds or pistachios on yogurt or ice cream.

Photo: Niamh Malcolm

Rose-Petal Jam with Cardamom

The most important consideration when making this jam is the quality of the rose petals, which must not come from roses that have been sprayed with chemicals. Choose pink, red, or variously colored petals from fully bloomed flowers with a lovely scent. Gather them in the morning, if possible, and not right after a rain. If they're perfectly ready to pick, the petals will simply fall into your hand when you cup each rose.

Makes 1½–2 cups.

2 cups loosely packed rose petals

¹⁄₃ cup water

²⁄₃ cup apple pectin (see p. 69)

¼ tsp ground cardamom

3 tbsp lemon juice (or 2 tbsp lemon juice and 1 tbsp lime juice)

2 cups sugar

Sterilize jars and warm lids. (See full instructions, p. 49, or Bare-bones Cheat Sheet, on flap.)

Rinse the petals in water as briefly as possible to remove any dirt. With scissors, snip a notch out of each petal to remove the firm, pale piece where it joins the flower; this can be bitter.

In a wide, deep non-reactive pot with a thick bottom, combine petals, water, apple pectin, and cardamom. Bring the liquid to a boil, turn heat down, cover and simmer for 30 minutes. Remove the rose petals and reserve them.

Stir in the citrus juice and add the sugar, stirring well until the sugar dissolves completely.

Turn the heat up and bring the mixture to a full, rolling boil that cannot be stirred down, and continue to boil, stirring frequently and skimming foam if necessary, until it reaches the setting point.

Turn the heat to low and add the rose petals, stirring gently until they are well distributed throughout the syrup.

Ladle into sterilized jars, leaving ¼ in (6 mm) of headspace. Seal with warm lids and process for 10 minutes at a rolling boil.

Remove the canner lid, turn off the heat, and allow the jars to sit in the hot water for another 5 minutes to cool down.

Mint Jelly

Some people like to add a drop or two of green food coloring to mint jelly so it has that vivid grasshopper-green color. However, when it's made with apple pectin, it has a pale rosy glow, which I much prefer. Mint jelly is a classic condiment for lamb, boiled new potatoes, and green peas.

Makes 3 cups.

4 cups coarsely chopped loosely packed spearmint or peppermint

4½ cups apple pectin (see p. 69) or 4 cups unsweetened apple juice plus 1 pouch (3 oz/85 mL) liquid pectin

3 tbsp lemon juice

4 cups sugar

Sterilize jars and warm lids. (See full instructions, p. 49, or Bare-bones Cheat Sheet, on flap.)

In a wide, deep non-reactive pot with a thick bottom, combine mint and apple pectin or apple juice. Bring to a boil, turn heat off, cover, and simmer for 30 minutes.

Strain out the mint leaves and measure out 4 cups of liquid.

In the same pot, combine the minty liquid and the lemon juice, then add the sugar, stirring well until it dissolves completely.

Turn the heat up and bring to a full, rolling boil that cannot be stirred down. (If you are using apple juice, add the liquid pectin at this point.) Boil the mixture, stirring frequently and skimming foam if necessary, until it reaches the setting point.

Ladle into sterilized jars, leaving ¼ in (6 mm) of headspace. Seal with warm lids and process for 10 minutes at a rolling boil (15 minutes for pint/500 mL jars).

Remove the canner lid, turn off the heat, and allow the jars to sit in the hot water for another 5 minutes to cool down.

Sumac Jelly

I read as a child that the pioneers made "lemonade" and jelly out of the cone-shaped, fuzzy red sumac "bobs" (fruit of the Smooth Sumac or Staghorn Sumac tree). This jelly is a rich brick-red with a tart, clean taste reminiscent of rosehips. Sumac can be harvested free in untended spots all over most of the US and Canada.

Makes 6 cups.

about 8 whole sumac bobs

5 cups water

¼ cup lemon juice

3 cups apple pectin (see p. 69)

6 cups sugar

Sterilize jars and warm lids. (See full instructions, p. 49, or Bare-bones Cheat Sheet, on flap.)

Rinse sumac bobs in cold water to remove dust and insects.

In a wide, deep non-reactive pot with a thick bottom, combine sumac and water. Bring to a boil for 5 minutes, breaking up the sumac as it boils. Turn heat to low, cover, and simmer for 30 minutes.

Strain out the sumac solids and pour the remaining liquid through a jelly bag. Measure out 3 cups of the strained liquid, which should be almost maroon in color.

In the same pot, combine the 3 cups of sumac liquid with lemon juice, apple pectin, and sugar, stirring well until the sugar dissolves completely.

Turn the heat up and bring to a full, rolling boil that cannot be stirred down. Boil the mixture, stirring frequently and skimming foam if necessary, until it reaches the setting point.

Ladle into sterilized jars, leaving ¼ in (6 mm) of headspace. Seal with warm lids and process for 10 minutes at a rolling boil (15 minutes for pint/500 mL jars).

Remove the canner lid, turn off the heat, and allow the jars to sit in the hot water for another 5 minutes to cool down.

Watermelon Jelly with Thai Sweet Basil Ribbons

From Paige Bayer of the blog Canning with Kids (San Jose, California)

Originally published at *canningwithkids.com/blog/2010/08/watermelon-jelly-with-thai-sweet-basil-ribbons.html*

Paige is a mom of two kids who, with her husband, restored an old home in Silicon Valley, and now grows persimmons, limes, lemons, tangerines, cherries, apples, grapes, blueberries, cherries, and blood oranges in her garden. Her blog invites readers to join her on her "journey to figure out how one girl, who was raised on TV dinners and macaroni and cheese, set out to learn the 'old ways of food' and pass it onto the next generation, before it's lost forever."

This summery, surprising taste combination is shown off well with cream cheese on crackers. Paige writes: "The hardest part of the process was tracking down the Thai sweet basil *[Ocimum basilicum* var. *thyrsiflora].* Search Asian grocery stores in your area." She warns not to replace it with Italian basil, which has a completely different flavor.

Makes 3 cups.

1 small watermelon (Sugar Babies are a great choice), to yield about 4 cups

3½ cups sugar

1¹/ boxes powdered pectin (each box is 2 oz/57 g)

3 tbsp lemon juice

18–20 leaves of Thai sweet basil, cut into narrow ribbons

Sterilize jars and warm lids. (See full instructions, p. 49, or Bare-bones Cheat Sheet, on flap.)

Chop watermelon, removing rind and all seeds.

Purée watermelon until smooth by running it through a strainer or using a food mill or, best of all, simply grate it coarsely over a strainer (this should yield 2 cups of juice or purée).

In a bowl, combine ½ cup of the sugar with pectin and reserve.

In a wide, deep non-reactive pot with a thick bottom on medium heat, combine the watermelon juice/purée, lemon juice, and pectin-sugar mixture, stirring well until the sugar dissolves completely. Bring the mixture to a full, rolling boil that cannot be stirred down.

Add the remaining 3 cups of sugar and bring the mixture back to a boil, stirring frequently, for 1 minute.

Remove from heat and allow the mixture to rest for 5 minutes.

Mix in the Thai basil ribbons.

Ladle into sterilized jars, dividing basil evenly among jars and leaving ¼ in (6 mm) of headspace. Seal with warm lids and process for 15 minutes at a rolling boil (20 minutes for pint/500 mL jars).

Remove the canner lid, turn off the heat, and allow the jars to sit in the hot water for another 5 minutes to cool down.

When lids have sealed firmly but the jelly is still warm, carefully grasp each jar without disturbing the lid and invert, twist, or rotate it to distribute basil throughout jelly.

Eldorado Habañero Pepper Jelly

From Tom Boyd (Toronto, not previously published.)

Tom is an avid urban vegetable gardener whose preserves have won numerous prizes at the Royal Agricultural Winter Fair held in Toronto. Habañeros are among the hottest known peppers, so this recipe packs a wallop! It is very attractive, with its bright red, orange, and green flecks suspended in golden jelly. Great with cheese and crackers.

Caution: When working with hot peppers, be very careful not to touch your face. Wet your knife before cutting into the peppers. Use a non-porous (e.g., glass, not wood) cutting surface if possible. Even after washing, the active oils will linger on your hands, knife, cutting board, and any other surface that has been exposed to them. Wearing disposable surgical gloves is a good idea. Pepper oils in the steam from the pot can burn your eyes and skin if you lean into it to smell the mixture, so exercise caution while cooking. Nonetheless, this delicious recipe is well worth the trouble.

Makes 3–3½ cups.

⅓ cup finely sliced dried apricots

¾ cup white vinegar (at least 5 percent acid)

¼ cup finely diced Vidalia or other sweet onion

¼ cup finely diced sweet yellow pepper

¼ cup finely diced (including seeds) habañero peppers

3 cups sugar

1 pouch (3 oz/85mL) liquid pectin

In a wide, deep non-reactive pot with a thick bottom, combine apricots and vinegar; let stand for 4 hours.

Sterilize jars and warm lids. (See full instructions, p. 49, or Bare-bones Cheat Sheet, on flap.)

Add diced onion, peppers, and sugar to the apricot-vinegar mixture, place pot on medium heat, stirring well until the sugar dissolves completely. (Note: Do not change the proportion of fruit and peppers to vinegar.)

Bring the mixture up to rolling boil that cannot be stirred down, and continue to boil, stirring frequently, for 1 minute.

Photo: Niamh Malcolm

Remove from heat. Immediately stir in pectin, mixing well.

Ladle into sterilized jars, dividing solids evenly among jars and leaving ¼ in (6 mm) of headspace.
Seal with warm lids and process for 10 minutes at a rolling boil (15 minutes for pint/500 mL jars).

Remove the canner lid, turn off the heat, and allow the jars to sit in the hot water for another 5 minutes
to cool down.

When lids have sealed firmly but the jelly is still warm, carefully grasp each jar without disturbing the lid
and invert, twist, or rotate it to distribute solids throughout jelly.

Herb or Flower-Petal Jelly with Citrus Pectin

This jelly will set so hard that when you turn it out of the jar onto a plate, it will retain its shape. When it is sliced it will even retain the tiny ridges from the knife blade.

Makes about 3 cups.

4 navel oranges

2 lemons

6 cups water

about 2 cups fresh aromatic edible flower petals or herbs or about ½ cup dried petals or herbs

about 6 cups sugar

Day 1:

Trim the oil-bearing outer skin off the oranges and lemons. Cut them in half. Juice the oranges and reserve the juice for drinking later. Reserve seeds.

In a non-reactive pot, combine the water, flowers or herbs, and juice of the lemons.

Finely chop all the remaining pith and pulp from the citrus fruits and the peel of half of one of the oranges.

Rinse the pith gently and briefly under cold water to remove any leftover juice or oils, and add it to the pot with the citrus seeds.

Bring to a boil, then reduce heat and keep at a low boil, stirring occasionally, for 90 minutes.

Hang mixture in a moistened jelly bag over a bowl and allow the liquid to drain off. (Do not squeeze it, or you'll get cloudier jelly.)

Day 2:

Sterilize jars and warm lids. (See full instructions, p. 49, or Bare-bones Cheat Sheet, on flap).

Measure the liquid, and add 1 cup of sugar for every cup of juice. Stir well until sugar dissolves completely.

In a wide, deep non-reactive pot, boil gently, stirring frequently and skimming off foam, until it reaches the setting point.

Ladle into sterilized jars leaving ¼ in (6 mm) of headspace. Seal with warm lids, and process for 10 minutes at a rolling boil (15 minutes for pint/500 mL jars).

Remove the canner lid, turn off the heat, and allow the jars to sit in the hot water for another 5 minutes to cool down.

French Cornichons

From David Ort of the blog Food With Legs (Toronto)
Originally published at *foodwithlegs.com/?p=1912*

David is a devoted food experimenter with a love of antique food traditions; he cures his own meats, and he's built an outdoor wood oven to roast meat and bake pizzas. When he discovered that fresh cornichon cucumbers (the tiny pickled ones that are in traditional French cuisine) can be very hard to find, he simply grew his own. "The Mathilde hybrid variety worked excellently," he writes.

Makes 2 cups.

2 cups cornichon (or similar) cucumbers (1 to 2 in/2.5 to 5 cm in length)

¼ cup kosher or ⅛ cup pickling salt

2 sprigs fresh tarragon

5 sprigs fresh thyme

1 dill head (umbrella-like part of a dill plant)

1 tbsp whole black peppercorns

¼ tsp freshly grated nutmeg

½ cinnamon stick

1 garlic clove, peeled and lightly crushed

1 piment d'Espelette (a hot pepper used in Basque cuisine) or 1 pinch red pepper flakes

about 2 cups white wine vinegar (at least 5 percent acid)

Day 1:

Trim off any blossom remnants from the cucumbers and gently rub the spines from their skins under cold running water.

In a non-reactive bowl, combine the rinsed cucumbers and salt and cover with water, stirring to dissolve the salt.

Cover with a heavy plate to submerge them and let stand at room temperature for 24 hours, visiting them occasionally for a quick stir (remembering to replace the plate).

Day 2:

After 24 hours, discard the brine, gently brush off any salt, and rinse the cucumbers in a solution of 1 part white wine vinegar to 3 parts water.

Sterilize 1 pint/500-mL jar and warm the lid. (See full instructions, p. 49, or Bare-bones Cheat Sheet, on flap.)

Tip:
Traditionally, these pickles were stored in a cool (below 50°F/10°C) dark place in sterile, covered ceramic or glass crocks with non-metallic lids. However, contemporary food-safety wisdom suggests that the safest way to store them is by processing in jars, as in this recipe.

In a wide, deep non-reactive pot with a thick bottom, combine the herbs, spices and wine vinegar. Bring to a simmer, and continue to simmer for 5 minutes.

Pack cucumbers tightly into the jar, leaving ¾ in (2 cm) of headspace.

Pour the liquid into the jars, leaving ½ in (1 cm) of headspace.

Run a plastic or wooden knife or chopstick around the inside of the jar to release any trapped air bubbles. Top up with more vinegar if necessary.

Seal with warm lids and process for 10 minutes at a rolling boil.

Remove the canner lid, turn off the heat, and allow the jar to sit in the hot water for another 5 minutes to cool down.

Wait at least 1 month before eating to allow flavors to develop fully.

Use a plastic lid after the jar is open to keep the vinegar from corroding the metal one.

Dill Pickled Green and Yellow Beans

From Jennifer MacKenzie (Buckhorn, Ontario)

Originally published in her book *The Complete Book of Pickling*

Here's a classic for veggie gardeners. Jennifer, a well-known pickling author who has also collaborated on a book about root-cellaring, writes, "If you prefer, you can use all green or all yellow beans instead of a mixture."

Makes about 12 cups (6 pint/500 mL jars).

3 lb (1.5 kg) mixed green and yellow (wax) beans

6 cups white vinegar (at least 5 percent acid)

⅓ cup sugar

2 tbsp kosher or pickling salt

2¾ cups water

6 cloves garlic, quartered

6 fresh dill sprigs

6 fresh dill heads (umbrella-like part of a dill plant)

1½ tsp fresh or dried dill seeds

{ **Tip from Jennifer:**
"Use mature beans for the best texture, but avoid tough, stringy ones. If the beans are too young, they may be limp after pickling. If they are over-mature (when the seeds bulge in the bean pod), they will be quite tough after pickling."

Sterilize jars and warm lids. (See full instructions, p. 49, or Bare-bones Cheat Sheet, on flap.)

Cut stems from green beans and discard any imperfect beans. Set aside.

In a wide, deep non-reactive pot with a thick bottom, combine the vinegar, sugar, salt, and water. Bring to a boil on medium heat, stirring well until the sugar and salt dissolve completely. Increase heat to medium-high. Add beans and return to a boil, pressing occasionally to immerse beans in liquid.

Remove from heat.

Place 4 pieces of garlic, 1 dill sprig, 1 dill head, and ¼ tsp dill seeds in each hot jar. Add beans, packing lightly and leaving 1 in (2.5 cm) of headspace.

Pour the liquid into the jars, leaving ½ in (1 cm) of headspace.

Run a plastic or wooden knife or chopstick around the inside of the jar to release any trapped air bubbles. Top up with more vinegar if necessary.

Seal with warm lids and process for 10 minutes at a rolling boil.

Remove the canner lid, turn off the heat, and allow the jars to sit in the hot water for another 5 minutes to cool down.

Use a plastic lid after the jar is open to keep the vinegar from corroding the metal one.

Indian-Spiced Zucchini Pickle

I live in a South Asian neighborhood, and thought it would be fun to make a pickle with one of the inexpensive boxes of premixed Indian spices that you can pick up in all the grocery stores for about a dollar. The result was a big success: a tasty pickle with a warming spicy afterglow.

Makes 6 cups.

2 lb (1 kg) zucchini (about 5 packed cups)

¼ cup salt

3 cups cider vinegar (al least 5 percent acid)

2 cups brown sugar

2 tbsp Indian spice mix of your choice (these come boxed in various mixtures in South Asian grocery stores for about $1 per box; if no such product is available in your neighborhood, look for pre-mixed *garam masala*)

Peel the zucchini and trim it to the height of a wide-mouth pint (500 mL) jar, less ¾–1 in (2–2.5 cm).

Slice the pieces into sticks not wider than ½ in (1 cm). (Alternately, you can slice a narrow zucchini into coins not thicker than ¼-in (½-cm).

In a non-reactive bowl, layer the zucchini and salt, add ice water, and cover with a heavy plate so the zucchinis stay submerged. Leave them in the brine for at least 2 hours.

Sterilize jars and warm lids. (See full instructions, p.49, or Bare-bones Cheat Sheet, on flap.)

Thoroughly rinse the salt off the zucchini sticks, covering and agitating them with fresh cold water, and pouring off, replenishing the rinse water at least 3 times. Then pat the zucchini dry and set on a dishtowel to air-dry completely.

In a wide, deep non-reactive pot with a thick bottom, combine the vinegar, brown sugar, and spices.

Bring to a simmer, and continue to simmer for 5 minutes.

Pack zucchini sticks tightly into the jars, leaving ¾ in (2 cm) of headspace.

Pour the liquid into the jars, leaving ½ in (1 cm) of headspace.

Run a plastic or wooden knife or chopstick around the inside of the jar to release any trapped air bubbles. Top up with more vinegar if necessary.

Seal with warm lids and process for 15 minutes at a rolling boil.

Remove the canner lid, turn off the heat, and allow the jars to sit in the hot water for another 5 minutes to cool down.

Wait at least a month before eating to allow flavors to develop fully.

Use a plastic lid after the jar is open to keep the vinegar from corroding the metal one.

Pickled **Beets with Fennel**

From Audra Wolfe of the blog Doris and Jilly Cook (Philadelphia)

Originally published at *dorisandjillycook.com/2010/06/29/pickled-beets-with-fennel/*

Audra writes: "Fennel and beets are a natural pair ... If you don't like fennel, no problem—just leave it out. If, on the other hand, you like a spicy pickled beet, feel free to add any of the following (but probably not all at once) to your pickling jars: peppercorns, cloves, allspice, star anise, dill heads, garlic, or strips of hot pepper." You can also reduce the amount of sugar, but not the vinegar, of course.

Fills 7 pint (500-mL) jars.

5 lb (2.2 kg) beets (about 15–20 small to medium)

1½ cups sugar

3½ cups distilled white vinegar (at least 5 percent acid)

1 long fennel frond, cut into 7 pieces

7 whole black peppercorns

1½ cups water

Sterilize jars and warm lids. (See full instructions, p. 49, or Bare-bones Cheat Sheet, on flap.)

Wash the beets well, leaving the roots and 1 in (2.5 cm) of the stems attached. Cook them until they are soft (by boiling, pressure cooking, roasting, or wrapping in foil and heating in a slow cooker).

Once cool enough to handle, skin the beets (if they are thoroughly cooked, the skins should slip right off) and trim roots and stems.

Leave small beets whole, but cut larger beets into bite-sized pieces, slices, or quarters.

In a wide, deep non-reactive pot with a thick bottom, combine the sugar and vinegar, stirring well until the sugar dissolves completely, and heat to the boiling point. Let boil until jars are ready to go.

Put a piece of fennel and a single peppercorn into each jar.

Fill jars with beets to within ¾–1 in (2–2.5 cm) of the top, and top up with vinegar, leaving ½ in (1 cm) headspace (this is double the headspace for jams or jellies). Run a plastic or wooden knife or chopstick around the inside of the jar to release any trapped air bubbles. Top up the vinegar if necessary.

Seal the jars with warm lids and process for 30 minutes at a full, rolling boil for pint/500 mL jars, 35 minutes for qt/L jars.

Remove the canner lid, turn off the heat, and allow the jars to sit in the hot water for another 5 minutes to cool down.

Wait at least six to eight weeks before eating.

Use a plastic lid after the jar is open to keep the vinegar from corroding the metal one.

Chiogga Beet Quickles

From Julia Sforza of the blog What Julia Ate (*whatjuliaate.blogspot.com*) (Esopus, New York; not previously published.)

This is not a true canning recipe; it's a shortcut for showing off the gorgeous beets you just plucked from your garden or bought from the farmer's market (or picked up at the corner grocer). If you can find them, Chiogga beets, with their ravishing pink-and-white rings, make breathtaking pickles. Julia writes: "You don't have to use Chiogga, of course, but I think they make a beautiful pink pickle. To me, they seem lighter in taste and texture than your more robust red varieties."

Makes about 4 cups.

7 or 8 small to medium beets

2 cups cider vinegar (at least 5 percent acid)

½ cup sugar

¼ cup kosher or pickling salt

about 2 cubic in (33 cubic cm) peeled fresh ginger, sliced in rounds

1 tsp whole coriander

½ tsp ground black pepper

Boil some water to rinse out a 1-qt (1-L) jar, but don't use soap.

Wash beets, leaving the roots and 1 in (2.5 cm) of the stems attached. Cook until it's easy to poke them with a fork (by boiling, pressure cooking, roasting, or wrapping in foil and heating in a slow cooker).

When cool enough to handle, skin the beets (if they are thoroughly cooked, the skins should slip right off), and slice them into rounds.

In a wide, deep non-reactive pot with a thick bottom, combine the remaining ingredients and bring the mixture to a simmer, stirring well to dissolve all the sugar and salt.

Pack the jar with the sliced beets and cover with the brine. Refrigerate. Will keep refrigerated for 1 month.

Use a plastic lid, since the vinegar will corrode a metal one.

Pickled **Sour Cherries**

These make a tart, refreshing complement to fatty meats like sausages, duck, or pork.

Fills 6 pint (500-mL) jars.

36 allspice berries

6–12 cinnamon sticks

6 bay leaves

24–36 cloves

1 cup sugar

4 cups white vinegar (at least 5 percent acid)

8 cups fresh or frozen (thawed) sour cherries

Sterilize jars and warm lids. (See full instructions, p. 49, or Bare-bones Cheat Sheet, on flap.)

In an ungreased cast-iron frying pan or the equivalent, toast spices until they become fragrant, being careful not to scorch or burn them.

In a wide, deep non-reactive pot with a thick bottom, combine the sugar and vinegar, stirring well until the sugar dissolves completely, and heat to the boiling point.

Put about 6 allspice berries, 1 or 2 cinnamon sticks, 1 bay leaf, and 4 to 6 cloves into each jar.

Fill jars with cherries to within ¾ in (2 cm) of the top, and top up with vinegar, leaving ½ in (1 cm) of headspace (this is double the headspace for jams or jellies). Run a plastic or wooden knife or chopstick around the inside of the jar to release any trapped air bubbles. Top up the vinegar if necessary.

Seal with warm lids and process for 25 minutes at a full, rolling boil.

Remove the canner lid, turn off the heat, and allow the jars to sit in the hot water for another 5 minutes to cool down.

Wait at least 6 to 8 weeks before eating to allow flavors to develop fully.

Use a plastic lid after the jar is open to keep the vinegar from corroding the metal one.

Pickled **Watermelon Rind**

Adapted from a recipe developed by the National Watermelon Promotion Board, originally posted at Watermelon.org/recipe_detail.asp?recipeDisp=350

When you serve watermelon on a scorching-hot day, save the rinds (they look pretty if you leave a little pink edge on them), and make pickles in the cool of the evening. I find it impossible to make this recipe without thinking about farming women during the Depression and other resourceful folks who would have made these because they needed to use every scrap of food. These days, we might serve watermelon pickles as a side dish at a barbecue, but I'm sure they've traditionally been used as a sweet, thirst-quenching pick-me-up for people working hard outdoors in the sun.

Makes about 7 cups.

8 cups sliced watermelon rind (the rind from a round one, about 10–12 in/25–30 cm in diameter)

8 cups water

2 tbsp kosher or pickling salt

3 cups cider vinegar (at least 5 percent acid)

1½ cups light brown sugar

1½ tsp cinq poivres (red, green, black, grey, and white peppercorns)

12 whole cloves

3 cinnamon sticks broken into pieces

about 2 cubic in (33 cubic cm) peeled fresh ginger, sliced

Sterilize jars and warm lids. (See full instructions, p. 49, or Bare-bones Cheat Sheet, on flap.)

Slice the rind into strips between ¾–1 in (2–2.5 cm) wide. Trim off the green parts, leaving as much white rind as you can. Slice into chunks between 1½–2 in (4–5 cm) long.

In a wide, deep non-reactive pot with a thick bottom, combine water and salt and bring to a boil. Add the watermelon chunks and boil for about 5 minutes, until all the pieces are translucent.

Strain the watermelon chunks and rinse in hot water, then drain very well in a colander or sieve, pressing down gently to remove extra water, without crushing them.

In a wide, deep non-reactive pot on medium heat, combine the vinegar, sugar, and all the spices. Stir well until the sugar dissolves completely and bring the mixture to a boil. Then turn the heat down and simmer for about 15 minutes until the spices have started to flavor the liquid.

Meanwhile, pack the drained watermelon chunks into the jars, leaving about ¾ in (2 cm) of head-space.

Cover the pickles with the vinegar mixture, leaving ¼ in (6 mm) of headspace. (It's fine if some of the spices end up in the jar, but remove the large chunk of ginger.)

Run a plastic or wooden knife or chopstick around the inside of the jar to release any trapped air bubbles. Top up with more vinegar if necessary.

Seal with warm lids and process for 15 minutes at a rolling boil.

Remove the canner lid, turn off the heat, and allow the jars to sit in the hot water for another 5 minutes to cool down.

Wait at least 1 week before eating to allow flavors to develop fully.

Use a plastic lid after the jar is open to keep the vinegar from corroding the metal one.

Pickled Watermelon Rind (page 160). Photo: National Watermelon Promotion Board

Southern-Style Pickled **Peaches**

From Sally McClelland (Toronto) (not previously published)

If you mention preserves to anyone from the southern US, it's likely that they'll start to swoon at the recollection of pickled peaches. This recipe comes from a cookbook belonging to Sally's southern family. It was listed under "Old Family Favorites," she says, "meaning submitted [by] anybody who could record how my grandmother made these things. I don't know that she ever wrote recipes down."

Makes 12–16 cups.

8 lb (3.5 kg) peaches (about 20 or 30, depending on size)

2 cloves for every peach

1 cup white vinegar (at least 5 percent acid)

2 cups water

8 cups brown sugar

3 tsp ground allspice

2 cinnamon sticks

Sterilize jars and warm lids. (See full instructions, p. 49, or Bare-bones Cheat Sheet, on flap.)

Skin the peaches by immersing them in boiling water for about a minute, then plunging them into cold water; the skins will then slip off easily.

Either stone the peaches and cut them in half, or leave them whole with the stone in. Stick a clove into each peach half (or two cloves per whole peach).

In a wide, deep non-reactive pot with a thick bottom, combine all ingredients except peaches and bring to a boil.

Turn the heat to low and simmer for about 5 minutes.

Pack peaches into sterilized jars, leaving ¾ in (2 cm) of headspace. Pour syrup over them, leaving ½ in (1 cm) of headspace.

Run a plastic or wooden knife or chopstick around the inside of the jar to release any trapped air bubbles. Top up with more syrup if necessary.

Seal with warm lids and process for 20 minutes (500 mL/pint) or 25 minutes (1 qt/L) at a rolling boil.

Remove the canner lid, turn off the heat, and allow the jars to sit in the hot water for another 5 minutes to cool down.

Wait at least 1 month before eating to allow flavors to develop fully.

Use a plastic lid after the jar is open to keep the vinegar from corroding the metal one.

Thai-Inspired Spicy Pickled **Veggies**

You can vary the proportions of vegetables to use whatever you happen to have on hand in the fridge or the garden. The mix of shapes and colors is very attractive in the jar.

Makes 8 cups.

3 cups small cauliflower florets

2 cups sliced carrot coins ¼ in (6 mm) or narrower

2 cups sliced zucchini coins ¼ in (6 mm) or narrower

1½ cups whole (peeled) pearl onions

2 cups rice wine vinegar (at least 5 percent acid)

½ cup water

½ cup sugar

about 2 cubic in (33 cubic cm) peeled fresh ginger, minced

1 tbsp pickling salt

2 whole Thai chilis per jar, with stems removed

2 star anise per jar

{ Tip:
Drag a fork along the edges of the carrots and zucchini before slicing them into coins to give them a decorative edge.

Sterilize jars and warm lids. (See full instructions, p. 49, or Bare-bones Cheat Sheet, on flap.)

Prepare the veggies as per the ingredients list (skin the pearl onions by immersing them in boiling water for about a minute, then plunging them into cold water; the skins will slip off easily).

In a wide, deep non-reactive pot with a thick bottom, combine vinegar, water, sugar, ginger, and salt, and bring up to a boil.

Turn the heat to low and simmer for about 5 minutes.

Pack vegetables tightly into sterilized jars with 2 Thai chilis and 2 star anise per jar, leaving ¾–1 in (2–2.5 cm) of headspace. Pour hot vinegar mixture over them, leaving ½ in (1 cm) of headspace.

Run a plastic or wooden knife or chopstick around the inside of the jar to release any trapped air bubbles. Top up with more vinegar if necessary.

Seal with warm lids and process for 10 minutes at a rolling boil.

Remove the canner lid, turn off the heat, and allow the jars to sit in the hot water for another 5 minutes to cool down.

Wait at least 1 month before eating to allow flavors to develop fully.

Use a plastic lid after the jar is open to keep the vinegar from corroding the metal one.

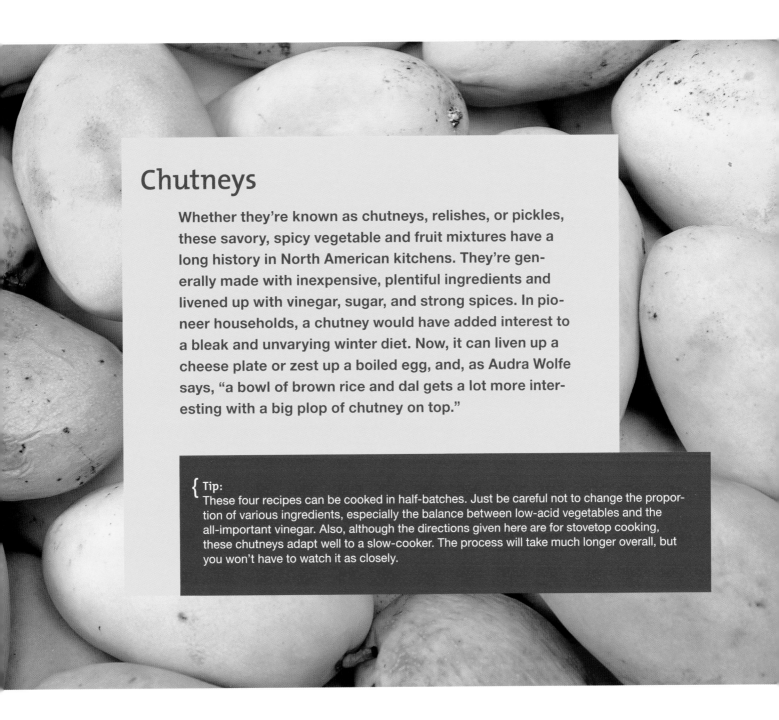

Chutneys

Whether they're known as chutneys, relishes, or pickles, these savory, spicy vegetable and fruit mixtures have a long history in North American kitchens. They're generally made with inexpensive, plentiful ingredients and livened up with vinegar, sugar, and strong spices. In pioneer households, a chutney would have added interest to a bleak and unvarying winter diet. Now, it can liven up a cheese plate or zest up a boiled egg, and, as Audra Wolfe says, "a bowl of brown rice and dal gets a lot more interesting with a big plop of chutney on top."

{ Tip:
These four recipes can be cooked in half-batches. Just be careful not to change the proportion of various ingredients, especially the balance between low-acid vegetables and the all-important vinegar. Also, although the directions given here are for stovetop cooking, these chutneys adapt well to a slow-cooker. The process will take much longer overall, but you won't have to watch it as closely.

Apple Chutney

From Audra Wolfe of the blog Doris and Jilly Cook (Philadelphia)

Originally published at *dorisandjillycook.com/2009/07/22/peach-chutney-with-lime/*

Audra originally designed this as a peach chutney, but her apple variation is extremely tasty.

Makes 8 cups.

5 lb (2.2 kg) apples (about 15 medium)

2 cups raisins

2½ cups cider vinegar (at least 5 percent acid)

2 cups brown sugar

2 tbsp mustard seeds

2 to 3 each: whole cloves, cinnamon sticks, small dried chili peppers

5 garlic cloves, minced

about 2 cubic in (33 cubic cm) peeled fresh ginger, minced

1 large onion, chopped

Sterilize jars and warm lids. (See full instructions, p. 49, or Bare-bones Cheat Sheet, on flap.)

In a large non-reactive pot with a thick bottom, combine all ingredients and bring to boil, stirring frequently.

Reduce heat; boil gently for 2 to 3 hours or until thickened, stirring frequently and adding more water if necessary.

Ladle into sterilized jars, leaving ¼ in (6 mm) of headspace. Seal with warm lids and process for 10 minutes at a rolling boil (15 minutes for pint/500 mL jars).

Remove the canner lid, turn off the heat, and allow the jars to sit in the hot water for another 5 minutes to cool down.

Use a plastic lid after the jar is open to keep the vinegar from corroding the metal one.

Mango Peach Chutney

Makes 6 cups.

4 cups chopped mangoes (about 3–4 medium)

4 cups peeled, pitted, and chopped peaches

1 large onion, diced

1 sweet red pepper, diced

2 large garlic cloves, minced

1½ cups packed brown sugar

1 cup cider vinegar (at least 5 percent acid)

½ cup seedless golden raisins

¼ cup lime juice

1 tsp each: salt, ground allspice, cinnamon

½ tsp each: ground ginger, turmeric

⅛ to ¼ tsp cayenne pepper or 1 or 2 jalapeño peppers, finely chopped, with seeds

From Yvonne Tremblay (Toronto)

Originally published in her book *250 Home Preserving Favorites*

Mango chutney is a classic, though hardly local to most North Americans; Yvonne Tremblay gives it a local twist with peaches. Its surprisingly dark, earthy, smoky taste pairs well with spicy South Asian cuisine, pork, or chicken.

Sterilize jars and warm lids. (See full instructions, p. 49, or Bare-bones Cheat Sheet, on flap.)

In a large non-reactive pot with a thick bottom, combine all ingredients and bring to boil, stirring frequently.

Reduce heat and boil gently for 1 to 1½ hours or until thickened, stirring frequently.

Reduce heat further and stir more often as it thickens. Test for doneness. (Place small amount of chutney on plate, then draw small spoon through center; it is done when no liquid seeps into the space. Chutney will thicken more as it cools.)

Ladle into sterilized jars, leaving ½ in (1 cm) of headspace. Seal with warm lids and process for 10 minutes at a rolling boil (15 minutes for pint/500 mL jars).

Remove the canner lid, turn off the heat, and allow the jars to sit in the hot water for another 5 minutes to cool down.

Use a plastic lid after the jar is open to keep the vinegar from corroding the metal one.

{ **Tip:**
In Toronto, we are lucky to have the "king of mangoes," the Alphonso from Pakistan or India, in season in late spring (before peaches). Other dependable varieties include the Mexican Ataulfo and the Caribbean Julie.

Gen's Pickle

From Katie Quinn-Jacobs of IthaCan (Ithaca, New York; not previously published)

I love this recipe because it's so representative of the most basic ingredients that thrive in the northeastern US and south-central Canada. Katie says: "My grandmother Genevieve Demarais Quinn, who came from northern Vermont near the Québec border, where she met and married my Irish grandfather, made these 'pickles' that were more like a chutney. My mother, Joan Rowe Quinn from the Catskill mountain region of New York, made them as well, and she passed the recipe down to me."

Katie says they can dress up or down, and are good in turkey sandwiches, burgers, and with baked fish. I look forward to trying a jar that's had a month or two to mellow. She also suggests a "Northeast Localvore Variation": substitute blueberries for raisins and maple syrup for brown sugar.

Makes about 10 cups.

5 lb (2.2 kg) tomatoes (about 15 to 20 medium)

4 green bell peppers

4 medium onions

6 medium tart apples, peeled and cored

2 cups white vinegar (at least 5 percent acid)

3 tsp salt

2 tsp mustard seed

2 tsp whole cloves

3 cinnamon sticks

2 cups brown sugar

1 cup raisins

Sterilize jars and warm lids. (See full instructions, p. 49, or Bare-bones Cheat Sheet, on flap.)

Chop the tomatoes, green peppers, onions, and apples into medium-sized pieces so the mixture is chunky. Peeling the tomatoes is optional.

In a wide, deep non-reactive pot with a thick bottom, combine all ingredients except the raisins and bring to boil.

Boil until liquids evaporate to the point where the mixture begins to thicken (at least 45 minutes).

Add raisins and boil for 15 minutes longer.

Ladle into sterilized jars, leaving ¼ in (6 mm) of headspace. Seal with warm lids and process for 10 minutes at a rolling boil (15 minutes for pint/500 mL jars).

Remove the canner lid, turn off the heat, and allow the jars to sit in the hot water for another 5 minutes to cool down.

Use a plastic lid after the jar is open to keep the vinegar from corroding the metal one.

Cottage Garden Pickle

From David Ort of the blog Food With Legs (Toronto)

Originally published at *foodwithlegs.com/?p=703*

I don't recommend this last chutney recipe for beginner canners; it would be too easy to go overboard with all these big, cheap, low-acid root vegetables and over-balance the acid content. Instead, either make a half-batch, refrigerate what you can use and share the rest (with the proviso that recipients refrigerate their gifts), or wait until you have access to a pressure canner.

That said, it's a delicious chutney. David writes: "My inspiration for this recipe was my desire to create a homemade Branston pickle. This British condiment is a necessary component to many versions of the Ploughman's Lunch (p. 256) and the perfect way to improve a grilled cheese sandwich. I was also trying to use up the odd bits of produce from the garden."

Makes about 6 pint (500 mL) jars.

1 medium rutabaga, peeled

1 medium cauliflower

3 small or 2 medium zucchini

about 5 small to medium carrots

10 small or 2 large beets, peeled

2 medium dill pickles

4 small or 3 medium tart apples, peeled

1 cup dried apricots

6 garlic cloves, finely minced

2 medium onions, peeled

2½ cups brown sugar

1 tsp kosher or pickling salt

2 tsp whole mustard seeds

2 tsp ground allspice

1 tsp cayenne

2 cups malt vinegar

½ cup lemon juice (juice of 1 large lemon)

Sterilize jars and warm lids. (See full instructions, p. 49, or Bare-bones Cheat Sheet, on flap.)

Dice all the vegetables, apples, and apricots finely for a smoother, more spreadable pickle, or more coarsely for a chunkier result.

In a wide, deep non-reactive pot with a thick bottom, combine all ingredients and boil—this is a British recipe, remember—until the rutabaga, cauliflower, and beets are softened but still hold their shape.

Ladle into sterilized jars, leaving ¼ in (6 mm) of headspace, but do not process unless you have access to a pressure canner (in which case, heat process pint/500 mL jars for 30 minutes and qt/L jars for 35 minutes at 10 lb [69 kPa] in a weighted gauge pressure canner). Otherwise, refrigerate the jars and use right away. Discard if it shows signs of mold or spoilage.

Use a plastic lid to keep the vinegar from corroding the metal one.

Recipes for Fall

The poet John Keats's "season of mists and mellow fruitfulness" brings some of the most important produce for preserving: plum tomatoes for sauce, pickling cucumbers, and the new crop of apples, rich with pectin and perfumed with their own tangy fragrance. As the temperature starts to dip, it's cozy to be in a warm kitchen next to a steaming pot of preserves.

Tomato Sauce

Makes 6 qt (L) jars.

18 lb (8 kg) paste tomatoes

1 large bunch fresh basil, finely chopped

(optional) dried herbs (e.g., thyme, oregano) to taste

2 tbsp sugar, or to taste

salt, to taste

ground black pepper, to taste

¾ cup lemon juice

> **Tip:**
> If you're canning tomatoes in quantity, wear gloves while handling them to protect your skin from the acidity. It won't actually burn you, of course, but after a while it really dries out your skin.

If you do no other canning, put up a few jars of tomatoes with this very simple sauce. You'll be delighted to be able to cook with fresh-tasting tomatoes in January. This recipe can be made in vast quantities, in which case it's fun to call in friends for help. If you get really serious about tomato sauce, consider investing in a machine that will skin and seed them for you.

Sterilize jars and warm lids. (See full instructions, p. 49, or Bare-bones Cheat Sheet, on flap.)

Skin the tomatoes by immersing them in boiling water for about a minute, then into cold water. The skins will slip off easily.

Quarter the tomatoes, remove the seeds (over a strainer, to save as much juice as possible) and chop them coarsely. (I use an old-fashioned meat grinder.)

In a wide, deep non-reactive pot with a thick bottom, combine the tomatoes, chopped basil, herbs (if using), sugar, salt, and pepper. Bring to a full, rolling boil, then turn down heat slightly and boil gently for 2 to 3 hours until the mixture has reached a meaty thickness.

Because tomatoes are on the borderline of safe acidity, add 2 tbsp of lemon juice to each qt/L jar (1 tbsp per pint/500 mL, or 3 tbsp per 1.5 qt [L] jar).

Ladle the sauce into sterilized jars, leaving ½ in (1cm) of headspace. Run a plastic or wooden knife or chopstick around the inside of the jar to release any trapped air bubbles. Top up if necessary.

Seal with warm lids and process at a rolling boil: 35 minutes for pint (500 mL) jars, 40 minutes for qt/L, or 50 minutes for 1.5 qt/L.

Remove the canner lid, turn off the heat, and allow the jars to sit in the hot water for another 5 minutes to cool down.

Aunt Edith's Chili Sauce 🎖

From Tom Boyd (Toronto; not previously published)

Like Gen's Pickle (p.168), this is a pioneer-style recipe, good for using up extra field tomatoes (not paste tomatoes). An old-fashioned "chili sauce," it has no hot spice. Tom, a dedicated cook of prize-winning preserves, says he enjoys it with cheese and crackers. It could be canned when it reaches a saucy consistency and used like a salsa dip, or finished to a much thicker consistency that would not drip off a cracker. The recipe can easily be halved or even quartered, but be careful not to change the proportion of vinegar to vegetables.

Makes 12 cups (thick consistency), or up to 18 (saucy consistency).

18 lb (8 kg) field tomatoes

6 medium onions

3–4 cups sugar (to taste)

2 cups white vinegar (at least 5 percent acid)

1 tsp ground cinnamon

1 tsp pickling salt

6 tsp pickling spice

Sterilize jars and warm lids. (See full instructions, p. 49, or Bare-bones Cheat Sheet, on flap.)

Skin and quarter the tomatoes and chop the onions.

In a wide, deep non-reactive pot with a thick bottom, combine the tomatoes, onions, sugar, vinegar, cinnamon, and salt. Add the pickling spice tied in a muslin or cheesecloth bag.

Boil until the liquids have been reduced by at least half and the mixture begins to thicken (at least 45 minutes).

Remove the spice bag and ladle the sauce into sterilized jars, leaving ½ in (1 cm) of headspace. Run a plastic or wooden knife or chopstick around the inside of the jar to release any trapped air bubbles. Top up if necessary.

Seal with warm lids and process for 10 minutes at a rolling boil (15 minutes for pint/500 mL jars). Remove the canner lid, turn off the heat, and allow the jars to sit in the hot water for another 5 minutes to cool down.

Use a plastic lid after the jar is open to keep the vinegar from corroding the metal one.

We Sure Can ... Tomatoes

Tomatoes are the great argument for canning. It takes some work to scald, peel, and seed them, but a jar of whole or crushed tomatoes, or tomato sauce, preserves that intoxicating summer scent all through the winter, at a cost that can be as little as one-third that of buying them at the grocery store. A jar of luscious, bright red, home-canned tomatoes beats the gray, woody winter tomato from the grocery store hands down, every time.

Furthermore, tomatoes are among the foods that can be raised (with a good growing season and a little luck) in considerable abundance in a small space. Even a balcony, an apartment rooftop, or a sunny backyard can produce a respectable harvest. These days, with the growing interest in preserving heirloom fruits, home gardeners can choose among varieties as small as quarters or as large as grapefruits. They may be yellow, green, orange, purple, black, or white as well as red, solid or striped, smooth or deeply ridged.

Mexico was the home to the ancestors of most of the plants that one might propagate today (the huge, deeply ridged Zapotec variety is an ancient one). The development of so much diversity is partly the result of investigations by commercial producers who need fruit that can be mechanically harvested and which travels well, partly to painstaking research by some very dedicated explorers and plant geneticists,

and partly to groups like Seeds of Diversity, who work to make sure older and rarer types are still being grown every year.

As a veggie gardener, I'm hooked on the tiny, yellow abundantly fruiting Blondköpfchen (which literally means "little blonde heads"), the very sweet, smooth, green-and-yellow striped Green Zebra, and the dark and meaty Purple Prince. All of these can be canned ... with just a grain of caution.

Tomatoes lie on the risky borderline between high- and low-acid fruit. Underripe, green tomatoes are more acidic than ripe ones. And apparently, commercial varieties have been bred for more sweetness and lower acid over the years, so the ones at your grocery store may be less acidic than the ones in your grandmother's garden. Furthermore, when it comes to heirloom varieties, the acid content is all over the map, so it's best to add extra acid when you can them: a tablespoon of lemon juice to a pint (500 mL) jar is the rule of thumb.

Some great books about tomatoes:

The Heirloom Tomato: From Garden to Table by Amy Goldman (a mouthwateringly photographed and enormously informative catalogue of tomato varieties by an expert in growing and cooking them).

Ripe: The Search for the Perfect Tomato by Allen Arthur (an absorbing history of tomato breeding that documents the work of the passionate and quirky botanical explorers and geneticists who have brought us the tomatoes we know and love).

We Sure Can ... Apples

When it comes to Red Delicious apples, which side of the debate are you on? Or were you hitherto unaware that this unassuming apple exemplifies the divide between large-scale farming and the local food movement?

A brief biology lesson is necessary first: The apple does not grow true to seed. This means that if you planted all the seeds from all the apples on a single McIntosh tree, you might not come up with a single McIntosh sapling. Depending on the pollen wafting through the air in your neighborhood, you'd likely get a field of apple mutts. Some might be good for eating, others not so much. Of course, you could discover the next great apple variety.

If you want to produce more McIntosh trees, you must graft McIntosh branches onto some other apple tree. All commercial varieties are propagated this way. The original McIntosh tree was a chance find in the field of a Dundela, Ontario, farmer named John McIntosh in 1811. Luckily, a visitor showed McIntosh how to take grafts from his tree—the world came close to missing out on one of its most popular and useful apples!

Among the other apples discovered by chance are the Russet, Northern Spy, and the comparatively recent Ambrosia, which appeared in Canada's Okanagan Valley in the 1980s. Many types—such as Cortland, Empire, Jonagold, Fuji, and Gala—were developed in agricultural research stations. Slow Food USA estimates that more than 15,000 apple varieties have been grown in North America. However, fewer than 3,000 are readily available today, and on my home turf of Ontario, only fifteen are commercially grown, with just three types—McIntosh, Empire and Red Delicious—making up the bulk of the crop.

Why is this a problem? Well, if you happen to sit down and taste a lot of different apples, you'll soon discover that some of the most commonly sold varieties (I'm looking at you, Red Delicious) actually taste bland and mealy, whereas some of the best cooking and eating apples (like Northern Spy, Newtown Pippin, and Russet) are becoming harder to find. This is because large commercial production favors other qualities over taste: a pretty appearance on the shelf, long storage potential, and the ability to resist bruising in transport.

The new crop of North American apples arrives between August and October every year. Many varieties can be stored for several months (some, like McIntoshes, are even said to improve over the first few weeks of storage). But by March, last fall's apples have lost their tangy scent, their taste is duller and sweeter, their skins are thicker and rubbery, and they have lost a great deal of their pectin. That vital pectin, the thing that makes jam cling to toast and jelly wobble, is crucial for home canning, so there's not much point in using spring and summer apples in preserves.

And think how many canning recipes call for apples! It's worth waiting for the new crop, when even the cheapest bag at the grocery store is perfumed and delicious, or begging neighbors for some fresh, hard green apples from their tree. It's also useful to get to know your local apples and help to maintain a market for the lesser-known varieties, because if farmers have no reason to graft that particular apple onto new stock, we risk losing it forever.

Some great books about apples:

Apples and Man by Fred Lape (a brilliant book by an environmentally aware scientist who loves the old apple varieties).

The Apple: A History of Canada's Perfect Fruit by Carol Martin (a chatty popular history crammed with photos).

The Botany of Desire: A Plant's-eye View of the World by Michael Pollan (the apple is one of four plants discussed; Pollan consistently misspells McIntosh—the computer way—however).

Apples to Oysters: A Food Lover's Tour of Canadian Farms by Margaret Webb (it has a chapter about the discovery of the Ambrosia apple).

Classic Apple Jelly

Besides being the basis for all kinds of herb, wine, and flower jellies, apple jelly is tasty on toast and lovely with sharp cheddar cheese or roast lamb. Use tart, crisp apples; they can even be underripe. Also, it doesn't really matter if the fruit is bruised or insect-damaged; just cut out any brown parts.

Makes about 6 cups.

6 lb (2¾ kg) apples (about 18 to 24 medium)

about 2 cubic in (33 cubic cm) peeled fresh ginger

4½ cups water

3 cinnamon sticks

about 8–10 whole cloves

about 6 cups sugar

{ **Note:**
The contents of the jelly bag will make great compost.

Day 1:

Wash the apples and chop them coarsely without peeling or coring them.

Roughly chop the ginger.

In a wide, deep non-reactive pot with a thick bottom, combine all the ingredients except the sugar, and bring to a boil. Turn heat to low and allow the mixture to simmer, stirring occasionally, until the apples have broken down (about 30 minutes).

Put the apple mixture into a jelly bag or 2 or 3 layers of cheesecloth or a wide-weave dishtowel.

{ **Tip:**
Wet the jelly bag or cloth with water first so it doesn't soak up a lot of valuable juice. Hang it over a bowl to drip overnight. (Do not squeeze the bag, or the jelly will be cloudy.)

Day 2:

Sterilize jars and warm lids. (See full instructions, p. 49, or Bare-bones Cheat Sheet, on flap.)

Measure the liquid, and add 2¼ cups of sugar for every 2½ cups of juice. Stir well until the sugar dissolves completely.

In a wide, deep non-reactive pot with a thick bottom, boil gently, stirring frequently and skimming off foam, until it reaches the setting point.

Ladle into sterilized jars, seal with warm lids, and process for 10 minutes at a rolling boil (15 minutes for pint/500 mL jars).

Remove the canner lid, turn off the heat, and allow the jars to sit in the hot water for another 5 minutes to cool down.

Crabapple Jelly

Dark pink crabapple jelly is not only pretty to look at, but tangy, fresh, and delicious with pork. All crabapple trees produce fruit that can be eaten; however, some varieties produce fruit that is too small, bitter, or mealy to be worth jellying.

Makes about 5 cups.

3 lb (1.5 kg) red crabapples

about 5 cups sugar

about ⅓ cup lemon juice

Wash the crabapples; you do not need to peel, core, or chop them.

In a pot, barely cover the crabapples with water and bring to a boil, stirring occasionally, until they have become soft (about 10 minutes).

Put the crabapple mixture into a jelly bag, 2 or 3 layers of cheesecloth, or a wide-weave dishtowel. Hang it over a bowl to drip for at least 2 hours or overnight. (Do not squeeze the bag or the jelly will be cloudy.)

Sterilize jars and warm lids. (See full instructions, p. 49, or Bare-bones Cheat Sheet on flap.)

Measure the crabapple juice and, in a wide, deep non-reactive pot with a thick bottom, bring it to a boil.

For every cup of boiling juice, add 1 cup of sugar and 1 tbsp of lemon juice. Stir well until the sugar dissolves completely.

Boil, stirring frequently and skimming off the very heavy, thick pink foam, until it reaches the setting point (about 20 minutes).

Ladle into sterilized jars, leaving ¼ in (6 mm) of headspace. Seal with warm lids and process for 10 minutes at a rolling boil (15 minutes for pint/500 mL jars).

Remove the canner lid, turn off the heat, and allow the jars to sit in the hot water for another 5 minutes to cool down.

Easy-Peasy Cranberry Sauce

This is a great recipe for newbies to make—and imagine the satisfaction of being able to tell Thanksgiving or Christmas dinner guests that if they liked it with the turkey, they can take a jar home with them!

Makes 4 cups.

4 cups fresh or frozen cranberries

1 cup water

(optional) 1 cinnamon stick

3 cups sugar

(optional) ¼ cup walnuts, chopped

Sterilize jars and warm lids. (See full instructions, p. 49, or Bare-bones Cheat Sheet, on flap.)

If using fresh berries, give them a rinse.

In a wide, deep non-reactive pot with a thick bottom, combine berries and water. Crush berries with a potato masher or the back of a slotted spoon. Add the cinnamon stick (if using).

Heat the berries just to the boiling point.

Remove from heat and add the sugar, stirring until it dissolves completely.

Return the mixture to the heat, bring to a full, rolling boil that cannot be stirred down, and continue to boil, stirring frequently and skimming off foam, until it reaches the setting point. This will happen much more quickly than with most jams; likely within 5 minutes.

Remove the cinnamon stick (if used). If you are using walnuts, add them now, and allow the cranberry sauce to sit for 5 minutes to incorporate them.

Ladle into sterilized jars, leaving ¼ in (6 mm) of headspace. Seal with warm lids and process for 10 minutes at a rolling boil (15 minutes for pint/500 mL jars).

Remove the canner lid, turn off the heat, and allow the jars to sit in the hot water for another 5 minutes to cool down.

Apple-Cranberry Jelly

A clean, fresh-tasting jelly to wake up an autumn breakfast or set off a rich meat dish such as pork chops or sausages.

Makes 3 cups.

2 cups fresh or frozen cranberries

2 cups water

about 1½ cups apple pectin (see p. 69)

3 cups sugar

1 cinnamon stick

Sterilize jars and warm lids. (See full instructions, p. 49, or Bare-bones Cheat Sheet, on flap.)

Wash the berries (if they're fresh).

In a wide, deep non-reactive pot with a thick bottom, combine cranberries and water. Crush berries with a potato masher or the back of a slotted spoon.

Heat the berries to the boiling point; reduce heat to medium and boil gently until the berries have dissolved into pulp (about 10 minutes).

When berries are cool enough to work with safely, run them through a sieve or food mill, then through a clean, dampened jelly bag. This should yield 1½ cups of juice.

Add enough apple pectin to the cranberry juice to make 3 cups in total. In a wide, deep non-reactive pot with a thick bottom, combine all ingredients. Stir until the sugar dissolves completely.

Return the mixture to the heat, bring to a full, rolling boil that cannot be stirred down, and continue to boil, stirring frequently and skimming off foam, until it reaches the setting point.

Remove the cinnamon stick and ladle into sterilized jars, leaving ¼ in (6 mm) of headspace. Seal with warm lids and process for 10 minutes at a rolling boil (15 minutes for pint/500 mL jars).

Remove the canner lid, turn off the heat, and allow the jars to sit in the hot water for another 5 minutes to cool down.

Left: Applesauce. Right: Orange Onion Jam with Sage and Thyme (p. 220). Photo: Niamh Malcolm

Applesauce

Experiment with various apple combinations until you find the perfect mix for your region. I recommend Northern Spy above all; also fine are McIntosh, Gravenstein, Jonagold, Macoun, and Honeycrisp, but don't waste time on Red Delicious. You can use a slow cooker instead of a stovetop pot if you like, but it will take a little longer.

Makes 4–5.

2 cinnamon sticks

6 cloves

10 allspice berries

4 lb (1.8 kg) apples (about 12–16 medium)

¼ cup lemon juice

1–2 cups sugar (to taste)

1 cup water

> **Tip:**
> In cake or muffin recipes, you can replace the oil with applesauce.

Sterilize jars and warm lids. (See full instructions, p. 49, or Bare-bones Cheat Sheet, on flap.)

In an ungreased frying pan on medium heat, combine the spices and toast them until they become fragrant, being careful not to scorch or burn them (about 5 minutes).

Wash, quarter and core the apples, but do not peel them. In a wide, deep non-reactive pot with a thick bottom, combine all ingredients. Heat to the boiling point, then reduce heat to low, cover, and simmer until the apples have dissolved to pulp (about 30 minutes). Remove the cover and cook on medium heat until the mixture is as thick as you like it (another 5 to 15 minutes).

When apples are cool enough to work with safely, pass them through a strainer or food mill to remove skins and whole spices. (If you like a finer texture, you can use an immersion blender to reduce them down even further.)

Ladle into sterilized jars, leaving ½ in (1 cm) of headspace. Seal with warm lids and process for 15 minutes at a rolling boil (20 minutes for pint/500 mL jars).

Remove the canner lid, turn off the heat, and allow the jars to sit in the hot water for another 5 minutes to cool down.

Persian-Inspired Quince Butter

The quince is apparently native to Persia (modern Iran), and is very high in pectin. Quince and apple preserves have been appreciated in Persia since at least the fourth century, when a literary character (a prince in disguise) names them as the best of desserts. Quince was the essential marmalade fruit before oranges. This quince butter has a very tart and tangy flavor.

Makes 4½ cups.

Sterilize jars and warm lids. (See full instructions, p. 49, or Bare-bones Cheat Sheet, on flap.)

3½ lb (1¾ kg) quinces

4 cups water

4½ cups sugar

3 tbsp lime juice

½ tsp ground cardamom (the seeds from 8 pods, finely ground)

Wash the quinces, quarter them, and remove the seeds and stems (don't worry about removing the hard shell that encases the seeds).

In a wide, deep non-reactive pot with a thick bottom, combine quinces and water. Boil for 10 minutes, then reduce heat and simmer, covered, until the mixture resembles the consistency of pea soup (about 25 minutes).

Run the mixture through a sieve or food mill and return it to the pot. Add the sugar, lime juice, and cardamom, stirring well until the sugar dissolves completely.

Boil on medium heat until the mixture thickens to the point where you can draw a spoon through it without seeing liquid seep from the sides (about 30–45 minutes). The mixture should turn quite dark red or red-brown. (Be very careful, because it will spit a lot while boiling. If you have glasses, wear them; long sleeves and an apron are also a good idea.)

Ladle into sterilized jars, leaving ½ in (1 cm) of headspace. Seal with warm lids and process for 10 minutes at a rolling boil (15 minutes for pint/500 mL jars).

Remove the canner lid, turn off the heat, and allow the jars to sit in the hot water for another 5 minutes to cool down.

{ Tip:
Be very careful when chopping the quinces; the very hard inner seed shell can turn the knife blade unexpectedly.

Grape Jelly

There is no more kid-friendly preserve than grape jelly. Concord grapes make the most delicious preserve, but Coronation grapes are also acceptable. The best jelly I ever made was from a chance blend of Concord and anonymous white grapes from a neighbor's backyard. (Wild grapes make fine jelly as well.)

Makes 5 cups.

10 cups grapes, stems and stalks removed

3 cups water

3 tbsp lemon juice

about 5 cups sugar

{ **Tip:**
It's worth being fussy about straining grape juice and letting it rest overnight, because otherwise it has a tendency to form crystals that will make your jelly crunchy. You won't remember the fuss while you're enjoying the jelly.

Day 1:

Wash grapes.

In a wide, deep non-reactive pot with a thick bottom, combine grapes and water, bring to a boil and boil for 5 minutes. Turn heat to low, cover, and simmer for 30 minutes.

Remove from heat and strain first through a food mill or a strainer, gently squeezing out the juice with the back of a spoon, and then through a jelly bag. Do not squeeze the jelly bag. If you have enough patience, pour it through a clean jelly bag a second time.

Refrigerate in tall glass jars overnight.

Day 2:

Sterilize jars and warm lids. (See full instructions, p. 49, or Bare-bones Cheat Sheet, on flap.)

Using a turkey baster or pouring or ladling carefully to avoid sediment, measure out 5 cups of juice.

In a wide, deep non-reactive pot with a thick bottom, combine the grape juice, lemon juice, and 1 cup of sugar for every cup of juice, stirring well until the sugar dissolves completely.

Turn the heat up and bring the mixture to a rapid boil, stirring frequently and skimming foam if necessary, until it reaches the setting point.

Ladle into sterilized jars, leaving ¼ in (6 mm) of headspace. Seal with warm lids and process for 10 minutes at a rolling boil.

Remove the canner lid, turn off the heat, and allow the jars to sit in the hot water for another 5 minutes to cool down.

Baba's Dill Pickles

From Elsie Petch (Toronto; not previously published)

Elsie writes: "This is a simple recipe which has been followed for four generations and perhaps longer. Most important is to get medium-small cucumbers as fresh off the vine as possible. Little hands can help by gently scrubbing the cukes before putting them end-down in the jars." The garlic in this recipe will probably turn blue in the jar; that's just fine.

Makes 6 qt/L jars.

about 6 lb (2 ¾ kg) small to medium pickling cucumbers (about 21 cucumbers, or 3 pint baskets)

10 cups water

3 cups white vinegar (at least 5 percent acid)

½ cup kosher or pickling salt

12 cloves whole garlic, peeled

12 heads fresh dill

(optional) 12 fresh (and unsprayed) oak or grape leaves

Sterilize jars and warm lids. (See full instructions, p. 49, or Bare-bones Cheat Sheet, on flap.)

Wash the cucumbers and take a thin slice off each end.

In a wide, deep non-reactive pot with a thick bottom, combine the water, vinegar, and salt, and bring to a boil.

Put 2 garlic cloves and 2 dill heads into each jar. (Some people put a couple of oak or grape leaves in as well because they contain tannin, which helps to keep the pickles crisp.

Pack the cucumbers as tightly as possible into the jars, leaving ¾ in (2 cm) of headspace.

Pour the brine into the jars, leaving ½ in (1 cm) of headspace.

Run a plastic or wooden knife or chopstick around the inside of the jar to release any trapped air bubbles. Top up with more brine if necessary.

Seal with warm lids and process for at a rolling boil: 10 minutes for pint (500 mL) jars, 15 minutes for 1 qt/L jars, and 20 minutes for 1.5 qt/L jars.

{ **Tip:**
Use a heatproof mug and a funnel to pour the hot brine into the jars.

Remove the canner lid, turn off the heat, and allow the jars to sit in the hot water for another 5 minutes to cool down.

Wait 4 to 6 weeks before eating to allow flavors to develop fully.

Use a plastic lid after the jar is open to keep the vinegar from corroding the metal one.

Photo: Tigress

Photo: José Machado

Recipes for Winter

In the cold months, North American cooks turn their eyes to the south, where citrus fruits and tropicals are thriving. For those of us who must put up with blizzards and below-zero cold snaps, the sunny flavors of the winter preserves are just what the doctor ordered.

Victorian-Style Seville Orange Marmalade

The best marmalade is made with bitter Seville oranges. They are only in season and available for a few weeks in January and February, but it is worth waiting for that special flavor. This recipe reflects the early nineteenth-century practice of discarding the water used to cook oranges to avoid a bitter flavor—a technique that changed after the gelling properties of citrus peel were better understood.

Makes about 6 cups.

3 lb (1.5 kg) Seville oranges (about 18)

6 cups sugar

3 cups water

Sterilize jars and warm lids. (See full instructions, p. 49, or Bare-bones Cheat Sheet, on flap.)

Scrub the oranges in warm, soapy water to remove any wax, pesticides, or dirt. Rinse thoroughly.

In a wide, deep non-reactive pot with a thick bottom, cover the oranges with water. Bring to a boil, then reduce heat to low, cover, and allow to simmer for 2½ to 3 hours. (An alternative: put the covered pot in the oven at 200° F/95° C for 2½ to 3 hours.) This will make the whole house smell wonderful.

Lift the soft poached oranges carefully out of the pot with a slotted spoon so they don't break apart, and put them into a sieve placed over a bowl to catch any drips. Discard the water they were poached in.

When the oranges are cool enough to handle, cut them in half. Scoop out the insides, strain out the juice and reserve it. Put the remaining pith, pulp, membranes, and seeds in a jelly bag or two or three layers of cheesecloth or muslin. Reserve the peel.

Cut the orange peel into thin matchsticks between ½-in and 2 in (1 to 5 cm) long, according to taste. In a wide, deep non-reactive pot with a thick bottom, combine the juice with the sugar and 3 cups of water.

Add the jelly bag with the orange pith and pips to the pot (I clip the top of the bag to the side of the pot

so it doesn't fall in), stirring well until the sugar dissolves completely, and bring to a full, rolling boil that cannot be stirred down.

Cook at a rolling boil, stirring frequently until it reaches the setting point. Discard the contents of the jelly bag.

Ladle into sterilized jars, leaving ¼ in (6mm) of headspace. Seal with warm lids and process for 10 minutes at a rolling boil (15 minutes for pint/500 mL jars).

Remove the canner lid, turn off the heat, and allow the jars to sit in the hot water for another 5 minutes to cool down.

Grapefruit Marmalade

From Elizabeth Baird (Toronto)

Originally published at *canadianliving.com/blogs/seasons/2009/04/06/why-make-marmalade*

This is a wonderful recipe from a woman who is revered across Canada not only for her wonderful food writing and recipe development as food editor of *Canadian Living* magazine for many years, but also for her very generous mentorship of many, many people in the food industry. My inaugural attempt at this marmalade won me a first prize in a marmalade competition. I would call it a double batch; you could divide it in half and either make each half one at a time (as she suggests), or daringly work with two pots boiling on the stove at once.

> **{ Tip from Elizabeth:**
> "To speed up the laborious task of chopping the citrus rind, I usually stack the lemon, then grapefruit halves, slicing through 3 or 4 at a time."

Makes about 12 cups.

3 large ruby red or pink grapefruit

4 lemons

15 cups cold water

12 cups sugar

Sterilize jars and warm lids. (See full instructions, p. 49, or Bare-Bones Cheat Sheet, on flap.)

Scrub the grapefruit and lemons in warm, soapy water to remove any wax, pesticides, or dirt. Rinse thoroughly.

Cut off stem and blossom ends, and pare off any surface blemishes. Discard these trimmings.

Halve grapefruit and lemons; squeeze out juice, reserving seeds separately. Using a spoon, scrape out and reserve all membranes from grapefruit and lemons. Loosely tie seeds and membranes in large double-thick piece of cheesecloth. Place in large non-reactive pot. Add juices and set aside.

Cut grapefruits and lemons into the thinnest possible slices, then cut slices into lengths no more than 2 in (5 cm) long.

Add water and peel to the pot with the juices, and bring to boil on medium-high heat, stirring occasionally. Remove cover and reduce heat so mixture simmers gently. From time to time, press the cheesecloth pouch to the side of the pan to extract its pectin-rich juices. Simmer until peel mashes easily with fingers, about 2 hours. Remove pouch; when cool enough to touch, press to extract juices and transfer them back into the pot.

Measure hot peel mixture; it should amount to 12 cups. If more, reduce further. If less, make up the difference with water.

In a wide, deep non-reactive pot with a thick bottom, combine 6 cups of peel mixture and 6 cups of sugar, stirring well until sugar dissolves completely. Place on high heat, bring to a full, rolling boil that cannot be stirred down, and continue to boil, stirring almost constantly, until it reaches the setting point (about 10 to 15 minutes).

Repeat with remaining peel mixture and sugar.

Ladle into sterilized jars, leaving ¼ in (6 mm) of headspace. Seal with warm lids and process for 10 minutes at a rolling boil (15 minutes for pint/500 mL jars).

Remove the canner lid, turn off the heat, and allow the jars to sit in the hot water for another 5 minutes to cool down.

Persian-Style Three-Fruit Marmalade

This delicious sweet-sour taste is inspired by Persian cuisine, which in the fourteenth century already featured recipes for sour-orange marmalade.

Makes about 3 cups.

6 Seville oranges

3 lemons

5 limes

10 cardamom pods

2½ cups sugar

Sterilize jars and warm lids. (See full instructions, p. 49, or Bare-bones Cheat Sheet, on flap.)

Scrub the oranges, lemons, and limes in warm, soapy water to remove any wax, pesticides, or dirt. Rinse thoroughly.

Cut fruits in half and squeeze the juice into a bowl through a sieve. Discard the half-limes, but use a spoon to scoop out the flesh, fibers, and pith of the oranges and lemons. Collect any extra juice through the sieve and reserve.

Put the orange and lemon pith, flesh, and seeds into a jelly bag. Squeeze it to extract any remaining juice through the sieve.

Cut the orange and lemon peels into very thin matchsticks, no longer than 2 in (5 cm), and set them in a pot of water to boil until they are tender (about an hour).

Crack open the cardamom pods on a cutting board or counter by pressing down with the ball of your hand on the flat of a knife blade covering the pods. Remove the dark seeds and reserve them.

When the peel is ready, pour it into a strainer or colander to drain away the water.

In a wide, deep non-reactive pot with a thick bottom, combine the sugar and citrus juice. Add the jelly bag full of pith and seeds. Bring the mixture to a boil, stirring frequently.

Squeeze the jelly bag against the side of the pot to remove any last juice and pectin; remove it, then add the orange and lemon peel and the cardamom.

Bring it to a gentle boil, stirring more or less constantly until the peel is transparent and the mixture has reached the setting point. Be careful not to let it boil over or burn.

Ladle into sterilized jars, leaving ¼ in (6 mm) of headspace. Seal with warm lids and process for 10 minutes at a rolling boil (15 minutes for pint/500 mL jars).

Remove the canner lid, turn off the heat, and allow the jars to sit in the hot water for another 5 minutes to cool down.

We Sure Can ... Citrus Fruit

The peel of citrus fruits is one of the best sources of pectin; citrus preserves have traditionally been so popular that they have their own name—marmalade—and inspire a peculiar devotion. The World's Original Marmalade Festival, held each February in Cumbria in the UK, attracts more than 500 entries into its competition. Imagine the excitement in 2010 when eleven-year-old Katie Mason so impressed the judges with her Pink Grapefruit Marmalade that a version has been put into production under Wilkin & Sons Limited's Tiptree brand. Her innovation? Nothing less than adding hand-cut orange-rind hearts to the mix.

Although Scotland's Janet Keiller (wife of James Keiller who founded the company that still bears his name) is often given credit for having "invented" orange marmalade in the late 1700s when she managed to salvage a shipload of overripe Seville oranges by putting them up in stoneware jars, it had already been around for a good while by then. If I were asked to give credit to any nation for creating marmalade, I would pick Persia (now Iran).

The Persians found out about sugar as a food preservative very early, and one text dating from around 1300 says: "Do not be grieved, O Sour Orange! Like the sweet orange, turn into preserves / And then your sourness will change into sweetness." So the Persians were probably making orange marmalade about 400 years before Janet Keiller's famous jam session. Traditional Persian jams tend to use spices like ginger, cloves, nutmeg, and cardamom.

Citrus fruits have several interesting characteristics besides their aromatic, pectin-rich skins. For one thing, they can remain on the tree in a state of ripeness for quite a long time, unlike apples and stone fruits, which quickly rot and fall off after ripening. Also, they have the amazing capacity to mutate into new colors, shapes, sizes, and flavors.

The earliest distinct types of citrus are thought to have been the mandarin (which gives us the tangerine and the Clementine, among other variants), the citron (oranges, lemons, and limes), the pomelo from southeast Asia (grapefruit), and the papeda (lesser known fruits like yuzu and Kaffir lime). Oranges have diversified into the bitter type, like Seville and sweet varieties such as the navel, Valencia, and the pink-fleshed Cara Cara (a type of navel). The Minneola is a cross between the grapefruit and tangerine; the tangelo is a hybrid of the tangerine and pomelo. Cooks around the world are becoming more familiar with the rarer citrus fruits, like the kumquat and Buddha's Hand, and new varieties are still appearing.

Large-scale citrus cultivation requires both extensive irrigation and elaborate measures for protection from cold, and it is mainly managed by very large corporations. Some types of citrus have an enormous carbon footprint, since they must be exported from Asia over long distances to other parts of the world, and although residents of California or Florida may have Meyer lemons or grapefruit growing in the backyard, for northerners, no citrus can really be counted as a local fruit.

So citrus fruit does come with a cost. As with coffee, chocolate, and vanilla, I hope and expect that citrus is a luxury that we will be able to keep in the sustainable shopping cart if we manage to balance out some of our other food-related extravagances.

Some great books about citrus fruits:

Citrus: A History by Laszlo Pierre (includes an eye-opening account of the seamy side of the orange juice business).

The Book of Marmalade by Anne C. Wilson (an absorbing scholarly history, with antique recipes).

Tangerine Marmalade

From Audra Wolfe of the blog Doris and Jilly Cook (Philadelphia)

Originally published at *dorisandjillycook.com/2009/12/16/tangerine-marmalade*

"This tastes like pure sunshine," Audra writes. "It makes a great gift, obviously. The serving suggestions are endless, too: bake it on a ham, put it on bruschetta, or, if you're feeling fancy, serve it with clotted cream for afternoon tea."

Makes about 6 cups.

3 lb (1.5 kg) tangerines (about 7 or 8 medium)

2 small lemons

1½ cups water

4½–6 cups sugar (to taste)

Day 1:

Scrub the tangerines and lemons in warm, soapy water to remove any wax, pesticides, or dirt. Rinse thoroughly.

Chop the fruit, peel and all, but remove seeds.

In a wide, deep non-reactive pot with a thick bottom, combine fruits and water and bring to a boil. Reduce heat and simmer for 5 minutes.

Remove from heat, cover, and let sit for 12 to 18 hours.

Day 2:

Sterilize jars and warm lids. (See full instructions, p. 49, or Bare-bones Cheat Sheet, on flap.)

Add the sugar to the citrus mixture and bring rapidly to a boil. Boil gently, stirring more or less constantly until the peel is transparent and the mixture has reached the setting point.

Ladle into sterilized jars, leaving ¼ in (6 mm) of headspace. Seal with warm lids and process for 10 minutes at a rolling boil (15 minutes for pint/500 mL jars).

Remove the canner lid, turn off the heat, and allow the jars to sit in the hot water for another 5 minutes to cool down.

Yuzu Marmalade

From Shirley Lum of A Taste of the World Tours (Toronto; not previously published)

Shirley leads culinary tours of Toronto, so she had no trouble sourcing the ingredients for this Asian-inspired preserve, which she refers to as "the Lexus of marmalades." The yuzu, a citrus, is popular in Japan; a single fruit can cost as much as $5, and the juice is about $25 for a Worcestershire sauce-size bottle. At these prices, few people will want to make a big enough batch to bother canning; this little taste is enough to dress up a dessert or add tang to a salad dressing. Shirley says her inspiration came from a recipe by Chef Josh DeChellis in *New York* magazine.

Makes just under 1 cup.

1 fresh yuzu

4 tbsp sugar

4 tbsp plus ½ tsp yuzu juice

2 tbsp light-colored liquid honey

2 tbsp water

½ tsp liquid pectin

Wash and peel the yuzu. Chop the peel into thin or very fine shreds. Chop the yuzu into small pieces, removing seeds.

In a non-reactive pot with a thick bottom, combine yuzu flesh and peel, sugar, 4 tbsp of the yuzu juice, honey, and water. Cook over a low heat until the peel is soft (about 8 minutes).

Add pectin and stir vigorously until it reaches the setting point.

Turn the heat off, add the remaining ½ tsp of yuzu juice, and allow the mixture to rest for 5 minutes, stirring occasionally.

Use immediately or store in the refrigerator for a few days.

Lime on Lime Shred Marmalade

{ **Tip from Tigress:**
"Warming the sugar is a technique that I often overlook in jam-making. It helps to ensure that it will dissolve, leaving no hard granules in the cooked jam."

From Tigress of the blogs Tigress in a Jam and Tigress in a Pickle (New York), adapted from *Sensational Preserves* by Hilaire Walden

Originally published at *tigressinajam.blogspot.com/2010/01/lime-on-lime-shred-marmalade.html*

Tigress writes: *"The use of Kaffir limes adds a depth of flavor and a strong hit of exoticism. If you're familiar with the taste of Kaffir limes, you will recognize its sweet-sour aroma right away ... It's an unexpected twist—that works—equal parts bitter and bright, like a good marmalade should be."*

Makes about 6 cups.

1 lb (500 g) Kaffir limes

1½ lb (750 g) limes

7 cups water

7 cups sugar

Sterilize jars and warm lids. (See full instructions, p. 49, or Bare-bones Cheat Sheet, p. on flap.)

Scrub the limes in warm, soapy water to remove any wax, pesticides, or dirt. Rinse thoroughly.

Peel the Kaffir limes thinly, leaving as much pith as you can. Slice the peel into very thin shreds.

Peel the "regular" limes (discard peel or save it for another use). Cut the lime flesh in half lengthwise, and slice each half into thin slices over a bowl to catch as much juice as possible.

In a wide, deep non-reactive pot with a thick bottom, combine sliced lime flesh, juice, shredded Kaffir lime peels, and water. Bring to a boil, then reduce the heat and simmer until it reduces by almost a half and the lime shreds are tender (about 1 hour).

Meanwhile, place sugar in a baking dish on low heat (about 130°F/55°C) in the oven and bake until warmed through (about 20 minutes).

Photo: Tigress

On low heat, add the sugar to the lime mix, stirring well until it dissolves completely.

Bring up to a full, rolling boil that cannot be stirred down and continue to boil, stirring frequently, until the mixture reaches the setting point (about 10 minutes.)

Turn the heat off and allow the mixture to rest for 10 minutes, stirring occasionally, until the shreds of peel are beginning to blend into the mixture.

Ladle into sterilized jars, leaving ¼ in (6 mm) of headspace. Seal with warm lids and process for 10 minutes at a rolling boil (15 minutes for pint/500 mL jars).

Remove the canner lid, turn off the heat, and allow the jars to sit in the hot water for another 5 minutes to cool down.

Buddha's Hand Marmalade

From José (Manny) Machado of the blog Café del Manolo (Toronto)
Originally published at *cafedelmanolo.com/2010/01/buddhas-hand-jam.html*

Manny writes: *"I have been intrigued by this fruit after seeing it used in an episode of* Iron Chef*, and it was once featured in an issue of* Cooks Illustrated*. I just had to have it, but what the hell was I going to do with it? It smelled amazing! The peel was so fragrant, and it perfumed my entire kitchen. I had to figure out a way to use it ... I was very happy with the end result ... The marmalade has the distinct fragrance that I love about the fruit."*

Makes about 5 cups.

1 Buddha's Hand citron

2 Meyer lemons

5 cups water

3 cups sugar

2 tbsp lemon juice

Sterilize jars and warm lids. (See full instructions, p. 49, or Bare-bones Cheat Sheet, on flap.)

Scrub the Buddha's Hand and lemons in warm, soapy water to remove any wax, pesticides, or dirt. Rinse thoroughly.

Break down the Buddha's Hand by cutting off each "finger" and cutting away the peel from the base. Thinly slice the Buddha's Hand and lemons. Reserve the seeds from the lemons (the Buddha's Hand has no seeds) and wrap them in cheesecloth. Place cheesecloth and sliced fruits into a bowl, cover with water, and let sit for about an hour.

In a wide, deep non-reactive pot with a thick bottom, heat the contents of the bowl. Bring to a gentle boil for about 30 to 45 minutes.

Remove the cheesecloth. When it is cool enough to handle, squeeze any remaining liquid back into the pot. Add the sugar, stirring well until it dissolves completely.

Bring up to a full, rolling boil that cannot be stirred down and boil, stirring frequently, until the mixture reaches the setting point (about 45 to 60 minutes).

Stir in the lemon juice about 10 minutes before cooking is complete.

Ladle into sterilized jars, leaving ¼ in (6 mm) of headspace. Seal with warm lids and process for 10 minutes at a rolling boil (15 minutes for pint/500 mL jars).

Remove the canner lid, turn off the heat, and allow the jars to sit in the hot water for another 5 minutes to cool down.

Lemongrass, Ginger, and Kaffir Lime Jelly with Pomona's Pectin

From Pamela MacDonald and Liako Dertilis of Red Rocket Coffee (Toronto; not previously published)

Toronto's Red Rocket Coffee is an icon of the east-end neighborhood known as "Leslieville," where specialty food shops, bakeries, and cafés rub shoulders with idiosyncratic fine dining establishments. Trained at the respected culinary school of George Brown College, Pamela and Liako have won international recognition for their baking creations, but they have also created in-house preserves, of which this is one of the most intriguing.

Makes about 7 cups.

5 tsp Pomona's calcium water

5 tsp Pomona's Pectin

4 cups sugar

about 3 cubic in (4.9 cubic cm) peeled fresh ginger

1–2 stalks lemongrass

6 large Kaffir lime leaves, washed

¼ cup water

5–5½ cups unsweetened apple juice

2 tbsp lemon juice

Sterilize jars and warm lids. (See full instructions, p. 49, or Bare-bones Cheat Sheet, on flap.)

Prepare calcium water in a small jar with a lid (½ tsp calcium powder from the Pomona's Pectin kit to ½ cup water). Store in the fridge between uses, but shake well to mix before using.

In a bowl, combine the pectin and 2 cups sugar and set it aside.

Using a blender or food processor, purée ginger, lemongrass, and Kaffir lime leaves in the water. Strain through a sieve, then through a jelly bag, cheesecloth, or muslin. Add enough apple juice to make 5½ cups of liquid in total.

In a wide, deep non-reactive pot with a thick bottom, combine apple juice liquid, lemon juice, and calcium water. (If you wish to intensify the flavors, you can put the strained pulp from the purée into a jelly bag and immerse it in the mixture.) Bring the mixture to a boil.

Add the pectin-sugar mixture to the pot and stir vigorously for 1 to 2 minutes to dissolve the pectin.

Jam Tarts (p. 236), filled with (clockwise, from top): Gooseberry-Ginger Jam (p. 116), Pineapple Jam with Honey and Pomona's Pectin (p. 208), Golden Raspberry Jam with Spearmint and Lemon Balm (p. 111), and Blackberry-Raspberry Jam (p. 114).

Photo: Niamh Malcolm

Add the remaining 2 cups sugar and stir to dissolve it. Return the mixture to a boil, then remove from heat immediately. Skim.

Remove the jelly bag if you have used one, and ladle into sterilized jars, leaving ¼ in (6 mm) of headspace. Seal with warm lids, and process for 10 minutes at a rolling boil (15 minutes for pint/500 mL jars).

Remove the canner lid, turn off the heat, and allow the jars to sit in the hot water for another 5 minutes to cool down.

Carrot Rhubarb Jam with Rosemary

From Tigress of the blogs Tigress in a Jam and Tigress in a Pickle (New York), adapted from *Well Preserved* by Mary Anne Dragan

Originally published at *tigressinajam.blogspot.com/2010/02/carrots-jammed-buttered.html*

Tigress writes: *"I'm excited about the idea of making a very worthwhile jam in the dead of winter, and with frozen rhubarb that I inevitably have picked by the bushel because, I swear, I have a field of rhubarb growing each spring."*

Makes about 5 cups.

2 Cara Cara oranges, juice and zest

2 Meyer lemons, juice and zest

2 heaping tbsp dried or 4 sprigs fresh rosemary

6 cups sugar

4 cups carrots, shredded

4 cups rhubarb, chopped into ¼ in (6 mm) pieces

Day 1:

Scrub the oranges and lemons in warm, soapy water to remove any wax, pesticides, or dirt. Rinse thoroughly.

With a vegetable peeler, take very thin slices of zest off of the oranges and lemons, leaving the pith behind. Chop the zest into a very small dice. Juice all the citrus fruit.

Place dried herbs into a tea ball, a jelly bag, or cheesecloth.

In a non-reactive bowl, combine sugar, citrus juice, zest, shredded carrots, and chopped rhubarb in a bowl and mix. Bury the tea ball or bag of rosemary in the mixture. If you are using fresh sprigs, mix them gently in, keeping them intact so you can fish them out later.

Cover the bowl with a cloth and refrigerate it to macerate overnight.

Day 2:

Sterilize jars and warm lids. (See full instructions, p. 49, or Bare-bones Cheat Sheet, on flap.)

In a wide, deep non-reactive pot with a thick bottom, heat the mixture from the bowl to a full, rolling boil that cannot be stirred down. Leave the rosemary in for 2 to 3 minutes, then remove it.

Boil, stirring frequently, until the mixture reaches the setting point (about 25 minutes). The carrots and rhubarb will remain somewhat intact.

Ladle into sterilized jars, leaving ¼ in (6 mm) of headspace. Seal with warm lids and process for 10 minutes at a rolling boil (15 minutes for pint/500 mL jars).

Remove the canner lid, turn off the heat, and allow the jars to sit in the hot water for another 5 minutes to cool down.

Pineapple Jam with Honey and Pomona's Pectin

This one's for my brother John. It's very tasty as a tart (p. 236), but would also be delicious glazed on a ham.

Makes about 4 cups.

Sterilize jars and warm lids. (See full instructions, p. 49, or Bare-bones Cheat Sheet, on flap.)

4 tsp calcium water

4 tsp Pomona's Pectin

2½ cups light-colored honey

4 cups chopped pineapple (1 medium pineapple with rind and core removed)

4 tbsp lemon juice

Prepare calcium water in a small jar with a lid (½ tsp calcium powder from the Pomona's Pectin kit to ½ cup water). Store in the fridge between uses, but shake well to mix before using.

In a bowl, combine the pectin and honey and reserve.

In a wide, deep non-reactive pot with a thick bottom, combine pineapple, lemon juice, and calcium water. Bring the mixture to a boil, mashing the pineapple with a potato masher or the back of a slotted spoon until the fruit has broken down into a jam-like texture.

Add the pectin-honey mixture and stir vigorously for 1 to 2 minutes to dissolve the pectin.

Return the mixture to a boil, then remove from heat immediately. Skim.

Ladle into sterilized jars, leaving ¼ in (6 mm) of headspace. Seal with warm lids and process for 10 minutes at a rolling boil (15 minutes for pint/500 mL jars).

Remove the canner lid, turn off the heat, and allow the jars to sit in the hot water for another 5 minutes to cool down.

When lids have sealed firmly but the jelly is still warm, carefully grasp each jar without disturbing the lid and invert, twist, or rotate it to distribute solids throughout jelly.

Recipes for All Seasons

There's no pressing need to pickle onion relatives, dried fruits, and root vegetables, since they keep well in storage, but they can produce such dramatic flavors that it's a shame to ignore them. At any time of year it's fun to bake up a batch of treats so you can put some of those jams and jellies to work as a dessert, with brunch, or as a teatime menu addition.

Spicy Pickled **Carrots**

Carrots have a gentle taste of their own, but they're also very good at absorbing spice flavors. This is a classic pickle-spice combination; try slicing these carrots thinly and serving them as a sandwich garnish with crisp lettuce.

Makes about 4 cups.

about 2 lb (1 kg) carrots

2 cups white wine vinegar (at least 5 percent acid)

1 cup white vinegar (at least 5 percent acid)

1½ cups sugar

1⅓ cups water

2 tsp kosher or pickling salt

about ½ tsp each: whole coriander, black peppercorns, whole cloves, whole allspice, cardamom seeds, and ground paprika (you can vary the mixture to taste and depending on what's in the kitchen)

1 whole dried hot pepper, crushed

about 2 cubic in (33 cubic cm) peeled fresh ginger

2 cinnamon sticks, broken into pieces

2 crushed bay leaves

Sterilize jars and warm lids. (See full instructions, p. 49, or Bare-bones Cheat Sheet, on flap.)

Peel the carrots, trim off the tops and bottoms, slice them into sticks, and trim them, if necessary, to fit in the jars leaving ¾ in (2 cm) of headspace.

In a wide, deep non-reactive pot with a thick bottom, combine all ingredients except the carrots. Stir well until the sugar dissolves completely, and then bring to a full, rolling boil.

Add carrots, and bring to a full, rolling boil again.

Pack carrots tightly into sterilized jars.

Pour the liquid and spices into the jars, leaving ½ in (1 cm) of headspace.

Run a plastic or wooden knife or chopstick around the inside of the jar to release any trapped air bubbles. Top up with more vinegar if necessary.

Seal with warm lids and process for 15 minutes at a rolling boil.

Remove the canner lid, turn off the heat, and allow the jars to sit in the hot water for another 5 minutes to cool down.

Wait 6 to 8 weeks before eating to allow flavors to develop fully.

Use a plastic lid after the jar is open to keep the vinegar from corroding the metal one.

Fiery **Carrots**

Makes 14 cups (7 pint/500 mL jars).

about 5 lb (2.2 kg) carrots (about 30 medium)

6 cups white vinegar

2 cups water

½ cup kosher or pickling salt

7 tsp dill seed

7 garlic cloves, finely chopped

about ²/₃ cup dried chilis

> **{ Tip:**
> Measure out the garlic, dill, and peppers into 7 little piles so they're ready for the 7 pint (500 mL) jars. Use 4 tsp of dried chilis (or 1 or 2 whole chili peppers) per jar.

From Joel MacCharles and Dana Harrison of the blog Well Preserved (Toronto)
Originally published at *wellpreserved.ca/2009/09/25/spicy-pickled-carrots/*

Joel and Dana write that this "extreme" recipe, which is not for the faint of palate, was the result of a mistake: they accidentally put 4 tsp of chili flakes into each jar. ("The recipe called for 4 tsp in total.") They recommend using the freshest possible carrots and experimenting with red or yellow heirloom varieties ("avoid the purple ones as they have a habit of changing the color of everything") and various types of chili peppers.

Sterilize jars and warm lids. (See full instructions, p. 49, or Bare-bones Cheat Sheet, on flap.)

Peel the carrots, trim off the tops and bottoms, slice them into sticks, and trim them as necessary to fit in the jars, leaving ¾ in (2 cm) of headspace.

In a wide, deep non-reactive pot with a thick bottom, combine the vinegar, water, and salt. Stir well to let the salt dissolve completely, then bring to a full, rolling boil.

Pack carrots tightly into sterilized jars, leaving ¾ in (2 cm) of headspace.

Add the dill, garlic, and chilis.

Pour the liquid into the jars, leaving ½ in (1 cm) of headspace.

Run a plastic or wooden knife or chopstick around the inside of the jar to release any trapped air bubbles. Top up with more vinegar if necessary.

Seal with warm lids and process for 10 minutes at a rolling boil.

Remove the canner lid, turn off the heat, and allow the jars to sit in the hot water for another 5 minutes to cool down.

Wait at least 1 month before eating to allow flavors to develop fully.

Use a plastic lid after the jar is open to keep the vinegar from corroding the metal one.

Pickled **Garlic**

From Dana Harrison and Joel MacCharles of the blog Well Preserved (Toronto)
A similar recipe is published at *wellpreserved.ca/2010/09/18/preserving-autumn-pickled-garlic/*

Pickled garlic can turn blue or bright green. Do not despair, say our friends at Well Preserved, who were chagrined "when the white bulbs met the hot vinegar and turned neon green." They have since learned that discoloration "can generally be avoided by quickly blanching your garlic [before adding it to the pickle jar], and the occasional discolored batch is completely edible (just turn your lights down lower)." Pair the finished garlic with cheddar cheese.

Makes 4 cups.

2 cups unpeeled garlic cloves (large ones can be cut in half)

3 cups white wine vinegar (at least 5 percent acid)

2 tsp kosher or pickling salt

4 dried chili peppers or 2 tsp chili flakes

2 tsp each of coriander and celery seeds

4 tsp ground black pepper

Sterilize jars and warm lids. (See full instructions, p. 49, or Bare-bones Cheat Sheet, on flap.)

In a large pot, boil enough water to completely immerse all the garlic. Blanch for about a minute, then immerse in cold water. Slip the skins off the garlic. (The hot water can be saved for soup stock.)

In a wide, deep non-reactive pot with a thick bottom, combine the vinegar and salt and bring to a boil.

Pack garlic and pre-measured spices into warm jars, leaving ¾ in (2 cm) of headspace.
Pour the liquid into the jars, leaving ½ in (1 cm) of headspace.

Run a plastic or wooden knife or chopstick around the inside of the jar to release any trapped air bubbles. Top up with more vinegar if necessary.

Seal with warm lids and process for 10 minutes at a rolling boil.

Remove the canner lid, turn off the heat, and allow the jars to sit in the hot water for another 5 minutes to cool down.

Wait at least 6 weeks before eating to allow flavors to develop fully.

Use a plastic lid after the jar is open to keep the vinegar from corroding the metal one.

Pickled **Shallots with Tarragon**

{ Tip:
Save any leftover vinegar to make a salad dressing.

Shallots taste like a mix of onion and garlic and are a staple of traditional French cooking. Unlike onions, they will not make you cry as you prepare them. These salty, tangy pickled shallots are sensational with beef; slice them thin and top a hot open-face sandwich with them, dump a jar over a roast of beef before cooking, chop a few to sizzle in a pan before cooking steak, or use them with Dijon mustard to dress a gourmet burger.

Makes about 6 cups.

2 lb (1 kg) shallots (about 24)

6 cups water

6 tbsp kosher or pickling salt

2½ cups red wine vinegar (at least 5 percent acid)

1½ cups white wine vinegar (at least 5 percent acid)

½ cup balsamic vinegar (at least 5 percent acid)

1 tbsp dried tarragon (in total) or 1 sprig fresh tarragon per jar

1 bay leaf per canning jar

½ teaspoon cinq poivres (red, green, black, gray, and white peppercorns) per jar

Day 1:
Trim off the tops of shallots and peel them. (You can blanch them first in boiling water, then plunge into cold water, to make this step easier.) If there's a papery skin between 2 bulb segments joined together, separate them and remove it.

Slightly shave the root ends to remove any dirt and root hairs, but leave most of it intact so the bulbs hold together.

In a non-reactive bowl, combine water and salt and stir. When the salt has dissolved completely, add the shallots and cover them with a heavy plate so they stay submerged. Leave them in the brine for 1 to 2 days, visiting them occasionally for a quick stir, remembering to replace the plate.

Day 2 or 3:
Sterilize jars and warm lids. (See full instructions, p. 49, or Bare-bones Cheat Sheet, on flap.)

Rinse the salt off the shallots very thoroughly by covering them with fresh cold water, agitating, pouring off, and refreshing the rinse water at least 3 times. Then pat shallots dry and set on a dishtowel to air-dry completely.

In a wide, deep non-reactive pot with a thick bottom, combine the vinegars and dry tarragon (if using), and bring to a boil.

Add the shallots and bring to a boil again.

Pack shallots tightly into the jars, and add the bay leaf, peppercorns, and fresh tarragon (if using) to each jar. Leave ¾ in (2 cm) of headspace.

Pour the liquid into the jars, leaving ½ in (1 cm) of headspace.

Run a plastic or wooden knife or chopstick around the inside of the jar to release any trapped air bubbles. Top up with more vinegar if necessary.

Seal with warm lids and process for 15 minutes at a rolling boil.

Remove the canner lid, turn off the heat, and allow the jars to sit in the hot water for another 5 minutes to cool down.

Wait 6 to 8 weeks before eating to allow flavors to develop fully.

Use a plastic lid after the jar is open to keep the vinegar from corroding the metal one.

Pickled **Leeks**

From Julia Sforza of the blog What Julia Ate *(whatjuliaate.blogspot.com/)*
(not previously published)

How beautiful these look in the jar, with their pale green-white colors!

Makes 4 cups.

3 large leeks

5 cups water

5 tbsp kosher or pickling salt

2 cups white vinegar (at least 5 percent acid)

2 bay leaves

1 tsp whole cloves

½ tsp whole allspice

½ tsp whole juniper berries

½ tsp black peppercorns

Day 1:

Clean the leeks well to remove any grit. Trim them to the height of a wide-mouth pint (500 mL) jar, less ¾–1 in (2–2.5 cm). Slice them into sticks, but don't separate the leaves.

In a non-reactive bowl, combine water and salt and stir. When the salt has dissolved completely, add the leeks and cover them with a heavy plate so they stay submerged. Leave them in the brine for 1 to 2 days, visiting them occasionally for a quick stir, remembering to replace the plate.

Day 2 or 3:

Sterilize jars and warm lids. (See full instructions, p. 49, or Bare-bones Cheat Sheet, on flap.)

Rinse the salt off the leeks, cover with fresh cold water, agitate, then pour off and refresh the rinse water at least 3 times. Pat dry and set leeks on a dishtowel to air-dry completely.

In a wide, deep non-reactive pot with a thick bottom, combine the vinegar and spices. Bring to a simmer, and continue to simmer for 5 minutes.

Pack leeks tightly into the jars, leaving ¾ in (2 cm) of headspace.

Pour the liquid into the jars, leaving ½ in (1 cm) of headspace.

Run a plastic or wooden knife or chopstick around the inside of the jar to release any trapped air

bubbles. Top up with more vinegar if necessary.

Seal with warm lids and process for 15 minutes at a rolling boil.

Remove the canner lid, turn off the heat, and allow the jars to sit in the hot water for another 5 minutes to cool down.

Use a plastic lid after the jar is open to keep the vinegar from corroding the metal one.

Wait 6 to 8 weeks before eating to allow flavors to develop fully.

Fire and Spice Pickled **Onions**

From Jennifer MacKenzie (Buckhorn, Ontario)

Originally published in her book *The Complete Book of Pickling*

Jennifer writes: "With plenty of kick, these pickles add spice to cocktail time, whether served on their own, on skewers broiled with bacon, or as garnish for cocktails."

Makes about 6 pint (500 mL) jars.

3½ lb (1¾ kg) of ¾–1 in (2–2.5 cm) pearl (pickling) onions (about 14 cups/3½ L)

¼ cup kosher or pickling salt

6 dried Thai chili peppers, crumbled

3 bay leaves, broken in half

1 tbsp mustard seeds

1 tsp coriander seeds

1 tsp cumin seeds (optional)

2 tbsp sugar

4½ cups white vinegar (at least 5 percent acid)

2 cups water

Day 1:

In a large pot of boiling water, in batches as necessary, blanch onions for 2 to 3 minutes or until skins start to loosen. Immediately plunge into a large bowl or sink of cold water.

Let stand until well chilled, about 15 minutes. Using a paring knife, trim off root end and slip off skins.

In a large non-reactive bowl, combine onions and salt. Add cold water to cover by at least 1 in (2.5 cm). Place a heavy plate on top to weigh down onions. Cover and let stand at a cool room temperature for at least 12 hours or up to 24 hours.

Day 2:

Sterilize jars and warm lids. (See full instructions, p. 49, or Bare-bones Cheat Sheet, on flap.)

In a colander, working in batches, drain onions and rinse well. Rinse again and set aside.

In a non-reactive pot, combine chili peppers, bay leaves, mustard seeds, coriander seeds, cumin seeds (if using), sugar, vinegar, and water.

{ Tip from Jennifer MacKenzie:

"Use only very fresh onions for pickling. The papery skins should be tight, with no signs of mold, and the onions should be plump and firm, with no sprouting in the center. Be sure not to blanch the onions too long; you don't want to cook them, only loosen the skins."

Bring to a boil on medium-high heat, stirring often until sugar is dissolved. Reduce heat to low, cover, and simmer for 5 minutes or until liquid is flavorful.

Working with one jar at a time, pack onions into hot jars, leaving 1 in (2.5 cm) of headspace. Pour in hot pickling liquid, leaving ½ in (1 cm) of headspace and dividing spices between jars as evenly as possible.

Run a plastic or wooden knife or chopstick around the inside of the jar to release any trapped air bubbles. Top up with more vinegar if necessary.

Seal with warm lids and process for 15 minutes at a rolling boil.

Remove the canner lid, turn off the heat, and allow the jars to sit in the hot water for another 5 minutes to cool down.

Use a plastic lid after the jar is open to keep the vinegar from corroding the metal one.

Wat at least a month before eating to allow flavors to develop fully.

Orange Onion Jam with Sage and Thyme

From Yvonne Tremblay (Toronto) Originally published in her book *250 Home Preserving Favorites*

Yvonne is arguably Toronto's top celebrity jammer; she has won the title of Grand Champion Jam and Jelly Maker five times at the Royal Agricultural Winter Fair and authored several popular cookbooks. She recommends adding this jam to sauces when deglazing the pan after cooking meats or using directly on roasted pork, lamb, chicken, or cooked vegetables. She writes: "Use a sweet onion such as Vidalia (Georgia) or Walla Walla (Washington), or use sweet red onions."

Makes about 5 cups.

5 cups thinly sliced sweet onions

$^1/_3$ cup water

1 large garlic clove, minced

3 cups finely chopped peeled oranges

2 tbsp finely chopped fresh sage (or 2 tsp dried)

1 tbsp finely chopped fresh lemon thyme or regular thyme (or 1 tsp dried)

$^1/_3$ cup white wine vinegar (at least 5 percent acid)

$^1/_2$ tsp salt

pinch freshly ground black pepper

1 box (2 oz/57 g) powdered pectin

3$^1/_4$ cups granulated sugar

$^3/_4$ cup packed brown sugar

Sterilize jars and warm lids. (See full instructions, p. 49, or Bare-bones Cheat Sheet, on flap.)

In a wide, deep non-reactive pot with a thick bottom on medium heat, combine onions and water. Reduce heat, cover, and simmer, stirring occasionally, for about 10 minutes or until very soft.

Stir in garlic, oranges, sage, and thyme. Increase heat to high and bring to a boil. Reduce heat, cover, and simmer for 8 more minutes or until oranges are softened.

Stir in vinegar, salt, and pepper.

Stir in pectin until dissolved. Bring to a full boil over high heat, stirring constantly.

Stir in granulated and brown sugar. Return to a full boil, stirring constantly to dissolve. Boil hard for 1 minute.

Remove from heat and skim off any foam. Stir 5 to 8 minutes to prevent floating fruit.

Ladle into sterilized jars, leaving ½ in (1 cm) of headspace, seal with warm lids, and process for 15 minutes at a rolling boil (20 minutes for pint/500 mL jars).

Remove the canner lid, turn off the heat, and allow the jars to sit in the hot water for another 5 minutes to cool down.

Rosemary Jelly

This fragrant herb jelly, with its pretty pale yellow-green color, is heavenly with lamb or chicken.

Makes 2 cups.

Sterilize jars and warm lids. (See full instructions, p. 49, or Bare-bones Cheat Sheet, on flap.)

2 cups loosely packed fresh rosemary stalks or ¼ cup dried rosemary

Rinse rosemary stalks if using fresh.

In a pot combine rosemary and water. Bring to a boil, then remove from heat and allow to steep for at least 4 hours.

2¼ cups water

½ cup lemon juice

Strain and measure the rosemary liquid (it should be about 2 cups).

1 pouch (3 oz/85 mL) liquid pectin

In a wide, deep non-reactive pot with a thick bottom, combine the rosemary, lemon juice, and pectin and bring the mixture to a boil.

about 4 cups sugar

Remove from heat and quickly stir in all the sugar. Return to the heat, stirring well until sugar dissolves completely.

Bring the mixture to a full, rolling boil that cannot be stirred down, and continue to boil, stirring frequently and skimming off foam, until it reaches the setting point.

Ladle into sterilized jars, leaving ¼ in (6 mm) of headspace. Seal with warm lids and process for 10 minutes at a rolling boil.

Remove the canner lid, turn off the heat, and allow the jars to sit in the hot water for another 5 minutes to cool down.

Jelly triangle.
Bottom row, left to right:
Dandelion Jelly (p. 95), Wild Violet Jelly (p. 96),
Masala Chai Jelly (p. 223), Sumac Jelly (p. 145).

2nd row: Chardonnay Jelly with Pomona's Pectin
(p. 229), Guava Jelly (p. 130), Rosemary Jelly
(p. 206).

3rd row: Apple Earl Grey Almond
Jelly (p. 224), Eldorado Habañero
Jelly (p.148).

Top: Watermelon Jelly with
Thai Sweet Basil Ribbons (p. 146).

Photo: Niamh Malcolm

Masala Chai Tea Jelly

Depending on the blend of tea you use, this jelly may be brownish or a lovely pink-ish-gold. Its subtly spicy flavor lends itself to exotic dessert concoctions—I like it paired with pistachio ice cream on a piece of pound cake.

Makes 2 cups.

Sterilize jars and warm lids. (See full instructions, p. 49, or Bare-bones Cheat Sheet, on flap.)

2 chai spice teabags

about 2¼ cups water

Brew a very strong tea with the teabags and water.

In a wide, deep non-reactive pot with a thick bottom, combine the tea, lemon juice, and pectin and bring the mixture to a boil.

½ cup lemon juice

1 pouch (3 oz/85mL) liquid pectin

Remove from heat and quickly stir in all the sugar. Return to heat, stirring well until sugar dissolves completely.

4 cups sugar

Bring the mixture to a full, rolling boil that cannot be stirred down, stirring frequently and skimming off foam until it reaches the setting point.

Ladle into sterilized jars, leaving ¼ in (6 mm) of headspace. Seal with warm lids and process for 10 minutes at a rolling boil.

Remove the canner lid, turn off the heat, and allow the jars to sit in the hot water for another 5 minutes to cool down.

Apple Earl Grey Almond Jelly 🎖

From Shae Irving of the blog Hitchhiking to Heaven (Fairfax, California)

Originally published at *hitchhikingtoheaven.com/2010/04/apple-earl-grey-almond-jelly.html*

This delicately flavored tea has a beautiful color. Shae says her inspirations were threefold: ingredients from Frances Bissell's Preserving the Harvest, techniques and proportions from Christine Ferber's Mes Confitures, and an Apple Apricot Almond Jelly made by Julia Sforza of the blog What Julia Ate.

Makes 2 cups.

3¼ lb (1.5 kg) Granny Smith or other tart apples (about 10–13)

6½ cups water, plus 1 cup for tea

3½ tbsp loose Earl Grey tea

4 cups sugar

2 tbsp lemon juice

¼ tsp almond extract

Day 1:

Wash and quarter the apples without peeling or coring them. Put them into a heavy pot, cover with 6½ cups of water, and simmer for ½ hour on low heat. The apples will become soft and pulpy.

Put the apple mixture into a jelly bag, 2 or 3 layers of cheesecloth, or a wide-weave dishtowel. Hang it over a bowl to drip overnight. (Do not squeeze the bag or the jelly will be cloudy.)

> **{ Tip:**
> Wet the jelly bag or cloth with water first so it doesn't soak up a lot of valuable juice.

Day 2:

Sterilize jars and warm lids. (See full instructions, p. 49, or Bare-bones Cheat Sheet, on flap.)

Measure out 4½ cups of the apple juice, using a turkey baster or scooping from the top of the bowl to avoid sediment.

Steep tea in 1 cup boiling water for 3 minutes, strain, and set aside.

In a wide, deep non-reactive pot with a thick bottom on medium heat, combine apple juice, sugar, and lemon juice, stirring well until the sugar dissolves completely. Bring the mixture to a full, rolling boil that cannot be stirred down.

Continue to boil, stirring frequently and skimming off foam until just before the setting point.

Add the tea and the almond extract. Boil to setting point.

Ladle into sterilized jars, leaving ¼ in (6 mm) of headspace. Seal with warm lids and process for 10 minutes at a rolling boil.

Remove the canner lid, turn off the heat, and allow the jars to sit in the hot water for another 5 minutes to cool down.

Photo: Gloria Nicol

Lemon, Fig, and Lavender Marmalade

From Gloria Nicol of the blog Laundry Etc (Forest of Dean, Gloucestershire, UK)
Originally published at *laundryetc.co.uk/2010/01/22/lost-in-translation*

This delicious, complex, grown-up preserve with a strong, tangy lemon flavor, will come to quite a firm set—be careful not to overcook it. When the lemons are added, it takes on a rose-pink undertone that is very attractive. Delicious with strong cheese, it would make a good a hostess gift. Gloria (author of the extravagantly gorgeous preserving book *Fruits of the Earth*) notes that it's worth shopping for the very best ingredients for this luxe marmalade. In particular, she recommends using "a really aromatic lavender," because if you use "dull" lavender, "it won't bring anything useful to the party."

(Audra Wolfe of the blog Doris and Jilly Cook in Philadelphia has had success with a simplified version of this recipe: Chop the lemon rinds and figs and combine them in one pot with all the water. Add a jelly bag with the lavender, lemon pith, and pits, bring it to a boil, turn off the heat, and leave it covered to steep overnight. Then proceed from the step that calls for adding sugar.)

Makes 6–7 cups.

5 lemons

**3½ cups water
(for lemons)**

**2 cups dried figs
(about 18)**

**3½ cups water
(for figs)**

**5 tbsp dried
lavender**

5 cups sugar

Scrub the lemons in warm, soapy water to remove any wax, pesticides, or dirt. Rinse thoroughly.

In a wide, deep non-reactive pot with a thick bottom on medium heat, combine the lemons with 3½ cups water. Bring to a boil on the stovetop, then reduce heat to low, cover, and allow to simmer for 2½ to 3 hours. (Or put the covered pot in the oven at 200°F /95°C for 2½ to 3 hours.)

Meanwhile, remove stems from the figs, chop them into small pieces (they will swell up as they reconstitute), and combine them, in a pot, with another 3½ cups water to soak.

Tie the lavender in a jelly bag and add it to the figs, then allow the mixture to steep until the lemons are ready.

Continued next page.

About 15 minutes before the lemons are ready, sterilize jars and warm lids. (See full instructions, p. 49, or Bare-bones Cheat Sheet, on flap.)

Carefully lift the soft poached lemons out of the water with a slotted spoon so they don't break apart, and put them into a sieve placed over a bowl to catch any drips. Add the remaining liquid from the lemons to the pot with the figs and lavender.

When the lemons are cool enough to handle, cut them in half. Scoop out the insides, strain out the juice and reserve. Put the remaining pith, pulp, membranes, and seeds in a jelly bag or 2 or 3 layers of cheesecloth or a wide-weave dishtowel. Reserve the peel.

Add the jelly bag with the lemon pith and seeds to the pot with the figs and lavender. Bring the pot to a boil, reduce the heat, and let simmer for 20 minutes.

Meanwhile, chop the reserved lemon peel very finely into strips.

Take the pot off the heat and remove the jelly bag with the lemon pith and seeds, but leave the lavender in the pot. Add the sugar, lemon juice, and lemon peel. Stir to make sure the sugar is completely dissolved.

Return the pot to the heat, bring it to a full, rolling boil that cannot be stirred down, and boil, stirring frequently, until it reaches the setting point (about 10 to 20 minutes).

Remove the jelly bag containing the lavender and ladle the liquid into sterilized jars, leaving ¼ in (6 mm) of headspace. Seal with warm lids and process for 10 minutes at a rolling boil (15 minutes for pint/500 mL jars).

Remove the canner lid, turn off the heat, and allow the jars to sit in the hot water for another 5 minutes to cool down.

Chardonnay Wine Jelly with Pomona's Pectin

From Pamela MacDonald and Liako Dertilis of Red Rocket Coffee (Toronto; not previously published)

Another recipe from the creative food wizards of Red Rocket Coffee. This one uses about 2 bottles of wine, with 2 glasses left over for the chef and sous-chef. Pamela and Liako initially used a Peach Chardonnay, which would be lovely if you can get one. Otherwise, use the most fruity and fragrant white wine you can find.

Makes 5 cups.

4 tsp calcium water

4 tsp Pomona's Pectin

2 cups sugar

4¾ cups Chardonnay or similar white wine

4 tbsp lemon juice

Sterilize jars and warm lids. (See full instructions, p. 49, or Bare-bones Cheat Sheet, on flap.)

Prepare calcium water in a small jar with a lid (½ tsp calcium powder from the Pomona's Pectin kit to ½ cup water). Store in the fridge between uses, but shake well to mix before using.

In a bowl, combine the pectin and sugar, and set aside.

In a wide, deep non-reactive pot with a thick bottom, combine wine, lemon juice, and calcium water. Bring the mixture to a boil.

Add the pectin-sugar mixture and stir vigorously for 1 to 2 minutes until completely dissolved.

Return the mixture to a boil and remove it from heat immediately. Skim off foam.

Ladle into sterilized jars, leaving ¼ in (6 mm) of headspace. Seal with warm lids and process for 10 minutes at a rolling boil.

Remove the canner lid, turn off the heat, and allow the jars to sit in the hot water for another 5 minutes to cool down.

Baco Noir Wine Jelly with Apple Pectin

{ Tip:
Wine jellies tend to become foamy and expand to as much as three times their original volume while boiling, so be sure to use a big enough pot.

Baco Noir is a hybrid between the Folle Blanche grape from France and a native North American grape, so it's hardy in the wine-growing regions of the northern US and Canada and fairly commonly grown around the Niagara area, the wine region closest to my home. I thought it would be fun to create a really local wine jelly, and this one is delicious with roast beef. I used a Niagara VQA Baco Noir, but the recipe would also work with most rich dark red wines.

Makes 2½ cups.

1 cup of apple pectin (see p. 69)

1½ cups Baco Noir (or similar dark red wine)

1½ tbsp lemon juice

1 tsp cracked black pepper

2 tsp dried thyme or about 6 stems of fresh thyme

2¼ cups sugar

Sterilize jars and warm lids. (See full instructions, p. 49, or Bare-bones Cheat Sheet, on flap.)

In a wide, deep non-reactive pot with a thick bottom, combine apple pectin, wine, and lemon juice.

Put the pepper and thyme into a jelly bag and immerse it in the pot, then bring the liquid to a boil, skimming off foam that rises to the surface. Reduce heat to low, cover and simmer for 10 minutes.

Skim the mixture again, then remove the seasonings and add the sugar, stirring well until the sugar dissolves completely.

Turn the heat up and bring the mixture to a full, rolling boil that cannot be stirred down, stirring frequently and skimming foam if necessary, until it reaches the setting point.

Ladle into sterilized jars, leaving ¼ in (6 mm) of headspace. Seal with warm lids and process for 10 minutes at a rolling boil.

Remove the canner lid, turn off the heat, and allow the jars to sit in the hot water for another 5 minutes to cool down.

Riesling Wine Jelly with Apple Pectin

Riesling is a traditional cold-weather grape that's fairly sweet, light, and fruity, and can taste of green apples, or peaches, or citrus. I used a Niagara VQA Riesling and my own simplified take on herbs de Provence.

Makes 2½ cups.

1 cup of apple pectin (see p. 69)

1½ cups Riesling (or similar light white wine)

1½ tbsp lemon juice

1 tsp each of dried oregano, lavender, and rosemary, or a stem each of fresh herbs

2¼ cups sugar

Sterilize jars and warm lids. (See full instructions, p. 49, or Bare-bones Cheat Sheet, on flap.)

In a wide, deep non-reactive pot with a thick bottom, combine apple pectin, wine, and lemon juice.

Put the herbs into a jelly bag and immerse them in the pot, then bring the liquid to a boil, skimming any foam that rises to the surface. Reduce heat to low, cover and simmer for 10 minutes.

Skim the mixture again, then remove the herbs and add the sugar, stirring well until the sugar dissolves completely.

Turn the heat up and bring the mixture to a rapid boil, stirring frequently and skimming foam if necessary, until it reaches the setting point.

Ladle into sterilized jars, leaving ¼ in (6 mm) of headspace. Seal with warm lids and process for 10 minutes at a rolling boil.

Remove the canner lid, turn off the heat, and allow the jars to sit in the hot water for another 5 minutes to cool down.

Tokaji Wine Jelly with Apple Pectin

Tokaji (pronounced "toe-kay") is a very sweet late-harvest dessert wine that is made from grapes grown only along the waterways of the Carpathian Mountains. It can be extremely expensive (the bottle I used cost between $25 and $30), but I know of no other flavor like it: a rich taste of orange marmalade, apricots, and other warm dried fruits that seem to match its strong orange-amber color.

Makes 2½ cups.

1 cup of apple pectin (see p. 69)

1½ cups Tokaji (or similar late-harvest dessert wine)

1½ tbsp lemon juice

1 tbsp orange zest

2 cups sugar

Sterilize jars and warm lids. (See full instructions, p. 49, or Bare-bones Cheat Sheet, on flap.)

In a wide, deep non-reactive pot with a thick bottom, combine all ingredients except the sugar and bring to a boil, skimming any foam that rises to the surface. Reduce heat to low, cover, and simmer for 10 minutes.

Skim the mixture again and add the sugar, stirring well until it dissolves completely.

Turn the heat up and bring the mixture to a full, rolling boil that cannot be stirred down, stirring frequently and skimming foam if necessary, until it reaches the setting point.

Ladle into sterilized jars, leaving ¼ in (6 mm) of headspace. Seal with warm lids and process for 10 minutes at a rolling boil.

Remove the canner lid, turn off the heat, and allow the jars to sit in the hot water for another 5 minutes to cool down.

Candied **Ginger**

This is not a canning recipe, it's true, but it's a thrifty way to make ginger for preserving and baking, and you can use the same process to make candied lemon or orange peel. Simply cut the citrus rinds into thick matchsticks about 3-in (8 cm) long, then cook them in the same way, although they need to be boiled and simmered only once.

Buy fresh ginger when you see it available; the skin should be wrinkle-free and have a silvery sheen. The candied ginger can be added to baking (Christmas fruitcakes!) or fruit preserves or dipped in melted chocolate. The syrup can be reserved in the fridge for a couple of weeks to use in lemonade, soda water, or cocktails, or to drizzle over desserts.

Makes about 4 cups.

2 lb (1 kg) ginger (about 2 very large roots)

6 cups water

6 cups sugar

½ tsp salt

extra sugar for coating ginger pieces

Peel the ginger and slice it into thin rounds or thin 2-in (5 cm) long sticks. (Thinner slices will be more like candy; thicker slices will have more bite.)

In a wide, deep non-reactive pot with a thick bottom, cover the ginger with water and bring it to the boiling point, then reduce the heat and let simmer for 10 minutes. (For fiery, chewier ginger, proceed to the next step. For sweeter, softer ginger, drain, cover with fresh water, boil, and simmer once or even twice more.)

Drain the ginger and, in a wide, deep non-reactive pot with a thick bottom, combine ginger, water, sugar, and salt. Stir well until the sugar dissolves completely, then bring to a full, rolling boil that cannot be stirred down.

Boil, stirring more or less constantly, until the mixture has reduced by half and the liquid has a frothy appearance like gently beaten egg whites. Its temperature should be 225°F (105°C) at this point. Be careful not to let it boil over or burn.

Do not seal ginger in jars; instead, roll the pieces in sugar and lay them out on cookie sheets covered with waxed paper or parchment paper. It will take several days for the ginger to dry completely; turn the pieces from time to time. Store candied ginger in an airtight jar or cookie tin.

Baked Treats

What to do with all your jams, jellies, pickles, and preserves? Here's a selection of simple recipes that will turn a humble jar of jam into a tea-party centerpiece or a brunch highlight.

Buttered Crepes (page 237). Photo: Ontario Tender Fruit Producers

Devonshire Scones

From Denise Gurney (Macclesfield, Cheshire, England; not previously published)

Freshly baked scones are the ultimate jam delivery vehicle. Many years ago, Denise took me into her kitchen and showed me how to make scones while I copied down the instructions. This is a classic recipe that can accommodate all sorts of variations. You can double the recipe, vary the shape or size of the scones, or add flavorings to the dry ingredients. Try a handful of seedless raisins, currants, dried cherries, cranberries, blueberries, walnuts, or a teaspoon of grated lemon zest in the dough. Just before baking, you can brush the tops with beaten egg or milk or dip them into sugar or a cinnamon-sugar mix.

Makes about 6 small scones.

1 cup all-purpose flour

2 tsp baking powder

¼ tsp salt

1–2 tbsp butter or vegetable shortening

about ¼ cup soured milk, buttermilk, or yogurt

Preheat oven to 450°F (230°C).

Grease and flour a cookie sheet or lay a sheet of parchment paper on it.

Into a large bowl, sift together flour, baking powder, and salt. (Add dried fruit, nuts, or zest now, if using)

With cool fingertips (run your hands under cold water, then dry them), rub in butter or shortening.

Add just enough milk or yogurt to make a light, springy dough—don't overwork it.

As soon as the dough will hold together but before it gets sticky, press into a loose ball and turn it onto a floured surface. Knead gently to remove cracks if necessary, then roll out lightly to about 1 in (2.5 cm) thick, and cut out rounds with a glass or cookie cutter. (You can re-roll and cut out the leftover bits, but they will be tougher and not quite so pretty.)

Place rounds on cookie sheet and bake near the top of the oven until they are pale golden with just a touch of brown (about 7 to 10 minutes).

Serve immediately with clotted cream and your favorite jam. If you make enough to keep, cool them on a wire rack before storing so they don't get soggy.

Jam Tarts

Jam tarts are an adorable dessert and beg to be taken to baby or bridal showers, children's birthday parties, and similar celebrations. They're also a great way to use up ends of jam jars and jams that have set too hard.

Makes about 24 small tarts.

1½ cups pastry flour

½ cup unsalted butter or vegetable shortening

1 tbsp sugar

½ tsp ground cinnamon (optional)

about ¼ cup ice water

about 1 cup of your favorite jam

Preheat oven to 350°F (180°C).

Grease and flour a mini-muffin tin (or use paper liners).

Using a pastry cutter, a couple of knives, or a fork, blend flour, butter, sugar (and cinnamon, if using) in a mixing bowl.

Add just enough ice water so the dough holds its shape.

With lightly floured hands, knead gently.

On a well-floured surface, roll out about ¼ in (6 mm) thick.

Cut into 2-in (5 cm) diameter rounds and tuck into muffin cups. Seal any holes in the dough so that the jam doesn't stick to the tray.

Drop about 1 tsp of jam into each shell.

Bake until edges are golden but not dark brown (10 to 15 minutes).

Cool on a wire rack before removing tarts from muffin tin.

Buttered Crêpes

From Chef Mark Picone (Vineland, Ontario)

Adapted from a recipe developed for the Ontario Tender Fruit Producers and originally published at *ontariotenderfruit.com/index.php?state=category% 7E8&node=3944*

This is an elegant way to serve any fruit preserves, especially Lavender Peach Preserve with Kirsch (p. 138) or Almond Apricot Preserves (p. 135). You could build a whole brunch around these crêpes; Chef Picone suggests serving them with fresh peaches and an ice wine.

Makes 4 crepes.

1 cup milk

2 eggs

¼ tsp salt

1 tsp sugar

½ tsp vanilla extract

⅔ cup all-purpose flour

1 tbsp melted butter

½ tsp ground cinnamon

pinch ground cloves

about ¼ cup canola oil

fruit preserves

(optional garnishes) toasted pecans, vanilla ice cream, whipped cream

In a large bowl, add milk, eggs, salt, sugar, vanilla, flour, butter, cinnamon, and cloves and whisk until smooth.

Allow batter to rest for 1 hour or overnight.

Over medium heat, lightly brush a small (8 in/20 cm) frying pan or crêpe pan with some of the canola oil. Add ¼ cup batter and quickly swirl to coat the bottom of the pan.

Cook until edges become dry and golden (about 1 minute). Using a spatula, flip the crêpe and cook until golden brown on the other side. Transfer to a plate and repeat with remaining batter.

Lay crêpes on work surface, spoon ¼ to ½ cup of preserves into the center of each crêpe and gently roll. Place crêpes on dessert plates and, if desired, garnish with pecans, ice cream, or whipped cream.

Serve immediately.

Galettes

A galette is simply a flat pie. This is a great recipe for the baking-challenged, because if it looks weird you can say it's "rustic." Some great combinations: Apricot Jam (p. 123) with Almond Apricot Preserves (p. 135), or Lavender Peach Preserves with Kirsch (p. 138), or Sour Cherry Jam (p. 122) with Vanilla Sour Cherry Preserves (p. 139). Fresh, ripe sliced apples, peaches, plums, cherries, or pears are delicious baked in a galette with a complementary jam; in the classic French tradition you'd glaze them with Apricot Jam.

Makes 2 large or 4 small galettes.

½ cup unsalted butter or vegetable shortening

2 tbsp sugar

1 cup pastry flour

(optional) ¼ tsp ground cinnamon

1–2 cups of your favorite jam and/or fruit preserves or fresh fruit

about 2 tbsp granulated sugar with (optional) 2 tsp ground cinnamon for dusting the tops

Preheat the oven to 350°F (180°C).

Grease and flour a cookie sheet or lay a sheet of parchment paper on it. Using a pastry cutter, a couple of knives, or a fork, blend butter and sugar in a mixing bowl until well mixed.

Add the flour (and cinnamon, if using), and blend it in well.

With lightly floured hands, knead lightly until the dough holds its shape.

On a well-floured surface, roll out to piecrust thickness, about ¼ in (6 mm).

Roughly cut the dough into 2 to 4 rectangles. Place each one on the cookie sheet.

Paint each galette thickly with jam or layer with fruit preserves (or paint with jam, then add preserves or fresh, sliced fruit). Leave about ¾ in (2 cm) of bare dough around the edges.

Photo: Niamh Malcolm

Fold the bare edges inward to make a sort of frame around the center of each galette. Sprinkle a little sugar (or sugar mixed with cinnamon) over the edges.

Bake until tops are light golden and edges have started to brown (20 to 25 minutes).

Serve immediately or cool on a wire rack first.

Vegan Thumbprint Cookies

From Roberta Schiff (Rhinebeck, New York; not previously published)

I met Roberta, vice-president of the Mid-Hudson Vegetarian Society, at Audra Wolfe's food-preserving workshop at the Omega Institute retreat center. She baked some of these and brought them in so other workshop participants could sample their jams in cookie form, and I knew right away that I wanted to use the recipe.

Makes 18 small cookies.

1¼ cups whole wheat pastry flour

1 tsp aluminum-free baking powder

½ cup organic sugar

3 tbsp grapeseed or other light vegan cooking oil

¼ cup fruit juice (apple, orange, or your choice)

1 tsp vanilla extract

⅛ tsp sea salt

about ¾ cup of your favorite jam or jelly

Preheat the oven to 375°F (190°C).

Grease and flour a cookie sheet or lay a sheet of parchment paper on it. In a large bowl, sift together the flour and baking powder.

In a measuring cup or small bowl, combine the remaining ingredients except the jam or jelly, and then add to the flour mixture, mixing well until all ingredients are moistened.

With moist hands, shape dough into 18 balls. Flatten each one slightly and place it on the cookie sheet.

Bake for 5 minutes, then remove the cookie sheet from the oven and (being careful not to burn yourself) press your thumb into the center of each cookie to make a small well.

Drop about a tsp of jam or jelly into each well, return the tray to the oven, and continue to bake until bottoms begin to brown (about another 7 to 10 minutes).

Cool on a wire rack before serving or storing.

4: Beyond the Stovetop

You've made your first-ever batch of apricot jam or pickled onions ... now what? In this chapter, you'll find ideas about embellishing and displaying your jars, creative gift-giving, wedding projects, serving ideas, and special occasions that present a chance to sample some homemade preserves with your friends.

Storing and Displaying Jars

The best way to store food in jars is to keep them in a dark, dry, cool place where, ideally, the temperature will not fluctuate too much throughout the seasons. A dry basement is great, but any cupboard or pantry will be fine as long as it is not right next to the oven, in an attic that overheats, or in an unheated porch or mudroom that may freeze.

Generally speaking, the jars should be stored upright and grouped in such a way that you can both find what you're looking for and use the oldest jars first. If you only have a few dozen jars, this will not be so hard; if you amass large quantities, you might want to think about keeping the cardboard boxes the jars were originally packed in and labeling them on the outside so you know exactly what types of preserves are stored in each.

I keep most of my preserves (along with things such as maturing Christmas cakes) in a cupboard with doors at the bottom of the steps into my basement. However, since it's nice to admire a shelf of jars while you think about what you're going to do with them, many enthusiastic home canners incorporate ingenious storage units into the design of their kitchens or dining rooms. These may be elaborate home carpentry projects or may simply involve creative rethinking of ready-built shelving units from home design or kitchen stores.

Ready-made shelving adapted for a dining-room jar display in the Toronto home of Dana Harrison and Joel MacCharles of the blog Well Preserved. Photo: Well Preserved

The inspiring wall of jars at Gilead Bistro and Café, created by Toronto's local-food hero, chef Jamie Kennedy.

I have a small pair of open shelves for jars over the main door into my kitchen. Exposed to bright light and rising heat from the oven, the contents of these jars will deteriorate and discolor a little more quickly than the others. However, since I plan to use most of them up within a year, this doesn't matter very much. And seeing them up there reminds me to use them; I make sure to reach for these jars before restocking from my basement supply cupboard.

If you would like to replicate my display shelves, here's what you will need to do.

Canning Jar Storage Shelf Project

Materials:

- tape measure or yardstick
- 2 vertical shelving tracks, 24 in (60 cm) long, or to fit your available space (I used a titanium-colored metal)
- small hacksaw (optional)
- stud finder (simple magnetic stud finders cost only a few dollars; more expensive electronic ones are also available, but in my experience, they don't necessarily do a better job)
- level (or string with a weight tied to it)

Photo: Peta Fry

Canning shelf (right). Photo: Niamh Malcolm

Home-preserved pears, apples, peaches, nectarines, plums, oranges, cumquats, and tomatoes in Australia's iconic Fowlers Vacola jars, displayed on extremely nifty built-in basement shelves, created by Trevor Collins and Joe Reid for Peta Fry of Kinglake, Victoria. Note that they're built to be exactly one jar deep (left).

- pencil
- 2 to 2½ in (5 to 6 cm) wood screws that will fit the holes in the shelving tracks
- screwdriver or drill with bit to match the screws
- electric drill (optional)
- hammer
- 4 matching snap-in shelf brackets that will accommodate a 9¼ in (24 cm) shelf
- pine or spruce trim measuring 1 in (2.5 cm) wide and ¼ (6 mm) thick (you will need 80 to 100 in [203 to 254 cm] in total, depending on your kitchen layout)
- 2 pine or spruce boards measuring 30 in (76 cm) long, 9¼ in (24 cm) wide and 5/8 in (1.5 cm) thick (you will most likely cut these from one 8 ft [2.4 m] length)

- saw (unless you pay to have the hardware shop cut the pieces to fit)
- 1 tr 1¼ in (2.5 to 3 cm) finishing nails (slim nails with almost no head)
- nail punch (a metal tool for sinking nail heads into wood; alternately, you can use a very large nail as a punch)
- white carpenter's glue
- sanding block (optional)
- sandpaper in coarse and fine grades
- paint, Varathane, or spar varnish (optional)
- small paint brush (optional)
- cleanup solvent for paint, Varathane, or spar varnish (optional)

Beyond the Stovetop   243

Installing the shelving tracks and brackets:

- First, measure the available wall space where you intend to hang the shelves. For two shelves, you will need a minimum area of 31 in (79 cm) wide by 22 in (55 cm) high.
- Use a stud finder to locate the studs (vertical wooden supports) inside your wall. In a standard modern home, these should be spaced with 16 in (40 cm) between centers. In some houses, they will be 12 or 24 in (30 or 60 cm) apart. (In my crazy little antique house, they were 14 in/35 cm apart!) Using a pencil, mark the position of two studs at three different levels with a small X.
- You may have to trim the tracks to fit your space. This is not difficult to do with a handheld hacksaw, but be careful not to give yourself a metal splinter. Before cutting, measure carefully and make sure you leave pre-drilled screw holes in the right places (there should be one right at the top of each track; it's less important to have a screw right at the bottom).
- With the help of a level or a weight tied to the end of a string, position one of the metal shelving tracks vertically on the wall over the center of a stud. Verify that it's the right way up by testing how the snap-in shelf will sit.
- Use a drill or hammer and nail to make a starter hole for your first screw, which should be near the top of the track. Holding the track into position, screw the first screw most of the way in. Use a level or your trusty piece of string to position the track vertically and loosely screw in the remaining screws.
- Now position the second track over the next stud. Make sure that it is exactly level with the first track or your shelves will slant. Attach it to the wall loosely; check the position of both tracks and tighten the screws all the way.
- Snap two shelf brackets into the lowest position. Measure up 10 in (25 cm) and position the second set. Make sure they snap firmly into place.

Building the shelves:

- If you are positioning your shelves in a corner, cut two pieces of the trim to the same width as the boards (9¼ in/24 cm). If the shelves are not in a corner, cut four pieces. (These will act as "railings" around the edges of your shelves to keep jars from slipping off the edge; you don't need one on an edge that's snug against another wall in the corner.) Reserve any sawdust.
- Spread glue thinly on the end of one board and onto the matching surface of the trim. Align the trim with the bottom of the board and press together. Then hammer finishing nails into each end of the trim, and add extras every 3 to 6 inches (8 to 15 cm). Wipe off excess glue. Repeat with the rest of the short trim pieces.
- Cut two pieces of trim to run along the length of each board. Attach them as with the short pieces.
- Using coarse sandpaper (with either a sanding block or your hand), gently smooth the boards, removing any unevenly joined edges and slightly rounding all sharp corners. Reserve any sawdust.
- Using fine sandpaper, give the shelves a smooth finish.
- Use the nail punch to drive the heads of all the nails just below the surface of the boards. Mix a tiny amount of glue with the leftover sawdust and use a nail to poke this mixture into the tiny holes so that each nail head is concealed under "wood."
- When the glue is dry, you may paint or varnish the shelves or leave them bare. If you choose to paint or varnish, allow enough time for each coat to dry out thoroughly according to the instructions on the can. (If the paint or varnish has not cured, the jars will stick to the paint and damage the surface.)
- Slot your shelves into the brackets so that there's a length of trim on any side not shielded by a wall.
- Display your jars with pride.

Jars by Shae Irving
of the blog
Hitchhiking to Heaven.
Photo: Shae Irving

Jar labels by LeAnn Locher
of the blog LeLo in NoPo;
LeAnn sells templates for
custom labels on Etsy.
Photo: LeAnn Locher

Styling Your Jars

Mason jars are pretty on their own, but it's fun to dress them up too. The classic traditional country-style fabric jar topper is still popular, but (like the preserves themselves) it's being re-imagined in every conceivable way.

Jar Toppers

The simplest way to dress up a jar is to cut out a square or circle of lightweight fabric that's about 6 in (15 cm) wide for a narrow-mouth jar, or about 8 in (20 cm) for a wide-mouth jar. Remove the screw-on ring from the jar, position the fabric over the top, and re-screw the ring to hold it on securely.

Here are some variations on the basic theme:

- Use an old-school gingham or floral print cotton, or a contemporary solid, striped, polka-dotted, or patterned fabric. You can also use newspaper or magazine pages, cellophane, plastic, or any other material that's fine enough to allow the jar ring to screw over it.
- Leave the fabric as is with raw cut edges, or scallop it with pinking shears, or sew a line of contrasting stitching about ¼ in (6 mm) from the edge.
- Tie a piece of ribbon, natural twine, decorative cord, lace, raffia, or rickrack over the ring.
- Affix a sprig of holly, a tiny fabric flower, a felt heart, a charm, a toy, a glass or ceramic bead or pendant, or any similar ornament to the ribbon knot.
- Use the ring to secure a tag or card that lies flat along the side of the jar.
- It's a bit fussier to do, but you can use a ribbon to secure the fabric topper instead of the ring—or fasten the material on with colorful stretchy hair ties.
- Vary the topping materials as much as you like: Martha Stewart ties inverted paper muffin cups to the tops of her jam jars.

{ **Tip:**
When choosing a printed fabric, remember that a very large pattern may not "read" when you cut it into smaller pieces. If you have taken on an immense project requiring dozens of jars, there are fabric- and paper-cutting tools that will allow you to cut exact circles in a trice; they're available in craft stores and online.

Labels and Tags

Even if you don't plan to present your jar as a gift, you should always label it with the contents and date so you don't end up with a cupboard full of mystery jars from the Pleistocene Era.

However, this raises a challenge that I call the Label Enigma: for some reason, until recently, no one had invented a label that looks great, is easy to write on, and will stay firmly on the jar while it's wanted and wash off like a snap when it's not. In 2010, a Toronto-based company called StickerYou (*stickeryou.com*) partnered with Bernardin, the Canadian manufacturers of canning jars, to produce customizable vinyl labels. They come in several sizes suitable for the tops or sides of the jars and cost $6.99 plus shipping for a sheet of 36 oval labels. Canners can design their own labels using an interface on the company website (which is tricky) or upload their own art. The labels are easy to peel off and reposition and leave no residue. If they end up in boiling water by mistake, they simply float off. The labels can be shipped outside Canada.

Otherwise, choices are somewhat limited. The labels that come with the jars usually don't win prizes for their appearance, and while they come off pretty easily after the first two or three months, they leave behind a persistent gummy residue if you try to remove them after a year. Places that sell scrap-booking supplies usually carry gorgeous labels, but often they either don't adhere very well to the glass or refuse to come off once they're on. The same problem applies to homemade designs printed onto blank labels.

There are several alternatives to sticking a label onto the side of the jar. The most straightforward and practical is to note the contents and date on the metal lid with a fine-point permanent marker. (Even if you are going to add a decorative wrapping, you may wish to do this so the recipient of a gift jar doesn't inadvertently discard the useful information with the ribbons.) But clearly, this leaves something to be desired in terms of decorative effect.

If you want to use a label despite the drawbacks, there are numerous online templates for circular and rectangular jar labels, many of which can be personalized with your name, the type of jam, or a special message. Visit *tipnut.com/canning-jar-labels* for a good starter list, or search online for "free canning jar labels." (Just make sure your virus protection is up-to-date because mischief-makers seem to love to install malicious trickery on links that promise free stuff online.) Etsy offers a good selection of customizable designs.

Because the lid of the jar will be discarded anyway, you may wish to stick your label there instead of to the jar itself. If you are planning to make a lot of matching gifts, be aware that some jars are molded with a horizontal oval indentation for a label. This oval may not match well with other label shapes. Be sure to examine a sample of the jars before you buy a lot of them if you already have a labeling idea in mind.

Apart from labels, there's the wonderful world of decorative tags. These may be purchased in bulk, printed from online templates, or handmade one at a time with your own calligraphy. They can be tied on with ribbon, raffia, or decorative string in a wide array of colors. And sometimes, more is more. There will be occasions when a fabric topper with a coordinated label *and* a gift tag will be the way to go.

Jars ready to be sent to the Royal Agricultural Winter Fair for judging.

Extra-special Wrapping and Presentation Ideas

- Remove the ring and lay a wide piece of ribbon over the top of the jar (iridescent chiffon is nice for this). Screw the ring back on and bring the ends of the ribbon up over the top of the jar, tie into a decorative bow, and add a tag. (As an extra gift, you could use this technique to tie on a jam spreader or spoon.)
- Cut one to three circles or squares of the stiff fabric netting known as tulle, about 9 in (23 cm) across for a half-pint (250 mL) jar. Stack them and seat the jar in the center of the fabric. Gather the tulle up and tie it like a sack over the top of the jar, using a ribbon to secure it. Add a tag, charm, or tiny fabric bouquet to finish it off.
- Enclose one to three jars in an iridescent chiffon gift bag with satin drawstrings or a cellophane bag fastened with decorative ribbon. Add a tag.
- Enclose a jar in tulle (or tissue or parchment paper) as described above, but leave the ends poking up in the air, and tie the ribbon around the rim of the jar to hold it in place. In this case, you may wish to affix a fairly large paper or fabric flower to the top of the jar with double-sided tape. Jars wrapped in this way can be massed together so they become a decorative element in a formal table setting.

Raspberry jam wedding favours created by Christina Friedrichsen of the blog Intimate Weddings. Photo: Christina Friedrichsen

- With or without a fabric jar topper or paper lid decoration, wrap a wide piece of ribbon or a strip of decorative paper around the jar and secure it with double-sided tape. Paste a gold foil seal over the join, or affix stamped sealing wax over the closure. Use holiday- and celebration-themed envelope labels (available in stationery shops and online) and emboss them with a personalized message or design.

If these types of presentation are too fussy for your taste, simply cut out a circle of paper or card stock the same size as the lid and screw the ring over it to hold it down. If you are preparing a large quantity of jars, you can download customizable circular labels for color printing or design your own or potato-print simple images onto circles of unbleached, recycled paper for a much more earth-friendly look. Again, look to Etsy for creative possibilities such as the attractive contemporary jar toppers created by designer LeAnn Locher of the canning blog LeLo in NoPo.

How to Remove a Jar Label

- Lift one corner of the label with a fingernail and try to pull it off very slowly.
- If that doesn't work, wet the label with warm water and let it soak through for a few minutes.
- Scrape the label with your thumbnail, a plastic knife, or a plastic scratchy dishwashing sponge. If you're lucky, the entire label will come off, or may only require a little further rubbing with a soapy non-metallic pot scrubber.
- If the first scraping only removes the top layer of paper and leaves a layer of sticky adhesive, try scrubbing with hot, soapy water.
- If the scrubbing fails to remove the stickiness, you'll probably have to resort to nail polish remover, lighter fluid, or a commercial product like Goo Gone. Then you'll have to wash the jar again very thoroughly with dish soap and hot water to remove all the solvent!
- Let the jar air dry, and you're done.

Wedding Projects and Other Thoughtful Preserving Gifts

DIY Wedding Favors

To judge from the evidence online, a remarkable number of engaged couples seem to be making their own homemade preserves as wedding favors for their guests. There's a lot to be said for the idea. A jar of tasty jam can cost as little as $2 to $3 to make (jar included), which is a lot less expensive and more likely to be used than many other wedding favors.

Besides being crafty, personal, and fairly earth-friendly, jam or jelly can easily be coordinated to most wedding themes and colors (brilliant red cranberry jelly for a December wedding; pink rose-petal jam for a Valentine's Day celebration; sunny marmalade for a June affair). The gift might communicate something about the family (fruit from a family garden or grandma's own raspberry jam recipe, packaged with a photo and an anecdote about the cook), or the location (Saskatoonberry jam for a Canadian prairie wedding; peach jam for a Georgia couple).

One person can reasonably make forty to sixty small jars in a couple of weekends; if any experienced jamming bridesmaids are willing to pitch in, as many as 200 jars might be knocked off—perhaps in one well-organized jam party—without causing any tears or bridezilla meltdowns. If the project seems too big, the bride and groom might choose to make preserves as gifts only for the immediate members of the wedding party.

The timing does have to be worked out. (Don't depend on making a recipe that calls for local fruit that's only available two weeks before the wedding day!) This can work in the couple's favor, however; they could prepare their favors several months ahead of the date.

The jars themselves can be decorated and placed at each guest's table setting or grouped as part of the centerpiece. Los Angeles-based graphic designer Kristina (of the blog A Lovely Morning) used oversized name tags on forty jars of her jam so they could double as place cards for the wedding-rehearsal dinner. Tags might also carry a light-hearted message like "Sweet thoughts," "Spread the love," "To help you 'preserve' the memory of our wedding day," or "Thank-you berry much."

Jam- and jelly-jar gifts may be stacked, pyramid-style, or presented on tiered cake plates on a buffet-type table. For a more rustic presentation, they can be arranged in bushel baskets or wooden crates.

Search online for terms like "jam wedding favors" for an astonishing range of other ideas.

Honeymoon Survival Basket Wedding Gift

Among other wedding-related ideas, a selection of luxurious handmade preserves could be part of a wedding present for the bride and groom who plan to drive from the reception directly to their honeymoon location. When they arrive exhausted, at their hotel, possibly after the restaurants have closed, imagine their pleasure at finding a Honeymoon Survival Basket that's been smuggled into the trunk!

Choose an appropriate receptacle (picnic basket, hiking backpack; whatever is appropriate for the couple) and fill it with fancy picnic items like bread, biscuits, or crackers; fresh or dried fruit; cheeses; chocolate, and champagne, wine, or sparkling water. Tuck in a pair of champagne flutes, mugs, or lovely wine or water glasses, as well as plates, napkins, and cutlery (these could be disposable, or they could be part of the gift: for instance, you might include two sets of reusable bamboo cutlery for the couple who do a lot of camping).

Top up your gift with the *pièce de resistance*: sample jars of your most special preserves, like Strawberry Jam with Black Pepper and Balsamic Vinegar (p. 93), Blackberry Lime Jam with Pomona's Pectin (p. 112), Victorian-Style Seville Orange Marmalade (p. 190), Brandied Sweet Cherry Preserves (p. 136), Eldorado Habañero Pepper Jelly (p. 148), Ashbridge's Garden Chive Blossom and Sage Jelly (p. 100), Thai-inspired Spicy Pickled Veggies (p. 164), Indian Spiced Zucchini Pickle (p. 155), Pickled Beets with Fennel (p. 156), or Pickled Asparagus and Fiddleheads (p. 106).

Student Survival Kit

Prize-winning Toronto jam- and pickle-maker Tom Boyd reports that his grandmother used to stock his college dorm room with a dozen jars of Aunt Edith's Chili Sauce (p. 173) every year, which he enjoyed with his friends throughout the term. Consider presenting your student relatives with a dozen jars of a favorite staple such as Tomato Sauce (p. 172), Baba's Dill Pickles (p. 186), a selection of jams, or a chutney. I'll bet Gen's Pickle (p. 168) goes great with packaged mac 'n' cheese.

Meal and Party-Planning Tips

Once you've amassed a few batches of jams, jellies, and pickles, make sure they don't sit on the shelf. Here's an array of ideas for breaking open those jars to celebrate holidays, birthdays, and all the days in between.

Big Girls' Tea Party: If you love Jane Austen, Beatrix Potter, and *Alice in Wonderland* (or if you've been saddled with organizing your best friend's baby or bridal shower), hold a tea party! Springtime is the obvious season, but as long as you have some pretty cups, fresh flowers—and homemade jam, of course—you can't really go wrong at any time of the year. (If you're wondering, teatime can be anywhere from about three to six p.m.—generally, the more formal the occasion, the later it will be.)

Cozy Tea Party: Choose two of your favorite teas (one with caffeine and one without) and serve them in pottery mugs at the kitchen table with the teabag still in them. For a centerpiece, stand a couple of wild roses or peonies in a Mason jar. Bake a batch of Vegan Thumbprint Cookies (p. 240) after your friends arrive (perhaps they can choose the jams or jellies you use). Let the chatting begin!

High Tea: Dress your tea table with a white linen cloth, a vase of pastel tulips, and the best china and silverware you can muster. Offer your guests a choice of unusual blends of loose teas (from Earl Grey to Lapsang souchong and beyond). Give each guest an individual mini-teapot of boiling water with the loose tea in it and a tiny strainer for pouring. If you can find one of those three-level cookie plates, use it to serve a mixture of Jam Tarts (p. 236), mini Devonshire Scones (p. 235), and other bite-sized sweets. With the scones, provide tiny jars of your best jam and little silver spoons. For a more substantial high tea, provide sandwiches made by buttering slices of sandwich bread, and adding a thin layer of filling (traditional fillings include thinly sliced cucumbers with cream cheese, watercress, meat or fish paste, or finely chopped egg or tuna salad), then trim off the crusts and cut them into quarters.

Photo: Donna Stines

Devonshire Cream Tea: Go with your most flowery chintz tablecloth, a bouquet of tea roses, and a china tea set, if you own one. See whether you can find genuine clotted cream anywhere in your area (possibly from a food specialty shop); if not, make do with very firmly whipped cream. Bake at least four Devonshire Scones (p. 235) for each guest. Serving them fresh and warm, invite each guest to cut her scone in half, spread it thickly with clotted cream, and top it with a dollop of Easy Victorian-Style Strawberry Jam (p. 91). You may substitute Easy Victorian-Style Raspberry Jam (p. 110)—and if you're using whipped cream, start with the jam layer and then top it with cream.

Bridal Shower Tea Party: Choose one of these tea-party variations, and create a gift to match the party theme. This might be a selection of homemade jams with a handwritten recipe book. Add a canning set if the guest of honor doesn't already own one. A nice surprise might be to give the bride-to-be the tea set or the china you use at the party, carefully washed and packed back in the original box. Or you could revive the old-fashioned custom of having each guest present the bride with one lovely teacup—matching is optional—so she can serve tea and coffee at her own parties. (The participants can add to the set on future wedding anniversaries or birthdays.)

Ploughman's Lunch Picnic

This is standard British pub fare, and it's based on the very simple meal that a farmer would have carried with him—knotted in his handkerchief, perhaps—when he went out to work in the fields. The contemporary pub-style version is a little more elaborate than the original heel of bread and knob of cheese, and it's certain to include a ramekin of chutney to spice up the mix.

Whether used as part of a real picnic, a simple lunch for friends, or a night curled up in front of the telly watching a BBC miniseries, a traditional Ploughman's Lunch is a chance to show off your pickle prowess. Arrange each diner's meal (suggested elements below) on a china plate, and supply your guests with big white napkins. The traditional accompanying beverage is dark beer, or, for youngsters, lemonade or ginger beer.

- sturdy slices of bread and butter
- a piece of good sharp cheddar, and, if you like it, some rich Stilton
- a few slices of a tart apple or ripe pear
- a mug of soup (optional)
- a dollop of chutney, such as Cottage Garden Pickle (p. 169) or Apple Chutney (p. 166), and a couple of pickles—perhaps French Cornichons (p. 152) or Pickled Beets with Fennel (p. 156)
- the obligatory pickled onion, like Fire and Spice Pickled Onions (p. 218), or a near relation, like Pickled Garlic (p. 212) or Pickled Shallots with Tarragon (p. 214)

Soirée Sophistiquée

Whether you're hosting a wine tasting or a *Mad Men*-style cocktail party, you'll be surprised how many canning projects have a place on an elegant canapé platter. Here are some ideas for both food and drinks.

- Serve a platter of about six soft, hard, and blue cheeses made from cow's, sheep's, and goat's milk along with bread or biscuits and a selection of small bowls containing Ashbridge's Garden Chive Blossom and Sage Jelly (p. 100), Lemon, Fig, and Lavender Marmalade (p. 227), Eldorado Habañero Pepper Jelly (p. 148), Chardonnay Wine Jelly with Pomona's Pectin (p. 229), or Riesling Jelly (p. 231).
- Serve a platter of charcuterie (smoked meats, patés, hams, sausages, and other deli specialties) with French Cornichons (p. 152), Thai-Inspired Spicy Pickled Veggies (p. 164), or other pickles, a scattering of walnut halves, and a ramekin of Crabapple Jelly (p. 179).
- Glaze a small pork tenderloin with Grapefruit Marmalade (p. 192) or Orange Onion Jam with Sage and Thyme (p. 220), grill it lightly and cut it into very thin slices. Serve on narrow toasted slices of a baguette garnished with a tiny spoonful of the jam and a snippet of fresh rosemary (for the Grapefruit Marmalade) or sage (for the Orange Onion Jam).
- Cut rare roast beef into paper-thin slices. Crumple each slice onto a plain cracker or a quartered piece of toast with the crusts cut off. Drop a small spoonful of Baco Noir Wine Jelly (p. 230) on each slice, and top with a tiny dot of horseradish.
- Spread plain crackers or Melba toast with cream cheese, garnish with Watermelon Jelly with Thai Sweet Basil Ribbons (p. 146), and top with a sprinkling of finely julienned cucumber or alfalfa sprouts.
- Serve classic Gibson Martinis: Toss 5 to 8 parts gin or vodka to 1 part vermouth with ice in a cocktail shaker and strain it into chilled martini glasses, then garnish each glass with two or three Fire and Spice Pickled Onions (p. 218).
- Experiment with cocktails; lots of online cocktail recipes call for candied ginger or citrus peel (p. 233), or fruit-flavored syrup. Several trendy Manhattan bars simply drop spoonfuls of jam right into their drinks.

Jamming Online

These ideas represent just a drop in the bucket of imaginative possibilities that lurk in every jar of jam or pickles. For more inspiration, you have but to visit some of the scores of sites posted by dedicated canners. Here, to end with, a selection that, at time of writing, were current, active, and more or less obsessed with putting up food in jars.

*   a recipe contributor

**   personal favorites

Anarchy in a Jar (anarchyinajar.com)

(Four Chickens and the) Art of Gluten-free Baking (artofglutenfreebaking.com)

Autumn Makes and Does (autumnmakesand-does.com)

*Backyard Farms (backyardfarms.blogspot.com)

Better Gardens Than Home (bettergardensthanhome.com)

Bigger Than a Breadbox (mimisbooks.blogspot.com)

A Bit of a Pickle (bitofapickle.wordpress.com)

*Café del Manolo (cafedelmanolo.com)

Café Libby (cafelibby.blogspot.com)

**Canning Across America (canningacrossamerica.com)

*Canning With Kids (canningwithkids.com)

Canning Jars Etc. (canningjarsetc.blogspot.com)

Catfish and Waffles (catfishandwaffles.com)

Consider the Pantry (considerthepantry.com)

Creative Canning (creativecanning.blogspot.com)

**David Lebovitz (davidlebovitz.com)

**Dawnabelle's (dawnabelle.ca)

**Diggin' the Dirt (kitchenjam.net)

Domestic Efforts (domesticefforts.blogspot.com)

*Doris and Jilly Cook (dorisandjillycook.com)

*Egg Day The Brunch Project (eggday.blogspot.com)

*Flamingo Musings (flamingomusings.com)

**Food in Jars (fooodinjars.com)

*Food With Legs (foodwithlegs.com)

For Better or Worsted (forbetterorworsted.blogspot.com)

Frugal Canning (frugalcanning.blogspot.com)

Gluten-free Girl (glutenfreegirl.blogspot.com)

Good Food. Eat Here (jobifood.blogspot.com)

Grow and Resist (growandresist.wordpress.com)

Hedonia (hedonia.seantimberlake.com)

**The Hip Girl's Guide to Homemaking (hipgirlshome.com)

*Hitchhiking to Heaven (hitchhikingtoheaven.com)

Hot Water Bath (hotwaterbath.blogspot.com)

Inn Brooklyn (innbrooklyn.com)

IthaCan (ithacanning.com)

Just the Right Size
(justtherightsize.blogspot.com)

*Laundry etc (laundryetc.co.uk)

Leena Eats This Blog (leenaeats.com/blog)

**LeLo in NoPo (lelonopo.com)

Leslie Land in Kitchen and Garden
(leslieland.com)

**Linda Ziedrich (lindaziedrich.com)

**Local Kitchen (localkitchen.wordpress.com)

Married ... With Dinner (marriedwithdinner.com)

Mother's Kitchen (motherskitchen.blogspot.com)

**Mrs. Wheelbarrow's Kitchen
(mrswheelbarrow.blogspot.com)

On a Little Land (onalittleland.blogspot.com)

The Pickle Blog (blog.rickspicksnyc.com)

Pickle Freak (picklefreak.com)

Planet Eve (planeteve.blogspot.com)

**Plot 22 (melamalie.wordpress.com)

The Practical Preserver (practicalpreserving.
blogspot.com)

*Prairieland Herbs
(prairielandherbs.blogspot.com)

PreserveNation (preservenation.blogspot.com)

Put-a-Lid-on-It (put-a-lid-on-it.blogspot.com)

Put Up or Shut Up! (putsup.com)

Putting By (puttingby.wordpress.com)

Rachel Eats (racheleats.wordpress.com)

**Rufus & Clementine (rufusandclementine.com)

Rurally Screwed (rurallyscrewed.com)

Saving the Season (savingtheseason.com)

Seasonal Menus (seasonal-menus.blogspot.com)

**Seasonal Ontario Food
(seasonalontariofood.blogspot.com)

Simply Canning (simplycanning.com)

**Small Measure (smallmeasure.blogspot.com)

**Stetted (stetted.com)

**Sugarcrafter (sugarcrafter.net)

**Sustainable Eats (sustainableeats.com)

Thinking Out Loud
(woodman-thinking-out-loud.blogspot.com)

A Thinking Stomach
(athinkingstomach.blogspot.com)

**Three Clever Sisters (threecleversisters.com)

*Tigress in a Jam (tigressinajam.blogspot.com)

*Tigress in a Pickle
(tigressinapickle.blogspot.com)

Toronto Tasting Notes [Sarah Hood's blog]
(totastings.blogspot.com)

Urban Hennery (urbanhennery.com)

*Well Preserved (wellpreserved.ca)

**Well-Preserved
(blogs.denverpost.com/preserved)

*What Julia Ate (whatjuliaate.blogspot.com)

Wine Book Girl (winebookgirl.blogspot.com)

*Yummy Supper (yummysupper.blogspot.com)

Sources

Abbott, Elizabeth. *Sugar: A Bittersweet History*. Toronto: Penguin Canada, 2008.

Allen, Arthur. *Ripe: The Search for the Perfect Tomato*. Berkeley: Counterpoint, 2010.

Alter, Lloyd. "Is There Bisphenol A in Your Home Canning?" *Treehugger*, July 13, 2009. http://www.treehugger.com/files/2009/07/is-there-bpa-in-your-home-canning.php.

Baird, Elizabeth. *Apples, Peaches & Pears*. Halifax: Formac, 2002.

————. *Summer Berries*. Halifax: Formac, 2002.

Baker, Charles L. and Neil L. Pennington. *Sugar: A User's Guide to Sucrose*. New York: Springer, 1990.

Ball Blue Book Guide to Preserving, [n.l.:] Alltrista Consumer Products, 2004.

Batmanglij, Najmieh K. *A Taste of Persia: An Introduction to Persian Cooking*. Waldorf, MD: Mage Publishers, 2003.

Bernardin Ltd. *Bernardin Guide to Home Preserving*. Oakville, ON: Bernardin, 2010.

Bone, Eugenia. *Well Preserved: Recipes and Techniques for Putting Up Small Batches of Seasonal Food*. New York: Clarkson-Potter Publishers, 2009.

Breckenridge, Muriel. *Every Day a Feast: Over 360 Delicious, Old-time, Special-occasion Recipes from Canadian Country Kitchens*. Toronto: McGraw-Hill Ryerson Limited, 1978.

————. *The Old Ontario Cookbook: over 420 Delicious and Authentic Recipes from Ontario Country Kitchens*. Toronto: McGraw-Hill Ryerson Limited, 1976.

Brillat-Savarin, Jean Anthelme. *Physiologie du goût*. Paris: Flammarion, 1982.

Buszek, Beatrice Ross. *The Blueberry Connection: Blueberry Cookery With Flavour, Fact And Folklore, from Memories, Libraries and Kitchens of Old and New Friends, and Strangers*. Halifax: Nimbus Publishing, 2007.

————. *The Cranberry Connection: Cranberry Cookery with Flavour, Fact and Folklore, from Memories, Libraries and Kitchens of Old and New Friends, and Strangers*. Granville Centre, NS: B.R. Ross, 1977.

Campoy, Ana. "Putting Up Produce: Yes, You Can." *Wall Street Journal* October 15, 2009. http://online.wsj.com/article/SB10001424052748703787204574449160079437536.html.

"Canners Across America, Can-A-Rama Home Canning Parties, 2010." *Canning Across America*. http://www.canningacrossamerica.com/can-a-rama-events/canners-across-america-can-a-rama-home-canning-parties-2010.

Click, Melissa A. and Ronit Ridberg. "Saving Food: Food Preservation as Alternative Food Activism." *Environmental Communication: A Journal of Nature and Culture* 4(3) (2010): 301—17. http://dx.doi.org/10.1080/17524032.2010.500461.

Cottrell, Annette. "Weather and How It Affects Hitting the Gel Stage." *Canning Across America* http://www.canningacrossamerica.com/resources/weather-and-how-it-affects-hitting-the-gel-stage/.

Crawford, Stanley. *A Garlic Testament: Seasons on a Small New Mexico Farm*. Albuquerque: University of New Mexico Press, 1998.

Dickerman, Sarah. "Can It: At-home Preserving Is Ridiculously Trendy." *Slate* March 10, 2010. http://www.slate.com/id/2246148/.

Diggs, Lawrence J. *Vinegar: The User friendly Standard Text, Reference, and Guide to Appreciating, Making, and Enjoying Vinegar*. San Francisco: Quiet Storm Trading Company, 1989.

Dragan, Mary Anne. *Well Preserved: Small Batch Preserving for the New Cook*, 3rd edition. Vancouver: Whitecap, 2009.

Elliot, Elaine. *Cranberries: Recipes from Canada's Best Chefs*. Halifax: Formac, 2005.

Elliot, Elaine and Virginia Lee. *Apples: Recipes from Canada's Best Chefs*. Halifax: Formac, 2006.

——— . *Blueberries: Recipes from Canada's Best Chefs*. Halifax: Formac, 2005.

Elton, Sarah. *Locavore: From Farmers' Fields to Rooftop Gardens: How Canadians are Changing the Way We Eat*. Toronto: HarperCollins, 2010.

English, Ashley. *Homemade Living: Canning & Preserving with Ashley English: All You Need to Know to Make Jams, Jellies, Chutneys & More*. New York: Lark Books, 2010.

Escoffier, Georges Auguste. *The Escoffier Cook Book: A Guide to the Fine Art of Cookery*. New York: Crown Publishers, 1969.

Ferber, Christine. *Mes Confitures: The Jams and Jellies of Christine Ferber*, translated by Virginia R. Phillips. East Lansing, MI: Michigan State University Press, 2002.

Freitus, Joe and Salli Haberman. *Wild Jams and Jellies: Delicious Recipes Using 75 Wild Edibles*. Mechanicsburg, PA: Stackpole Books, 2005.

Friedrichsen, Christina. "How to Make Raspberry Jam: Ooooh La La! It's Music to Your Lips!," *Intimate Weddings*, July 27, 2009. http://www.intimateweddings.com/blog/how-to-make-raspberry-jam-ooooh-la-la-its-music-to-your-lips/

Garrett, Blanche Pownall. *Canadian Country Preserves and Wines*. Toronto: James Lewis & Samuel, 1974.

Goetzman, Keith. "Home Canning: Pickles, Peppers, and a Dash of BPA?" *Utne Reader* (online) October 23, 2009. http://www.utne.com/Environment/Home-Canning-Pickles-Peppers-and-a-Dash-of-BPA-5673.aspx.

Goldman, Amy. *The Heirloom Tomato: From Garden to Table: Recipes, Portraits, and History of the World's Most Beautiful Fruit*. New York: Bloomsbury, 2008.

Gollner, Adam Leith. "Spreading the Word." *Wall Street Journal* (online) September 9, 2010. http://magazine.wsj.com/gatherer/the-specialist/spreading-the-word/2.

Hale, Todd. "Gardening, Canning Categories Capitalize on Economy." *Nielsenwire* May 18, 2009. http://blog.nielsen.com/nielsenwire/consumer/gardening-canning-categories-capitalize-on-economy.

Hedrick, Kristina. "DIY Jam Jar Placecards." *Beautiful Morning* October 16, 2008. http://alovelymorning.blogspot.com/2008/10/diy-jam-jar-placecards.html.

Hekmat, Forough-es-Saltanah. *The Art of Persian Cooking*. Garden City, NY: Doubleday, 1961.

Jeanroy, Amelia and Karen Ward. *Canning & Preserving for Dummies*, 2nd ed. Edison, NJ: For Dummies, 2009.

Johnson, Lorraine. *City Farmer: Adventures in Urban Food Growing*. Toronto: Greystone Books, 2010.

Kingry, Judi and Lauren Devine. *Ball Complete Book of Home Preserving: 400 Delicious and Creative Recipes for Today*. Toronto: Robert Rose, 2006.

Kurlansky, Mark. *Salt: A World History*. Vancouver/Toronto: Vintage Canada, 2002.

Ladies of Toronto and Chief Cities and Towns in Canada. *The Home Cook Book*. Toronto: The Musson Book Co., 1877.

Lape, Fred. *Apples & Man*. New York: Van Nostrand Reinhold, 1979.

Laszlo, Pierre. *Citrus: A History*. Chicago: University of Chicago Press, 2007.

MacKenzie, Jennifer. *The Complete Book of Pickling: 250 Recipes from Pickles to Chutneys to Salsa*. Toronto: Robert Rose, 2009.

Martin, Carol. *The Apple: A History of Canada's Perfect Fruit*. Toronto: McArthur & Co., 2007.

Maxwell, Steve and Jennifer MacKenzie. *The Complete Root Cellar Book: Building Plans, Uses and 100 Recipes*. Toronto: Robert Rose, 2010.

McClellan, Marisa. "Canning 101: Preserving with Tattler's Reusable Lids." *Food in Jars* September 21, 2010. http://www.foodinjars.com/2010/09/canning-101-preserving-with-tattlers-reusable-lids/.

Mick, Hayley. "We Be Jamming." *The Globe and Mail* (online) September 4, 2009. http://www.theglobeandmail.com/life/food-and-wine/we-be-jamming/article1276356/.

Moskin, Julia. "Preserving Time in a Bottle (or Jar)." *The New York Times* (online) May 26, 2009. http://www.nytimes.com/2009/05/27/dining/27cann.html.

"The Nielsen Company Issues Top Ten U.S. Lists for 2009." December, 2009. http://www.nielsen.com/content/dam/nielsen/en_us/documents/pdf/Press Releases/2009/December/The Nielsen Company Issues Top Ten U.S. Lists for 2009.pdf

Nicol, Gloria. *Fruits of the Earth: 100 Recipes for Jams, Jellies, Pickles, and Preserves*. London, UK: Cico Books, 2009.

"October Retail Sales: Americans Pare Down, Stay Home." *Nielsenwire* December 10, 2008. http://blog.nielsen.com/nielsenwire/consumer/october-retail-sales-americans-pare-down-stay-home.

O'Donnel, Kim. "The United States of Canning." *The Huffington Post* August 24, 2009. http://www.huffingtonpost.com/kim-odonnel/the-united-states-of-cann_b_267583html.

Pollan, Michael. *The Botany of Desire: A Plant's-eye View of the World*. New York: Random House, 2002.

Saunders, Rachel. *The Blue Chair Jam Cookbook*. Kansas City, MO: Andrews McMeel Publishing, 2010.

Shackford, Stacey. "Ithacans Are Turning to Home-preserving, Home-grown Food." *The Ithaca Journal* (online) May 29, 2009. http://www.theithacajournal.com/article/20091129/NEWS01/911290333/Ithacans are turning to home-preserving home-grown food (link no longer available to non-subscribers).

Shephard, Sue. *Pickled, Potted, and Canned: How the Art and Science of Food preserving changed the world*. New York: Simon and Schuster, 2000.

Swann, Amelia. *The Victorian Kitchen Book of Jams and Jellies*. Godalming, Surrey, UK: Island Books for S. Webb & Son, 1995.

Topp, Ellie and Margaret Howard. *The Complete Book of Small-Batch Preserving: Over 300 Recipes to Use Year-Round.* Toronto: Firefly Books, 2007.

Trail, Gayla. *Grow Great Grub: Organic Food from Small Spaces*. New York: Clarkson Potter, 2010.

Tremblay, Yvonne. *250 Home Preserving Favorites: From Jams & Jellies to Marmalades & Chutneys*. Toronto: Robert Rose, 2010.

Vinton, Sherri Brooks. *Put 'em Up: A Comprehensive Home Preserving Guide for the Creative Cook, from Drying and Freezing to Canning and Pickling*. North Adams, MA: Storey Publishing, 2010.

Walden, Hilaire. *Perfect Preserves*. New York: Wiley, 2002.

Webb, Margaret. *Apples to Oysters: A Food Lover's Tour of Canadian Farms*. Toronto: Viking Canada, 2008.

Wilson, C. Anne. *The Book of Marmalade*. London: Constable, 1985.

Wolfe, Audra. "Jars and Lids." Doris and Jilly Cook March 2, 2010. http://dorisandjillycook.com/2010/03/02/jars-and-lids/.

Ziedrich, Linda. *The Joy of Jams, Jellies, and Other Sweet Preserves: 200 Classic and Contemporary Recipes Showcasing the Fabulous Flavors of Fresh Fruits*. Boston: Harvard Common Press, 2009.

———. *The Joy of Pickling, 250 flavor-packed recipes for vegetables and more from garden or market*. Boston: Harvard Common Press, 2009.

Index

SARAH B. HOOD is a freelance food writer who has been canning for more than a decade. Her preserves have won prizes from Canada's Royal Agricultural Winter Fair and the Culinary Historians of Canada. She is a contributor to the uTOpia Book Series (Coach House Books) and numerous publications, including *The National Post, The Globe and Mail,* and *Spacing,* and has been shortlisted for Canada's National Magazine Awards and the Kenneth R. Wilson Awards for business writing. She lives in Toronto.